MW00358514

TARANTINO AND THEOLOGY

This collection pops with the panache that QT deserves. Tarantino and Theology pours the firebrand filmmaker's blood, music, and humor into a tasty philosophical stew seasoned with timeless truths. A great merger of style and substance, provocation and profundity.

Craig Detweiler, PhD
Director
Center For Entertainment, Media and Culture
Pepperdine University
Author, *iGods*

Few books engage film and the Christian faith in ways that enhance our understanding of both disciplines. *Tarantino and Theology* is one. Highly recommended not only for Tarantino fans (and detractors), but for all interested in religion and popular culture.

Robert K. Johnston, PhD
Professor of Theology and Culture
Fuller Seminary
Author, *Reel Spirituality*

I love Tarantino movies. As it so happens, I love God too. While some may find these loves to be contradictory, I assure you they are not—and this book is proof. With each chapter, *Tarantino and Theology* dares to dig deeper into the sometimes brutal, sometimes profane, often hilarious, and always meaningful world of Quentin's films—and finds within them the truths that hold our own world together, and point us to that greater love.

Zach Hoag
Author, *Nothing But The Blood: The Gospel According to Dexter*
Writer at zhoag.com

The tradition of theology dialoging with the popular culture goes back to the Church Fathers who gave considered thought to great poets and thinkers of their age. Jonathan and Jerry Walls contribute an excellent volume here to that tradition, engaging with one of the most important creators of culture in our time. *Tarantino and Theology* is a must read for anyone who wishes to see how culture and theology can seriously engage with each other.

Joshua Wise
Author, *Past The Sky's Rim: The Elder Scrolls & Theology*

To Jones, Best wishes as you plumb the depths of theology with Q.T.!
Jerry L. Walls
6/26/16

TARANTINO AND THEOLOGY

Edited by Jonathan L. Walls and Jerry L. Walls

TARANTINO

AND

THEOLOGY

Edited by
Jonathan L. Walls
and Jerry L. Walls

GRAY MATTER BOOKS

GRAY MATTER BOOKS / LOS ANGELES

Tarantino and Theology
Edited by Jonathan L. Walls and Jerry L. Walls
Gray Matter Books
Copyright © 2015
ISBN: 9780988930575

Contents

To Headley and Zunker, my longest-running partners in crime

SPECIAL THANKS

Special Thanks

Thanks to Aaron Champion for the encouragement and inspiration to take on another book project. This book simply wouldn't exist without him. Thanks to my mom for accidentally and unknowingly introducing me to *Pulp Fiction* so many years ago. Thanks to my wife, Emily, for her proofreading, her constant advice and feedback along the way, and of course her cute face.

INTRODUCTION

Jonathan L. Walls

I first watched *Pulp Fiction* when I was 14 years old. And then I watched it again, and again, and again, until I lost count of the viewings. I couldn't, at the time, pinpoint what it was about that film that so captured my imagination. It was energetic, honest, and brutal, but above all, it was a lot of *fun*. To take a ride on any of Tarantino's narrative rollercoasters is to take a ride of pleasure and excitement. It's a lot of fun.

Some would surely argue that I was a few years too young for the "mature" language and imagery offered by Tarantino's breakout hit, and maybe they're right. But then again, maybe they're wrong. At 14 I had certainly not yet reached the level of mental and emotional maturity required to fully appreciate *Pulp Fiction* for all of its nuance in character development, structural bravado, and, of course, weighty theological implications. But on the other hand, it introduced me to a style of storytelling and a brand of cinematic flair quite foreign to my undeveloped cinematic palate. I can even say that my meeting this film at that particular point in my life was one of the most important artistic revelations I will ever have, as it directly shaped my journey toward becoming a filmmaker. Without question, coming across *Pulp Fiction* at age 14 was good for me.

As I said, some may disagree with this assertion on pure principle. The profanity and violence presented to my adolescent eyes should have been, at the very least, reserved for a more mature heart and mind, if not avoided altogether, they may suggest. This opinion may even lie with some of the contributing authors of this book. But even if that were the case (I haven't asked, so I can't be sure), I'm sure that none would argue that a great deal of good at least accompanied my early encounter with *Pulp Fiction*, even if they argue that it was outweighed by potential bad.

Therein lies one of the many friction points of our culture's relationship with Tarantino that, in part, makes him the scintillating public figure and artist that he is. For better or worse, his films evoke passionate discussion, deep critical thinking, and serious artistic analysis, even from his biggest detractors (whether they own it or not). Some say his artistic brilliance makes it worth the task of wading through the grit to uncover it, while some say it is not. Some say his artistic ability is compromised *because* of the ubiquitous violence and profanity blanketing his films, while others say that this controversial content is itself an integral ingredient in his brilliant storytelling. In other words, the two are part of the same beast. It will be no surprise that I align myself firmly with the latter group.

No matter your stance, one thing is certain: Tarantino's films will make you react, and that reaction will make you think. Often, it will make you think hard about issues in a way you have not thought about them before. Further, it is the belief of my fellow contributors and myself that Tarantino's films will make you think *theologically*. While no clear religious or theological affiliation (or anything like one) can be pinned to Tarantino's greater cinematic repertoire, theological implications, suggestions, and intimations abound throughout the Tarantino-verse. This is where my fellow contributors and I simultaneously take our liberties with Tarantino's material, and where we acknowledge our own limitations.

The purpose of this book *is* to examine how Tarantino's cinematic universe may be employed to illuminate many different aspects of Christian theology. It is *not* to claim any level of intent toward Christian beliefs for Tarantino or his movies. The purpose of this book *is* to see how various corners of Christian theology appear when viewed through the lens of Tarantino's camera. It is *not* to superimpose Christian beliefs onto any of his films. There is a fine line between what this book is and what it is not, but the distinction is crucial. The wrong side of that line would be to claim that our analyses convey the "correct" interpretation, or the actual theological beliefs, found in Tarantino's movies. The right side of that line is to discourse on the numerous theological issues that can be extrapolated organically from Tarantino's fiction, by merit of its sheer depth and complexity alone. Indeed, Tarantino's films could well be used also as a backdrop for a wide array of theological and philosophical studies outside the realm of Christian thought, and they surely are. But Christian theology is right there in the thick of them, and that's why we wrote this book. Furthermore, if Christian theology is correct in its fundamental assumption that God exists and created all things, then there will be traces of theological truth to be found everywhere, including some surprising places. Sometimes those traces appear as mere residue, other times they strike like a bullet in the chest. Tarantino's films contain both varieties and everything in between.

It is our hope that fans of Tarantino and fans of theological studies—be they curious, entry-level seekers or seasoned academics, well-watched cinephiles or eager newcomers in the ways of cinema—will find much to enjoy and ponder in these pages. Whether your theological beliefs align with some or none of those found within this book is immaterial. It is our simple hope to represent our points of view honestly and clearly, and give readers a new way and a fresh lens to view Tarantino's work and the theological ideas on display.

A quick glance at our table of contents and authors' bios will reveal what an accomplished and varied group of thinkers we have assembled for this volume. Differing backgrounds, and with them, differing opinions, will be found within these essays. It will be evident even from this introduction and my own essay that I don't align perfectly with every opinion on the bill here, and that's just fine. Perhaps Tarantino's greatest ability, beyond the prodigious visual and narrative skill that permeates his work, is his ability to generate impassioned discussion and even disagreement. Embrace it. It's all part of the fun.

THE INCARNATIONAL AESTHETIC OF QUENTIN TARANTINO

Brett McCracken

If you're reading this, you've likely sat through at least one Quentin Tarantino film. But have you ever sat through one of his films without closing your eyes at least once? Or without peeking through your hands while grimacing in horror? If so, you've got a strong stomach and nerves of steel. Tarantino's films are notable for many things, but perhaps mostly for their in-your-face violence and heart-pumping tension. There's something uniquely visceral about Tarantino's cinema, and it's part of what makes the *auteur*'s films so popular with audiences and so critically acclaimed.

What is it about Tarantino's films that makes them so memorable? There are many possible answers to that question: the colorful characters, the extravagant violence, the fight scenes, the music, the pop culture references, the cathartic revenge fantasies, and on and on. But one thing that seems consistent in Tarantino's cinema is a deep fondness for this world in all of its human physicality, eccentricity, and sometimes grotesque vulnerability. His films manifest a childlike awe and fascination with the smallest details of human culture, conflict, and mythology. In their fixation on bodies (both fierce and frail), curious interest in food and drink, and focus on the sights, sounds, smells and textures of the material world, Tarantino's films represent an aesthetic that could be called "incarnational." In so doing, they help the Christian viewer re-sensitize to the physical, fleshy world in which Christ lived, breathed, died, and rose. By paying attention to the incarnational aesthetics of Tarantino's films, we push against the increasing disembodiment of our digital world, as well as our western Christian tendency to etherealize our faith, divorcing it from a material and embodied context.

Flying Limbs, Exploding Hearts, and the Centrality of the Body

One of the things that makes Tarantino films so simultaneously compelling and horrifying, so "can't-turn-away" attractive and "I-have-to-close-my-eyes" repulsive, is the director's skill at visceral communication of human embodiment.

His heroes and villains are full of life: they are quick with their hands, expressive with their eyes, clever in their speech, and lethal in their skill with samurai swords, baseball bats, shotguns, and bare knuckles. And yet unlike the super-human heroes and villains of much of Hollywood fiction, Tarantino's characters are also decidedly mortal. They bleed, they groan, they die. And they do so frequently in his films.

For almost the entirety of Tarantino's first film, *Reservoir Dogs* (1992), the breakability of Mr. Orange (Tim Roth) is on shocking display as he bleeds, wheezes, cries, squeals, and squirms in gruesome agony — in the backseat of a car at first and then on a warehouse floor.

As he bleeds from the stomach and writhes on the floor, others suffer around him, including a hostage cop who is tortured and killed in what becomes the film's most controversial display of violence.

Bodies go through quite a lot of punishment in Tarantino films. Limbs are frequently severed and maimed victims left convulsing and screaming in pain (see the "House of Blue Leaves" sequence in *Kill Bill: Vol. 1*); legs are severed and fly through the air like projectiles (see the car crash scene in *Death Proof*); bones are viciously broken (the mandingo fighting match in *Django Unchained*); eyeballs squished and hearts exploded (*Kill Bill: Vol. 2*); heads scalped, carved, or bashed in via baseball bat (*Inglourious Basterds*), and so on.

The explicit carnage and creative array of injuries inflicted on bodies in the Tarantino *oeuvre* is more than a shock tactic or trademark, however. It's certainly up for dispute, but I don't believe that Tarantino is a sadist or bloodthirsty lover of violence for its own sake. Rather, I believe that the director recognizes that the human body is innately dramatic, charged by the reality of its vulnerability. Without the ever present possibility of injury or death, there would be no drama. No fight. No stakes. Tarantino uses violence — even foregrounds it via exaggeration (e.g. "spray blood") — because he wants the audience to feel uneasy and squeamish about the reality of embodiment, at once a glorious and tenuous thing. Our heart rates rise, we wince, our white-knuckled fingers cover our eyes, because we see our own contingency in that of these characters.

Whereas in most Hollywood action films the protagonists are almost universally invincible (see the filmography of Steven Seagal or Sylvester Stallone), surviving all manner of violence, time and time again, with nary a scratch or broken bone, the survival of Tarantino's heroes is never a given. In *Inglourious Basterds*, several sympathetic characters are shown to be skilled survivors and yet don't survive to the end of the film. Killing machine Stiglitz (Til Schweiger), British spy Archie Hicox (Michael Fassbender), even heroine Shosanna (Melanie Laurent) are no match, in the end, for the lethal force of a few bullets. In *Django Unchained*, bounty hunter protagonist Dr. Schultz (Chistoph Waltz) is also killed off by an unceremonious shotgun blast near the end of the film.

Even when Tarantino's characters seem super-human in their skill with weaponry and bad-guy thwarting, they are revealed to be decidedly breakable and prone to the same pangs of embodiment as the rest of us. Django (Jamie Foxx) is incredibly vulnerable at various points in *Django Unchained*. As the film opens he is in chains as a slave, ankles bloodied and whip scars all over his back. Later in the film he is hung naked, upside down, captive of one of Calvin Candie's henchmen.

Uma Thurman's character (the Bride) in *Kill Bill* is arguably the fiercest, most powerful figure in any of Tarantino's films. And yet even she has a body that is easily broken. As *Vol. 1* opens we see a close-up of her bloodied, beaten face, before she is shot at point blank range and left for dead. We then see her wake up from a four-year coma, struggling to regain movement in her atrophied legs and feet. In *Vol. 2* we again see her shot and left for dead, this time buried alive in a wooden casket. The agonizing, claustrophobic scene once again shows her body's vulnerability. She screams, cries, kicks, and writhes in the confined space, ultimately punching her way out (though not without bloodying her knuckles).

Tarantino's insistence on the vulnerability and mortality of his characters is just one aspect of his high view of human embodiment. The director's camera also focuses quite a bit of attention on the movement, gestures, and mannerisms of his characters. Whether it's the walking of Pam Grier at the opening of *Jackie Brown* (1997), the famous dance scene between Uma Thurman and John Travolta in *Pulp Fiction*, or the way Leonardo DiCaprio holds a cigarette in *Django Unchained*, Tarantino seems to relish the way his actors embody their characters. His films are always full of close-ups on faces and frequently on hands and feet.

You'll also notice that a preferred camera vantage point in Tarantino films is from below, looking up at characters looking down.[1] From this perspective, actors loom large in the frame, appearing imposing, powerful, dominant. It's a visual way of communicating the grandeur of the human form, while also hinting at its ever-present vulnerability (e.g. looking up at Ordell and Beaumont from the perspective of a car trunk in *Jackie Brown*, followed soon after by Ordell's unceremonious killing of Beaumont).

In all of this, Tarantino is establishing a decidedly incarnational aesthetic. He is at least as interested in the embodiment and fleshiness of his characters as he is with what they say and the ideas they espouse. Even in their dialogue with one another, which often dominates long, 10- to 20-minute stretches of his films, Tarantino seems less interested in the substance of *what* they are discussing (which is often random and mundane, and only about plot exposition when necessary) than with the fact that they *are* discussing. Talking is something humans do. It is the chattiness itself that seems more interesting to Tarantino than the topics of chatter.

Tarantino's films celebrate the human-ness of humanity: the way we talk, move, dance, fight, sweat, bleed, and die. And also the way that we eat.

---

[1] See video essay "Tarantino // From Below," by user kogonada (February 27, 2012): http://vimeo.com/37540504

"Royale With Cheese": Food in the Films of Tarantino

Food and drink are noticeably present in the films of Quentin Tarantino, and they often establish themselves very early on in the films. Both *Reservoir Dogs* and *Pulp Fiction* open in diner-type restaurants, with characters dialoguing over coffee, beer, and breakfast. The memorably tense opening scene of *Inglourious Basterds* features the most ominous milk drinking in the history of cinema, followed later by the white-knuckle scene of Shosanna and Hans Landa eating a delicious-looking apple strudel with cream.

Who can forget the famous dinner scene in *Pulp Fiction*, at Jackrabbit Slim's, where John Travolta and Uma Thurman order menu items like the Douglas Sirk steak (prepared "bloody as hell"), the Durwood Kirby burger, and the $5 Martin and Lewis shake? Or the climactic encounter between the Bride and Bill in *Kill Bill: Vol. 2*, which prominently features Bill making a sandwich, complete with mayo, mustard, and Bimbo bread *sans* crust? Or the fabulously wrought tavern scene in *Inglourious Basterds*, where beer, biersteins, and bubbly abound?

It's one thing to include food as a prop in a film; almost every film has it somewhere, usually sitting on tables uneaten during dialogue scenes. But Tarantino's camera takes special notice of food. It pauses for a close-up on the delectable apple strudel and then pauses again when the waiter plops a dollop of cream on it. In *Jackie Brown* the camera takes special notice of coffee being poured into a mug. In *Django* the camera takes a moment to zoom in on Dr. Schultz pouring a golden, refreshing looking draft beer and then scraping off the excess head.

Sometimes food is just a conversation piece, as in the famous "Royale with Cheese" dialogue scene between Jules (Samuel L. Jackson) and Vincent (Travolta) in *Pulp Fiction*. Other times it is a character's trademark, as in Ordell's cocktail of choice (the screwdriver) in *Jackie*

Brown, or Calvin Candie's white cake and coconut cocktail, or Stuntman Mike's greasy nachos in *Death Proof*. Frequently food is associated with the unique ethnicity or piece of pop culture being mined at the moment: sushi in the Tokyo sequence of *Kill Bill: Vol. 1*; rice during the Pai Mei training sequence in *Kill Bill: Vol. 2;* apple strudel with the Nazis and 33-year Scotch with Lt. Hicox in *Inglourious Basterds*; sweet tea and bourbon cocktails in *Django Unchained*; and so on. Food is a vivid, sensuous part of culture, and Tarantino loves culture.

The Colors and Cultures of the World

In addition to the prominence of the body and the prevalence of food, another aspect of Tarantino's incarnational aesthetic is the director's general interest in visuals, color, buildings, costumes, and characters that reflect the vibrancy and diversity of human culture.

One way this is expressed is simply the ubiquity of literal color in Tarantino's films. It's everywhere. The man loves primary colors especially, whether yellow motorcycles (*Kill Bill: Vol. 1*), bright blue flight attendant uniforms (*Jackie Brown*), or red dresses (*Inglourious Basterds*) and (of course) flowing red blood. As if the colorful walls, cars, and costumes weren't enough, Tarantino also gives his characters and settings colorful names: Misters Brown, Blonde, Pink, White, and Orange in *Reservoir Dogs*, Vernita Green and the House of Blue Leaves in *Kill Bill: Vol. 1*, and then, of course, Jackie Brown.

Color also manifests itself in the diversity of ethnicities and nationalities represented. In the same way that Tarantino's films are each a pastiche of genres and pop culture anachronisms, they are also mosaics of race and nationality: Caucasian, Asian, African, Hispanic, Jew, Gentile, European, American, and so on. Tarantino makes a point of rendering this diversity in sharp relief. In *Kill Bill: Vol. 1* he calls attention to O-Ren Ishii's half-

Japanese and half-Chinese background, as well as Sophie Fatale's French/ Japanese heritage. In *Inglourious Basterds* he exaggerates the Britishness of his British characters (see Mike Myers and Michael Fassbender in the "Operation Kino" briefing scene), the Frenchness of his French characters (see cinephile Shosanna looking bohemian while reading and smoking in a Paris café) and the Germanness of his German characters (see the sloshy beer-drinking of the Nazis in the Tavern scene). Tarantino's characters' names also reflect this celebration of culture at its most whimsically exaggerated. You can almost smell the magnolia blossoms in a Southern belle name like Lara Lee Candie-Fitzwilly (*Django*), and you can almost picture the dirndl dress and blonde braids in a Bavarian name like Bridget von Hammersmark.

Tarantino's globetrotting films relish the anthropology of place, even if it is "place" as filtered through the fantasies and genres of cinema and pulp fiction. His films are about Los Angeles through the lens of hardboiled crime novels and 1950s Hollywood; Tokyo through the lens of anime, samurai, and yakuza crime films; Europe through the lens of spy and war films; the American frontier as filtered through John Ford and spaghetti westerns, and so on. It's not that Tarantino isn't enamored with the places and cultures themselves—he is—but he's even more enamored with the way that cinema has explored, exaggerated, remixed, and mythologized them.

Tarantino's love of place and culture also manifests itself on a more material level in his love of buildings, production design, and memorable set pieces. The director's preference for episodic narrative lends itself to the building of elaborate scenes and sequences (or "chapters" as he often calls them) that are supported by the scaffolding of memorable physical spaces. From *Pulp Fiction* we vividly remember the bright colors and Hollywood pastiche of Jackrabbit Slim's. From *Inglourious Basterds* we recall the "Operation Kino" tavern and the movie theater that is the setting for the film's explosive climax. In *Django* we have the epic "Candieland" plantation, where the final fifty or so minutes of the film play out (before the plantation is spectacularly blown to smithereens).

In a manner similar to that of Wes Anderson, Tarantino often takes time to explore the spaces of these set pieces with his camera, floating through walls, above ceilings, and below floors to immerse the viewer in the space. In the House of Blue Leaves in *Kill Bill: Vol. 1*, Tarantino establishes the space at length by following various characters around, giving us a tour of the Japanese restaurant/bar before the bloodbath begins. A similar thing happens in the climactic chapter of *Inglourious Basterds*, when Tarantino's camera watches Shosanna put on her makeup and then (from above) sees her walking from her apartment out to the balcony overlooking the foyer bustling with doomed Nazi revelers.

Whether it be Col. Sanders white suits, cotton fields, and Spanish moss paying homage to the Antebellum South, the music of Ennio Morricone celebrating Sergio Leone spaghetti westerns, or prolonged car chases glorying in 1970s grindhouse cinema, Tarantino's films are full of a vibrant, exuberant embrace of the eccentricities and diversities of human culture. More than just a celebration of pastiche, reflexivity, and irony, Tarantino's films are earnestly in love with the quirks, colors, songs, sayings, celebrities, superheroes, myths, histories, and imperfections of man. In this they are deeply human, grounded in the messiness of life, death, and everything in between.

What is the Incarnation Anyway?

All of the above is an attempt to outline the incarnational aspects of Tarantino's films, but what do we mean by "Incarnation"?

The Christian theology of the Incarnation begins with the notion that Jesus Christ, as the second person of the Trinity, became flesh when he was born of the Virgin Mary. It's the idea that Jesus Christ was fully divine but also fully human. He wasn't just an ethereal deity or super-human God-man. He sweated, bled, talked, walked, cried, and yelled like the rest of us. He experienced pain. He died a brutal, bloody death, agonizing in pain throughout the torture and execution, just like so many Tarantino characters do.

Also like so many Tarantino characters, Jesus ate and drank. He "came eating and drinking," notes Luke 7:34. What kind of God needs food and drink? As if to emphasize the human-ness of Jesus and his need to participate in such banal human activities as eating and drinking, the Gospels actually seem to highlight this part of Jesus' life. In the Gospel of Luke, there are numerous mentions of Jesus fellowshipping at the tables of others: at a banquet in the house of Levi (Luke 5:27–39), at dinner in the house of Simon the Pharisee (7:36–50), breaking bread at Bethsaida (9:10–17), enjoying hospitality at the home of Martha (10:38–42) or Zacchaeus (19:1–10), dining at the homes of Pharisees (11:37–54, 14:1–24), culminating in the breaking of bread at Emmaus (24:30), in which the disciples' "eyes were opened" (24:31) and "he was known to them" (24:35) in the act of the breaking of bread. Jesus loved doing ministry over long meals. Food was part of his "mission strategy," notes Tim Chester in *A Meal With Jesus*. "He did evangelism and discipleship round a table with some grilled fish, a loaf of bread, and a pitcher of wine."[2]

When we eat, we are thus participating in an activity that God incarnate participated in daily. Jesus didn't just talk about eating. He ate. He ate bread, fish, honey, and figs, among other things we also eat.

---

[2] Tim Chester, *A Meal With Jesus* (Wheaton: Crossway, 2011), 13.

The reality of his human fleshiness should cause us to feel the majesty of his incarnation all the more clearly. Never is this more evident than in the Eucharist, the very physical ritual of eating bread and drinking wine, which brings us right back there to the Upper Room and the "he came eating and drinking" Savior who trod the same physical world as we do and ate of the same grains and grapes. As Jamie Smith points out in *Desiring the Kingdom*, the "rhythms and rituals" of our Christian habits of worship "invoke and feed off of our embodiment and traffic in the stuff of a material world: water, bread, wine, each of which point us to their earthy emergence: the curvature of the riverbed, the shimmering fields that give forth grain, the grapes that hint of a unique *terroir.*"[3]

The act of worship, like the Christ we worship, is thus bodily material, concrete, earthy. But it is also cultural. We see this as well in the Eucharist:

> The Lord's Supper does not only hallow and sanctify nature's biological processes that bring forth grain and grapes and compel us to eat and drink. After all, it's not wheat and grapes that are on the table; it's bread and wine. These are not naturally occurring phenomena; they are the fruit of culture, the products of human making. In blessing the bread and giving thanks for it, Jesus not only hallows the stuff of the earth, but he also hallows the stuff of our hands. The affirmation of the goodness of creation includes not just the furniture of "nature" but also the whole panoply of cultural phenomena that humanity, by its cultural labor, teases out of creation.[4]

Jesus wasn't acultural. Just as he did not shun his embodiment, so

---

[3] James K.A. Smith, *Desiring the Kingdom* (Grand Rapids: Baker Academic, 2009), 139.
[4] Ibid., 200.

also did he not downplay his culture. On the contrary, throughout his ministry he incorporated culture in his parables and teachings, drawing upon "various [cultural] artifacts (coins, clothing, implements, tools), conventions (language, holy days, instructional methods), and institutions (kingdoms, marriage, civil and religious authority structures) as illustrations or vehicles through which to assert his unique callings and pursue the unfolding of the kingdom of God."[5]

What this means for Christians is that the world—in all its muddy, harsh, jagged physicality and cultural color and oddity—is not just kindle for an eventual fire; it's the chosen medium of God's revelation. In Christ, God came to meet us on our own turf. He ate our food, suffered the same temptations, and thirsted after the same water as he toiled under the same sun. We must thus adopt a sacramental understanding of the world: "that the physical, material stuff of creation and embodiment is the means by which God's grace meets us and gets hold of us."[6]

Towards an Incarnational Aesthetic of Cinema

So what, then, might an incarnational aesthetic look like in cinema? It is my contention that the aesthetic of Quentin Tarantino gets pretty close. In labeling Tarantino's films "incarnational," the question of whether or not Tarantino believes in Jesus Christ's physical life, ministry, and death is secondary to the fact that his view of the world is decidedly sacramental. As we have seen, his cinema embraces the fleshiness of flesh, the embodiment of bodies (both at their most magnificent and frail), the intensity of man's contingency, the glories of quotidian life (namely eating and drinking), and a visceral manifestation of the colors, rituals, and icons of culture.

---

[5] T. M. Moore, Culture Matters: A Call for Consensus on Christian Cultural Engagement (Grand Rapids: Brazos Press, 2007), 20.
[6] Smith, 141.

Some might argue that Tarantino's films are more about artifice than realism, which may very well be true. The exaggerated violence (does anyone bleed like Sophie Fatale bleeds when her arm is cut off in *Kill Bill: Vol. 1*?) and over-the-top pop culture pastiche often evoke a world that feels more like a celebration of movies than a celebration of life. But even a slightly off-kilter, hyperbolized world can still be a visceral expression of the human-ness of humanity and the vibrancy of culture. Even though we know Tarantino's films are fake (they often call special attention to their fakery), they still pack a physical punch: they get our blood boiling, our hearts racing, our senses heightened. Why? Because they understand cinema's unique power to zoom in on the incarnate wonders and horrors of this life.

Other films and filmmakers embrace cinema's artifice and yet fail to engage the bodily senses in the way Tarantino does. Advances in technologies such as CGI (computer-generated imagery) have allowed filmmakers to create "more realistic" things like explosions, dinosaurs, aliens, robot war machines, and cities being obliterated by some combination of natural disasters or man-made carnage. Yet ironically, CGI further distances the viewer from the real-ness of reality and drains cinema of its visceral power. Granted, CGI has made large-scale fantasy and superhero action films possible (see Peter Jackson's *Lord of the Rings* or Joss Whedon's *The Avengers*), and many of those films have done a fair job balancing in-the-flesh action with CGI theatrics. But in general, CGI creates unnecessary and distracting fakery that saps a film of its incarnational beauty. It's one thing for filmmakers to use CGI to render creatures that do not exist in reality (dragons, dinosaurs, King Kong, whatever that beast-out-of-the-sea was in *Cloverfield*), but why create CGI versions of things that do exist, such as deer (see *I Am Legend*), gophers (see *Indiana Jones and the Crystal Skull*) or humans (see *The Matrix: Reloaded*)? Celebrating fantasy and artifice is fine, but why not use flesh-in-blood actors, real-life built sets, makeup, costumes, and good-old-fashioned fake blood rather than digital replicas? Tarantino goes this route, and his films are better for it.

"The only time you're allowed to use CGI," noted Tarantino in a 2013 interview with the *Daily Mail*, "is where you would kill the actor if you did the stunt for real. Otherwise, if you want to impress me as a viewer, you've got to do it."[7] Tarantino goes to extremes to ensure the "realism" of the action he is shooting, such as famously shooting the high-speed climactic chase in *Death Proof* with stuntwoman Zoe Bell on the roof of the car *for real*. In *Django Unchained*, for example, Tarantino went to extremes to capture the coldness of the wintertime opening sequence:

> I needed it to be so cold you could see the actors' breath; I didn't want to add the breath later. It was -8F. People were collapsing, going face down in the snow. People would start crying and were having nervous breakdowns because it was so brutally, frigidly cold. But if I can shoot the real thing, I will.[8]

Tarantino's insistence on going to great lengths to shoot things "for real" may likely be more time-consuming, expensive, and rigorous for actors, but it pays dividends in its affective force on the viewer. Tarantino's sweaty, bloody, bone-crunching foregrounding of embodiment is far more riveting to watch than the dead-eye characters of CGI action getting battered in digitally altered ways (see *Avatar*, or almost everything Zack Snyder has directed).

---

[7] Quentin Tarantino, "Go ahead, take your best shot: Quentin Tarantino on the story behind his Western *Django Unchained*," *Mail Online*, January 12, 2013, http://www.dailymail.co.uk/home/moslive/article-2260197/Quentin-Tarantino-Django-Unchained-The-story-Western.html.
[8] Ibid.

Tarantino isn't the only one making these sorts of hyper-embodied, physical, incarnational films, of course. Martin Scorsese (excerpt perhaps in *Hugo*), Kathryn Bigelow, David Cronenberg, and Nicholas Winding Refn are all known for their visceral violence and bodily carnage. Filmmakers like Wes Anderson, Sofia Coppola, and David Lynch share Tarantino's love of colors, costumes, set pieces, sound design, and cultural iconography. Then there are those filmmakers — like Terrence Malick, Werner Herzog, and Kelly Reichardt — who focus on human embodiment as just one among many material phenomena populating the natural universe. These filmmakers and their films, like Tarantino's, are as interested in material ambience as cerebral exploration.

In contrast to the incarnational cinema of which Tarantino (among others) is exemplar, there are other filmmakers whose cinema favors the more cerebral, ethereal, almost disembodied end of the spectrum. Filmmakers like Michael Haneke, Lars von Trier, Ingmar Bergman, and Woody Allen tend to create chatty, idea-rich films that downplay materiality. Lars von Trier's *Dogville* (2003) and *Manderlay* (2005) are so much about the words and ideas that the action actually takes place on a soundstage, with no sets and few props to speak of. Woody Allen's films, while often set in locations (Manhattan, Paris, London, Rome) that become characters unto themselves, are also similarly skewed toward ideas and dialogue rather than visual, aural, or physical impact.

Still other directors manage a nice balance between the material and cerebral. The repertoire of Richard Linklater is perhaps the best example of a cinema that is at once intellectual and idea-rich (his films are largely people chatting with one another about existential matters) while also cinematic and material. The way his camera treats the beautiful buildings, boulevards, and iconic spaces of Vienna, Paris, and Greece in the *Before*[9] films almost

---

[9] Before Sunrise (1995), Before Sunset (2004), and Before Midnight (2013)

upstages the compelling dialogue that is the series' ostensible star.

But if we are talking about a bona fide incarnational cinema—one in which embodiment, materiality, and the richness of human culture is foregrounded and integral to the film's overall impact—the cinema of Tarantino is second-to-none.

It's not necessarily that such a style is inherently better, more effective, or more cinematic than other styles (though one could argue this… perhaps in another essay), but perhaps it is a style that our increasingly disembodied, digitized world needs more than ever. At a time in history when formerly ubiquitous artifacts of analog culture (books, handwritten letters, physical music records, to name a few) are rendered obsolete, when face-to-face, incarnational community is being replaced by screen-to-screen communication, and when globalization continues to gradually erode cultural specificity, Tarantino fights tooth-and-nail to preserve the irreplaceable beauty of life incarnate. His cinema rattles us, shakes us, sensitizes us to the glories of the fleshiness of flesh and the earthiness of earth.

For Christians—who have sometimes been prone to Gnostic tendencies to deemphasize the body and its attendant this-worldly habitats and cultures—the incarnational aesthetic of Quentin Tarantino is a helpful reminder that medium and message are intimately linked. And in the case of the gospel we profess, the medium is material: a physical man who entered a dusty, rocky terrain; who ministered to others around tables with fish, bread, and wine; whose body was broken, battered, buried, and ultimately resurrected; and who lives today not in philosophical ideas or discourse but in the lives of his human followers, the church, the body of Christ.

RIDDLED BY BULLETS: THE MYSTERY OF DIVINE INTERVENTION IN *PULP FICTION*

Jonathan L. Walls

" We should be fuckin' dead, man. **"**

Multiple bullet holes riddle the wall just behind the standing figures of Jules Winnfield and Vincent Vega. Seconds earlier, a "hand-cannon" wielding man had burst out of the bathroom unexpectedly and unloaded at them from point blank range. In this situation, one would normally expect to be dead as fried chicken. But this is Quentin Tarantino's universe, and in the Tarantino-verse, things don't usually play out as expected. Indeed, Jules and Vincent remain unscathed, and it is this event that sets their lives on two very different paths, though they will end the same way.

As great storytellers have the ability to do, Tarantino and *Pulp Fiction* co-writer Roger Avary channel two distinct, and even opposing, voices of our culture through the characters of Jules and Vincent and this series of events. Jules, played brilliantly by Samuel L. Jackson, believes that in their seemingly inexplicable escape from certain death, he has witnessed a miracle. Vincent, portrayed perfectly by John Travolta, sees things differently. Still shell-shocked, the two share this exchange:

> **Jules:** This was divine intervention. Do you know what divine intervention is?
>
> **Vincent:** I think so. That means that God came down from heaven and stopped the bullets?
>
> **Jules:** That's right. That's exactly what it means. God came down from heaven and stopped these mother fuckin' bullets.

Vincent, on the other hand, believes that they witnessed nothing more than a random, albeit unlikely, occurrence. His half-hearted admission (which he later denies) that they had indeed witnessed a miracle serves only to pacify Jules so they can leave the crime scene and continue their "theological discussion," as Vince puts it, in their car rather than "in a jailhouse with the cops." Satisfied, Jules allows them to leave, now with Marvin (the mysterious man in the corner of the apartment, who seems to be familiar with Jules) in tow.

Mere minutes later, in the car, the gun in Vincent's hand will unexpectedly go off and send a bullet right into the face of poor Marvin, splattering both Vincent and Jules with Marvin's blood and brain, temporarily sidetracking their heated disagreement about the nature of miracles.

Perhaps it's another miracle that Jules and Vincent find a safe house, get cleaned up, and, aided by The Wolf (famously played by Harvey

Keitel), dispose of poor Marvin's body without attracting the cops or causing any domestic unrest for Jimmy, the unsuspecting acquaintance whose home they seize as a base of operations.

If nothing else, the Marvin incident shows that miracles, or freak occurrences, can cut both ways. One minute a gunman, feet away and with intent to kill, misses multiple times from point blank range, sparing Jules and Vincent's lives, murderers whose line of work suggest that they are likely to eventually meet their deaths in a similar fashion anyway. Minutes later, the gun in Vincent's hand mysteriously discharges when it shouldn't, and Marvin, a man who, as far as we know, is completely innocent, meets his demise. Vincent, after all, is a skilled and experienced gunman and insists he doesn't know how or why the gun goes off. Perhaps Tarantino aligns these two events in such close proximity to suggest that the seemingly incredible events of the universe are indeed random; that is, no greater intelligent force can be attributed to them. On the other hand, perhaps Tarantino merely means to suggest that the very thing that makes miracles the extraordinary things they are is the fact that they occur in a sometimes arbitrary world, *but they still really happen.* It's a question worth exploring, as the reality (or non-reality) of miracles and divine intervention suggest two very different but important things about our universe and, as Jules and Vincent will show us, how we live in it.

American philosopher William Hasker says in *The Cambridge Companion to Theology* that there are

> ...four major types of variables that determine the shape of a doctrine of providence. There are the divine intentions—what God is doing or trying to do. There is divine power, God's ability to bring about what he desires. There is divine knowledge, the kind and extent of which conditions the exercise of his power. And there is human freedom: to

what extent do human beings (and other rational creatures, if there are any) possess the capacity either to freely respond and cooperate with God's intentions, or to resist them?[10]

Miracles and *direct* divine intervention, like the bullets incident in *Pulp Fiction*, are one way in which God brings about what he desires, and his power, knowledge of the future, and human beings' free will all play major roles in how we view the nature and identity of such acts in our world. But before we can jump into all of that, we need to get something straight. What exactly constitutes a miracle, anyway?

Webster's Dictionary Defines a Miracle as…Just Kidding

After a wild morning dealing with the Marvin situation, Jules and Vincent finally find a few moments to relax over breakfast in a diner and, continuing their banter over the nature of the bullets incident, Jules prompts Vincent:

> **Jules:** What is a miracle, Vincent?
> **Vincent:** An act of God.
> **Jules:** And what is an act of God?
> **Vincent:** When God makes the impossible possible.

In our hyperbole-prone modern vernacular, the term "miracle" is often used to describe events that are amazing or unlikely, such as an underdog victory in the sports world or the survival of a highly dangerous situation like a violent car wreck. Furthermore, "miracle" is often used to describe events that are not only natural, but common, everyday occurrences, like childbirth. The truest understanding of the term "miracle," however, is closer to Vincent's, whether he believes

---

[10] William Hasker, "Eternity and Providence" in *The Cambridge Companion to Christian Philosophical Theology*, ed. Charles Talliaferro and Chad Meister (Cambridge: Cambridge University Press, 2010), 86.

they're real or not: An occurrence that alters, breaks, or goes above and beyond the natural order, having been brought forth by some sort of deity or supernatural power.

So how do we know where to begin with these varying definitions of the term? Luckily, a very distinct fork in the road presents itself here to clear things up a bit. We'll call the first split of the fork the "Vincent path," the path designated for those inclined not to believe in any supernatural power. Now, to be fair to Vincent, he never explicitly denies the possibility or existence of miracles. However, he obviously utterly denies that the bullets incident was a miracle, and registers great skepticism toward the concept as a whole, more than once remarking that unusual stuff "just happens." Therefore, it is safe to assume that Vincent represents those who disbelieve in the phenomenon of miracles, or who are at the very least highly skeptical. For Vincent and those on his path, the possibility for any miracle in the truest definition disappears. These people may still believe in "soft" miracles in the two more inclusive senses mentioned above, of course, but true miracles are out of the question.

It's worth noting, however, that it does seem puzzling in some sense that such awe would be so consistently provoked by ordinary events like childbirth. Childbirth is, after all, completely explainable from a biological standpoint, and is furthermore woven into the very nature of our existence, suggesting that it should carry an inextricable air of the everyday and common. Yet the experience can, and often does, feel life changing, even transcendent. Of course this can all be written off to mere misleading feelings or lack of scientific knowledge, but then again, one can make a strong argument that the very existence of the universe is a bona fide miracle,[11] so maybe there is something to all of this "miracle of life" business after all.

---

[11] The term *Creatio Ex-Nihilo*, which means "Creation out of nothing," reflects the intuition that it is hard to believe that matter of any sort can come to being from "nothing," and that only a Creator of some sort, who is not made of matter and therefore not dependent on matter to exist, must have the power to create "ex nihilo," or "out of nothing."

For the second group, who take the "Jules path," miracles are at least *possible.* For them, if there is a God to perform miracles (which they believe there is), miracles are at least in the cards. But understanding exactly what they involve is still at issue. For all of us on the Jules path, C. S. Lewis offers a caveat that applies even to the truest sense of the term "miracle," and suggests that the common, theistic understanding of this definition still falls a bit short.

In his aptly titled book *Miracles*, Lewis argues that a miracle requires outside involvement from God, but it does *not* break the laws of nature. Lewis says, "A miracle is emphatically not an event without cause or without results. Its cause is the activity of God: its results follow according to Natural Law."[12]

So, since the Christian believes that the very beginning of nature sprang from the lips of God, Lewis reckons a miracle falls in line with that as well.[13] However, this is not an attempt to neutralize specific miracles that take place in a defined moment in time and paint them into the mural of ordinary history. Lewis explains that a miracle will still require God to get directly involved and alter the course of nature, that is, alter the way nature *would* have gone (according to the original laws of nature, which He himself set up) *had He not intervened.* It is after this occurrence, however, that whatever was affected by a given miracle will thence fall directly back in line with the original laws of nature.

> If God annihilates or creates or deflects a unit of matter He has created a new situation at that point. Immediately all Nature domiciles this new situation, makes it at home in her realm, adapts all other events to it. It finds itself conforming to all the laws. If God creates a miraculous spermatozoon in the body of a virgin, it does

---

[12] C. S. Lewis, *Miracles* (New York: HarperCollins, 2001), 95.
[13] Ibid., 96.

not proceed to break any laws. The laws at once take it over. Nature is ready. Pregnancy follows, according to all the normal laws, and nine months later a child is born.[14]

Lewis further elaborates the point by giving us a few more examples:

> Miraculous wine will intoxicate, miraculous conception will lead to pregnancy, inspired books will suffer all the ordinary processes of textual corruption, miraculous bread will be digested. The divine art of miracle is not an art of suspending the pattern to which events conform but of feeding new events into that pattern.[15]

The bullets incident certainly seems to fit Lewis' definition of a miracle, at least. God "deflects a unit of matter" (or multiple units, in this case) when He redirects the bullets around Vincent and Jules. Indeed, some bullet holes seen in the wall are placed directly behind Jules so that they would have had to travel directly through Jules' abdomen, or around him, in order to get there. And, according to Jules at least, it does signify direct involvement of God. He tells Vincent, "Whether or not what we experienced was an according-to-Hoyle miracle is insignificant, but what is significant is I felt the touch of God. God got involved."

God feeds an extraordinary new event into the normal pattern of Jules' life, and as a result, a fresh pattern emerges.

Too Important for a Footnote

Before we continue, I feel we must clear the air, as there is a rather large elephant in the room that must be shooed out. That elephant, as is so often the case, is The Problem of Evil. Every tough theological issue swings back this way at one point or another, as The Problem of Evil is, itself, the single most difficult theological hurdle for those who believe

---

[14] Ibid., 94.
[15] Ibid., 95.

in a good God. However, we can't get much meat out of a debate on the existence or purpose of miracles and divine intervention if we are hung up on The Problem of Evil, because it would be like discussing the nature of the Trinity without basic belief in God. Of course, there is a time and place for every discussion, but for us to have a chance of getting anywhere near the core of miracles and divine intervention, we must assume some common ground. I have no wish to brush the issue aside or dodge it. On the contrary, I believe that a strong case can and has been made for the rationality of belief in a good God in a universe that contains suffering, and I urge anyone who is unconvinced on the topic to look further into the matter. So, while we will grab an item or two off of the multi-layered and crowded shelf of The Problem of Evil issue before the end of this essay, we can hardly engage that issue in depth here. Let us soldier on with the assumption that there can be an all powerful, good God, even in our broken world full of pain.[16]

Water into Wine? Why Not?

If we accept Lewis' definition of miracles, we are free to move on to the issue of why God may have reason to intervene and bring miracles about, which is a supremely perplexing issue. And more perplexing (and vexing) still: why does He often *not* do so? Moments before storming out of the bathroom, weapon ablaze, the gunman who shoots at Jules and Vincent prays, "Oh God please, I don't want to die." When his clip empties harmlessly into the wall, Jules and Vincent don't hesitate to gun him down alongside his already fallen apartment-mates. So it would seem, in this case, God ignores one prayer and

---

[16] For readers who would like more, see C. S. Lewis, *The Problem of Pain* (San Francisco: HarperSanFrancisco, 2001). If you want something more academic, see Marilyn McCord Adams, *Horrendous Evils and the Goodness of God* (Ithaca: Cornell University Press, 1999); Philip Tallon, *The Poetics of Evil* (New York: Oxford University Press, 2012).

I also comment more deeply, though hardly extensively, on the problem of evil in my essay "Trouble in the Golden Realm: Ganondorf and Hyrule's Problem of Evil in Ocarina of Time," in *The Legend of Zelda and Theology* (Los Angeles: Gray Matter Books, 2011).

answers a non-existent one. The reason God may have for this can't be known for sure, but in this case, as we will see, the apparent fruits of His decision come to be known in time.

Now, taking one group of men who apparently knowingly involved themselves with the mob (the men in the apartment) and pitting them against the mob itself (represented by Jules and Vincent) for the benefits of God's assistance seems to give God a lot of morally gray elbow room to work. However, an instance where a pure desire is brought before God by a normal, law-abiding citizen who generally respects his fellow man makes things a bit trickier. For example, why would God heal one disease-stricken child and not another? After all, as most Christians would agree, disease, misery, and pain are not God's desire for us.

One common answer, based on an overly simplistic misreading of a number of Bible verses, suggests that enough faith, coupled with the right type of prayer, can and will yield the desired results every time, at least when something pure is requested.[17] In essence, according to this view, there *is* no problem to figure out regarding the presence or lack of divine intervention in our broken world. According to this line of thinking, the issue is easily explained by the amount and strength of faith and prayer involved in a given situation. As such, if the people praying for disease-stricken child "A" have enough faith, that child will be healed. If those praying for disease-stricken child "B" do not have enough faith, however, God will not intervene, and Child B will not be saved from death.

Circumstantial evidence would certainly seem to suggest otherwise, as numerous prayers, offered with seemingly genuine faith and for perfectly righteous desires (as the riddance of disease for an innocent child would surely be), have gone unanswered[18] time and again over

---

[17] Matthew 21:21, John 15:7, Luke 8:50, Matthew 17:14-20
[18] "Unanswered" at least in the sense that the specific requested result, namely, the healing of the child, does not come about.

the years. But those who hold fast to this way of thinking will insist that this circumstantial evidence is lacking, as we could never prove that one group's set of prayers and faith is as genuine as others, despite how much one may wish or believe it to be.

However, this belief runs into a surprisingly simple and evident roadblock that renders it highly dubious: Everyone dies. Everyone. Even those whose diseases are miraculously healed, die. If a grieving family member of a disease victim insists that disease is not God's plan, this same family member must also remember that neither is death God's original or ultimate plan for us. If you believe that any disease can be prayed away through faith, then so too must death itself. If not, we find ourselves picking and choosing which sin-induced maladies God ought to save us from, and assigning an age at which it finally becomes "God's will" for us to be allowed to die. It is hard to avoid an arbitrary answer here, and this is a serious problem for this view.

It may *feel* less sad for a loved one to die at an old age than it would for one to die, disease-ridden, at a young age, and this feeling is perfectly reasonable, of course, but death, even occurring in one's sleep at age 105, is just as much of a breach on God's vision for Eden as is violent death in the prime of youth. Our cells decay and our hearts stop beating no matter the cause, so to suggest that God saving us from one kind of earthly death only to leave us quite helpless to another is highly suspect.

God *has* saved us from eternal death, which is at the heart of the gospel, but the hard reality remains that we must go through earthly death first. There is no imperative on God to perform miracles to preserve our lives in the meantime, and the nature of our sinful, fallen world means that we will all die.

But He Does Do Miracles Sometimes, Right?

Just because God has no imperative to save us from painful and horrific worldly perils like disease does not mean that He can't, or won't, on some occasions. As Tarantino suggests with the "bullets" scene, God does sometimes intervene, even if His reasons can't be fully understood. However, it's necessary to adjust our line of thinking on what such miracles achieve. As pointed out, if God miraculously heals someone from a deadly disease, it is not done to save that person from the death we all must face. Still, it's reasonable to believe that such acts may be done as a chance for God to show His power and goodness, and likely shift history in such a way that God's plan is brought forth.

If we look at the way the bullets incident affects Jules' life, we get a glimpse into one of the possible reasons that God may have for bringing about miracles. In the car directly after the bullets incident, only moments before Marvin's death, Jules is so shaken by the bullets incident that he has already made the decision to leave his life of crime. He quickly arrives at this resolution, but Vincent, ever the skeptic, finds this new resolve absurd. Of course, the conversation is quickly derailed by Marvin's unexpected death.

Later, in the diner scene, if we remember, Jules and Vincent's conversation rounds back to the bullets incident. Here in the safety of the diner and with more time to debate, Vincent renounces his empty admission from earlier and dismisses the phenomenon by saying, "No, [it was] the miracle *you* witnessed. I witnessed a freak occurrence." Not to be deterred, Jules then reveals that he meant what he said in the car about leaving "the life" (of crime and violence), and that he will dedicate his existence to God. He will simply walk the earth, "like Caine, from Kung Fu."

Vincent: How long do you intend to walk the earth?

Jules: Until God puts me where He wants me to be.

Vincent: And what if He don't do that?

Jules: If it takes forever then I'll walk forever.

As Jules lays out his plan to leave his and Vincent's chosen vocation, Vincent grows increasingly vexed, from skeptical to annoyed to patronizing. He eventually tells Jules that the life he claims to seek, one of a wandering nomad of sorts, will reduce him to little more than a bum. Clearly, Vincent, in his non-belief, will choose a different path from Jules, one of continuing crime and violence. As Tarantino understands, what we believe about God, and whether (and how) He interacts with us, matters.

Minutes later, "Pumpkin" and "Honey Bunny", two characters we met earlier in the film in what we now see to have been this very same scene, will pull out their guns and attempt to hold up the diner. Evidently, it's just one of those days for Jules and Vincent.

After a few tense moments, Pumpkin will foolishly stick his gun in Jules' face, who will easily disarm Pumpkin, hold him at gunpoint, and tell him about his newly found outlook on life, while the other diners lie on the floor, scared witless. (Vincent has made a timely visit to the restroom and has not yet returned.) Honey Bunny naturally leaps to Pumpkin's aid, pointing her gun at Jules and promising that if he hurts Pumpkin, she will kill him. Fortunately, that end may not be in the cards, as Jules says: "Normally both your asses would be dead as fuckin' fried chicken, but you happened to pull this shit while I'm in a transitional period and I don't want to kill you. I want to help you."

Jules then voluntarily surrenders the contents of his wallet, around $1,500, to Pumpkin, who Jules has taken to calling "Ringo," even though Jules could easily keep it for himself and simply give the two would-be robbers their marching orders. However, Vincent, who has recently emerged from the bathroom to find this bizarre standoff in progress and now has his gun trained on Honey Bunny, states that he will shoot Pumpkin on principle if Jules gives him $1,500. But Jules, with his newfound sagacity and even disposition, to boot, simply responds: "I ain't givin' it to him, Vincent. I'm buying something for my money. You wanna know what I'm buying, Ringo? Your life. I'm giving you that money so I don't have to kill your ass."

Even in this situation, we clearly see the difference that belief in the miracle makes for our two protagonists. The Jules path and Vincent path lead to very different reactions to this event from their respective patrons.

Jules then recites his now famous made-up mishmash of Bible verses at Ringo, and we wonder if this is actually the end for Ringo, as we had earlier seen Jules recite this same bit to his two victims only moments before taking their lives. Jules says:

"The path of the righteous man is beset on all sides by the iniquities of the selfish and the tyranny of evil men. Blessed is he who in the name of charity and goodwill shepherds the weak through the valley of darkness, for he is truly his brother's keeper and the finder of lost children. And I will strike down upon thee, with great vengeance and furious anger, those who attempt to poison and destroy my brothers. And you will know I am The Lord when I lay my vengeance upon you." I been saying that shit for years, and if you heard it, that meant your ass. I never gave much thought to what it meant. I just thought it was some cold-blooded shit to say to a motherfucker before I popped a cap in his ass. But I saw some shit this morning [that] made me think twice. See now I'm thinking maybe it means: you're the evil man, and I'm the righteous man, and Mr. 9 mm here, he's the shepherd protecting my righteous ass in the valley of darkness. Or it could mean: you're the righteous man and I'm the shepherd, and it's the world that's evil and selfish. I'd like that. But that shit ain't the truth. The truth is: you're the weak, and I'm the tyranny of evil men. But I'm trying, Ringo. I'm trying real hard to be the shepherd."

He then releases Ringo and Honey Bunny, who, although leaving with their ill-gotten wares, also leave with a much higher outlook on life. In just a few short hours of Jules' life, we've already gotten a good picture of the effects of God's decision not only to spare Jules' life, but to do so in a miraculous way. A gangster has made the decision to abandon his life of crime, and two other criminals may well be rethinking their lives of crime as well.

It's tempting to observe the fact that Jules just *happens* to be in the right place at the right time to confront Ringo and Honey Bunny and couple that with the fact that Jules has *just* found a new outlook on life which very well may lead to reformation for the criminal couple, and call that a miracle. Jules certainly believes it is all part of God's plan. But that isn't the miracle, as Jules seems to understand. Recall that he says, "You *happened* to pull this shit while I'm in a transitional period."

Certainly the situation has the resin of God's influence all over it, but we must remember that every event and chance meeting is dependent on, and preceded by, an extraordinarily large number of occurrences that have made them possible. In fact, this truth is a major theme in the larger tale of *Pulp Fiction,* which includes more than the story of Jules and Vincent, and involves many other characters and outlandish events, all nearly as unlikely as this one. That is the nature of our world, and coincidences shouldn't be confused with miracles, even if they are set in motion by God. But it was the hand of God *stopping* those bullets that was the miracle; *that* was the moment when God threw a wrench into the natural course of things, *that* was the Holy incident that demanded action from the one who saw and believed, and it was *then* used to steer history to achieve God's will, even though from that point history continues once again to play out naturally, or as Lewis would say it, "Nature domiciles this new situation, makes it at home in her realm, adapts all other events to it."

Jules the Prophet?

All of this may sound good upon further scrutiny, but there is one giant issue that still seems to be hindering our bid to make any sense of divine intervention: If God is really all powerful, why would He ever feel the need to perform miracles at all? If He didn't want the bullets to pierce Jules and Vincent, why didn't he simply orchestrate the events of history so that the two hit-men were never in harm's way at all? Better yet, why doesn't God just orchestrate history in such a way that Jules, Vincent, Honey Bunny and Pumpkin never enter a life of crime at all? After all, He could use his infinite power and knowledge to make it so that they all lead lives of respect and love toward their fellow human beings. But if God is going to do that, why doesn't He just do that for *everyone*? And why doesn't He just eradicate disease and earthquakes and, as long as we're at it, why is there death at all?

Just like that we find ourselves back at The Problem of Evil. Unfortunately, not much has changed since a few pages ago, and we still haven't the time or space to dive fully into this issue. However, there is one large principle upon which the "answer" to the Problem of Evil hinges, which you will undoubtedly read all about if you delve into further study on the issue. This principle is Free Will, which is also fundamental in our understanding of divine intervention. If our choices are undetermined, and we are to be given Free Will, *genuine, libertarian* free will, which is vital for human beings to have the richest, best possible loving relationship with God,[19] then the possibility for sin *must* exist.

[19] This debate, which goes back a few hundred years, has become something of a hot top-

Given this view of the existence and importance of Free Will, theologian John Hick offers some insight into why God may choose to use miraculous violation of natural law rather than simply creating said laws so that His desired events are brought about. Hick says there are two main reasons, the first of which is to respond to human actions such as praying for something righteous, or even choosing bad actions. Hick elaborates as follows:

> An entirely regular world in which everything (apart from human choices) occurred in accordance with natural laws would not be a world in which God had any living interaction with human beings. It would be a world in which God had planned in advance what would happen if some human did this or if some human did that, and he would have so arranged natural laws that his responses to human actions and situations were built into the laws. He would never respond to the sins of humans as they committed them, their requests and acts of worship as they made them...[20]

Hick's second reason applies more to the "resins" of God's work that become apparent, much like the events that occur after the bullets incident.

> The second kind of reason why God might intervene in the natural order is just occasionally to put his signature on the work or teaching of some prophet in order to show that that work or teaching was God's work or teaching. In these cases God has reason to provide some (not necessarily enormously strong) evidence that he has violated natural

---

ic debate among Christian circles. A vocal but *decidedly* minority movement, commonly known as Calvinism, denies that humans possess libertarian free will (that our choices are truly up to us and could be made otherwise). This essay assumes the existence of libertarian free will, which is by far the most common belief stemming through all of church history. For further details, see Jerry L. Walls and Joseph R. Dongell, *Why I Am Not a Calvinist* (Downers Grove: InterVarsity Press, 2004). See especially chapters 3-4.

[20] John Hick, *Evil and the God of Love* (London: MacMillan and Company Limited, 1966), 284-286.

laws. He could do this by causing the prophet's life's work to achieve its goals or his teaching to be propagated on a large scale, as the result of an apparent violation of natural laws.[21]

Certainly God may decide for Himself when and when not to intervene, but according to this logic it is not hard to imagine why He would, at least sometimes. If our free will is to be upheld, these miraculous incidents may, in God's perfect wisdom, be the perfect opportunities to steer history the way He sees fit and to leave the evidence of his presence throughout history. Perhaps Jules has become a prophet tasked with spreading the news about God's wonder. He certainly wastes no time getting started.

Caught in the Middle

We've made some progress, it seems, in painting a picture of a world where it is at least *reasonable* to think that God would sometimes choose to intervene and perform miracles. However, if we recall, one variable that determines the shape of a doctrine of providence that has gone largely unmentioned up until now is Divine Knowledge. The following three options give us a good, albeit broad, look at the spectrum of contemporary thought on this issue.

Imagine Tarantino with his script for *Pulp Fiction*, the day before principal photography began. He already knew what would happen to Jules and Vincent on that fateful day in the apartment, as the timeline for his own fictional universe was laid out before him in black and white. In fact, Tarantino even lets us, the viewers, in on a little of his omniscience, as he chooses to tell the story in a non-linear fashion. As such, at the end of the movie, when Jules and Vincent leave the diner together, we know that Vincent's decision to stay the course on his life of crime will end with him dead, caught on the wrong end of his own gun.

---

[21] Ibid.

It's tempting to believe that Divine Knowledge must work something like this: that God, being all-knowing, knows the entire future like Tarantino knows what will happen in every scene of the movie. (Of course, no analogy is perfect. In our analogy, the Tarantino "God" figure is the sole author of every event, which is closer to a Calvinist, "determinist" view of foreknowledge. However, we are suggesting a scenario in which God *knows* the entirety of the future, but due to free will, did not determine, or "write" all of it word for word.) This first view of God's knowledge is perhaps the most common view on the matter, but it is hardly without its problems. One of them, as Hasker points out, is that perhaps knowledge of the future on this account isn't actually very useful to God. Why? Because it's already "there," so to speak, like Tarantino's script. Such foreknowledge is simply reading what is already written.

> Knowledge of the actual future is of no use whatever to God in devising his plan for the world. To see this, ask yourself what God could do if, looking into the future, he were to see something occurring that was contrary to his desire and intention. The answer is, God could do nothing whatever to prevent such an event, because (by hypothesis) he knows this is an event of the actual future, and it is contradictory to suppose that God foresees that occurrence in the actual future, and yet acts with the result that the event is not part of the future.[22]

Our second option comes in the form of a possible solution to this brain teasing issue. It was formulated by the sixteenth century Jesuit Luis de Molina, and is aptly known as Molinism. A key idea in Molina's theory is the idea of "middle knowledge," which has gotten a lot of attention in recent philosophy of religion.

Middle knowledge is not, as such, knowledge of the actual future;

---

[22] Hasker, 88.

rather, it is knowledge concerning what actions free creatures would perform under any conceivable circumstances in which they might exercise libertarian free will in choosing a course of action.[23]

The idea here is that God draws on this knowledge when he creates the world. He has control over the world because he has different options to choose from, and he exercises this control by putting people in the circumstances in which he knows they will freely do what he wants them to do.

We can't engage this fascinating theory in detail, but it is worth noting that critics see problems with it. Hasker, one prominent critic, notes some of them.

> ...it has been argued that the kind of control afforded by middle knowledge would actually be undesirable: God's interaction with his creatures, given this knowledge, would not be a genuine interpersonal relationship but, rather, a kind of manipulation.[24]

Moreover, as Hasker goes on to note, this also means God has planned each of the evil things that occur, which obviously poses problems.

So, Molinism sees God as a super-genius of sorts, who sees all ends to technically skirt any breach on Free Will, but on closer scrutiny it may leave us with a less meaningful account of genuine choice and genuine, freely chosen personal relationships.

However, our third option, non-traditional though it may be, opens itself up for consideration, namely, the view known as "Open Theism." This is the idea that the future is open to God in an important sense, as well as to us.

This view requires a certain revision of the traditional doctrine that God is omniscient, that he knows all things, including the future, in exhaustive detail. The revision in question is that omniscience doesn't necessarily mean

---

[23] Ibid.
[24] Ibid., 90.

knowing the future if there is *nothing yet to know, or if certain things about the future may simply be unknowable in principle.* Future free actions in particular may be the sort of things that are simply unknowable in principle, even by God. Advocates of open theism argue that this qualification on omniscience is no more of a problem than the traditional qualification on God's omnipotence, or his supreme power. Not even omnipotence can *do* the logically impossible, such as make a square circle or a married bachelor. If recognizing this is no problem, there should be no problem admitting that some things may be impossible to *know.*

Still, some balk at this presumption, believing it would assign risk to God's decision to create, which they call a sign of weakness and which, by definition, cannot apply to an all powerful God. Hasker addresses this concern as follows:

> God has the wisdom, power, and resourcefulness to accomplish his ultimate purposes in the world, even in the face of creaturely resistance…God willingly assumes the risk that his creation of the world will result in evil as well as good; however, the specific instances of evil that occur are neither intended nor approved by God, even though he can and does work in the world to bring good out of evil.[25]

It certainly feels unintuitive at first to *take away* specific bits of knowledge from God and then turn around and call Him more powerful as a result, but perhaps the ability to leave the future truly open in certain respects, and still have *absolute, unquestioned* power to accomplish his ultimate purposes, suggests an even more creative and powerful deity than one who needs to determine or control the choices of his creatures

[25]Ibid. It's also worth noting here that the author openly admits that the problem of evil then becomes less severe, but is by no means negligible. I have, of course, only sketched some of the main views of divine foreknowledge and omniscience. For a discussion of these issues that is more sympathetic to more traditional views of foreknowledge, and in particular, Molinism, see William Lane Craig, *The Only Wise God: The Compatibility of Divine Foreknowledge and Human Freedom,* (Grand Rapids: Baker Books, 1987).

in order to have His way.

If this is indeed the case, then a world in which miracles serve a purpose and are logically possible remains completely intact. In essence, Jules may not be walking away from his lucrative life of crime for no good reason.

Conclusion

Perhaps it would be over-thinking the issue to actually call Jules a prophet of sorts, but if we look closely, Jules is undoubtedly tethered to the great biblical story that he poetically mangles before murdering his victims. Recall that in the cafe, as Jules tells Vincent of his desire to leave a life of crime and walk the earth, he compares himself to "Caine from Kung-Fu," a clear reference to Kwai Chang Caine, a wandering Monk from *Kung Fu*, a '70s television show. This character, like Jules, shares a few not-likely-coincidental similarities with Cain from the Bible. After Cain from the Bible commits the murder of his brother, God banishes him to roam the earth as a restless wanderer. However, as an act of mercy, God marks him with protection, promising that should anyone bring death upon Cain, that person would have vengeance brought sevenfold upon himself.[26]

Note that, as mentioned earlier, despite God's decision to spare Vincent and Jules from the bullets in that apartment, which sends their lives in two different directions, their lives will both end the same way. Unsurprisingly, as Vincent chooses to continue in his life of crime and violence, he finds himself impaled on his own sword: He is shot down on a stakeout by the very victim he is there to murder. Jules' fate comes later, and may only be apparent to sharp-eyed Tarantino fans. In *Kill Bill*, Tarantino's modern-day samurai/western/anime mashup revenge tale, which was released in 2003, nine years after *Pulp Fiction*, a mysterious, drifting piano player who bears a suspicious resemblance to Jules, even beyond the fact that he is played by Samuel L. Jackson, is murdered by Bill

---

[26] See the book of Genesis, chapter 4.

and his henchmen (and women) along with the rest of Beatrix's friends at the wedding slaughter. Bill, the main perpetrator of this act, lives to see every one of his henchmen, and even his brother, systematically destroyed by *Kill Bill's* protagonist, Beatrix, before she brings death upon Bill himself. Though this is not done specifically in retaliation for Jules' murder, it is certainly an intriguing series of events when held up next to the obvious ties Tarantino makes between Jules and Cain. More intriguing still (and undoubtedly scintillating for film nerds), is that Bill is played by David Carradine, who also played Kwai Chang Caine, the very character to whom Jules compares himself in the cafe. Perhaps this all throws Beatrix's plight for vengeance in *Kill Bill* into a different light. Perhaps she is an unknowing instrument of God's justice.

When we distill the nature of our sinful world down, we find it to be a place much in need of miracles, and a place in which God's divine hand can be used as a guiding tool for history, not only through general omniscience, but in individual, specific miracles that show God's wonder and strike belief into the hearts of those who witness them. At least that's what appears to happen for Jules. But then again, maybe the gunman was just a really poor shot.

IT GOES TO SHOW YOU NEVER CAN TELL: UNEXPECTED SOUNDS— A THEOLOGICAL READING OF THE PULP FICTION SOUNDTRACK

Emma Hinds-Greenaway

Can you describe the complex sensation of experiencing a film in just two words? Is it possible? Perhaps not, but if we were asked to describe such a thing through the medium of sound, you might be more successful. A person only need hear the first two notes of the *Jaws* theme tune, and the ominous timbre of the whole film is accomplished in a second. In the first two notes (incidentally they are a C and a C#), a listener understands a tone that might take reels and reels of film to convey. We have come to understand music as emotional cues, and this is due, at least in part, to years of training as viewers. K. J. Donnelly suggests that:

> while it may be argued that these reactions are fully dependent
> upon the narrative and identifactory processes of films themselves,

53

an emotional reaction, although unspecific to music on its own, is most definitely a reality, and the effect of music with film amplifies reaction exponentially.[27]

Donnelly's conception of how society hears music in film is a passive one, understanding the emotional triggers that affect us (such as a swell of strings at a romantic moment, or a loud, harsh sound to indicate fear) as the product of the semi-subconscious.[28] They represent an internal correlation between sound and image that we are partially aware of but also instinctively respond to. For a large portion of cinematic history, music has thus been utilized as a manipulative tool only, something consigned to a supportive role rather than an active one, and a filmic ingredient we passively digest.

Much has been made of how music might serve a film,[29] but recently, film music has been experiencing something of a critical renaissance. Pauline Reay suggests that more and more it is becoming "important to realize that music is just one element of the soundtrack and that the dividing lines between all three elements are becoming increasingly blurred."[30] This development in thought has been partially due to the accelerated production of films that have reversed the classic order of film-music production. Rather than have a score written for the finished

[27] K. J. Donnelly, *The Spectre of Sound: Music in Film and Television* (London: The British Film Institute, 2005), 6.
[28] Ibid. Donnelly says, "Sound and music can be, and often are, dealt with in an unconscious or semi-conscious manner," referring to the experiments of a notable musical theorist, Annabel Cohen, who deduced that the level of consciousness recognized in film audiences is variable. While they might fail to notice music missing from a film, a viewer who is not convinced by the subject matter might become more aware of the musicality of the piece. p 6-7.
[29] For an explicit explanation, one might look at *Music in Film—Soundtrack and Synergy* by Pauline Reay (London: Wallflower Press, 2004). She has helpful summaries of the five areas of the functions of music in film proposed by Aaron Copland, and Claudia Gorbman's seven principles of music in film (p 32-33). Both theorists reinforce a hierarchical understanding of music in film, understanding non-diegetic sound to be the subordinate.
[30] Reay, 32.

film, contemporary filmmakers are more and more following the lead of directors who set their films to soundtracks of popular music. This includes Tarantino, who admits to finding his initial inspiration for some scenes in a piece of music. When asked how he chooses music for his films, Tarantino said: "A good majority of them I come up with beforehand. More or less the way my method works is you have got to find the opening credit sequence first. That starts it off from me."[31]

The future of how we understand films is not in their visual capacity alone, but as a conglomeration of sound and picture, a total experience that will allow music to have its full impact on this art form. By progressing chronologically through the film *Pulp Fiction,* this essay will illustrate how Tarantino's use of music explores the development of this potential accomplishment. The goal particularly will be to map the use of music as a transcendent ascension, elevating it beyond an aural tool to a moment of spiritual kenosis where music becomes "the interface between heaven and earth, and the sublime and banal, and is accordingly powerful."[32] The questions we will be asking and hoping to answer are the following: How does music engage with a theological reading, and what does it mean for music to be "theological" anyway? Any assertions that we make about Tarantino's material's theological capacity will be a reflection of the inherent themes of the texts presented, and not a presumption of Tarantino's own motives as a film-maker. Our concern is less about the religious intention of the creator, but rather what is sub-created by the marriage of music and text, a unique product with its own, separate, theological potential. By outlining the thesis of some of the more prevalent imaginative theologians of today, we will see

---

[31] Quentin Tarantino Interview (II) with Pam Grier, Robert Forster, and Lawrence Bender. *The Guardian,* January 5, 1998, http://www.theguardian.com/film/1998/jan/05/quentintarantino.guardianinterviewsatbfisouthbank3 (accessed September 1, 2014).
[32] Donnelly, 5.

how imaginative theology of the Theological Fantastic influences how we might come to perceive film, particularly film soundtrack, and the possibilities that emerge from that.

Constant Alienation: Expect the Unexpected

"Now look, I've given a million ladies a million foot massages, and they all meant something. We act like they don't, but they do."
—*Vincent Vega*

Let us consider that the opening moments of this highly regarded film soundtrack are made up of purely diegetic sound. That is to say, it is entirely music-less. Defying our common conceptions of film beginnings, which are usually musically driven, *Pulp Fiction*'s beginning offers no non-diegetic sound whatsoever. However, the sounds we do hear engender within us a certain type of expectation. The scene is set in a diner with a young couple in love, who are planning a heist of some kind. The sounds are benign: the tinkle of coffee being poured and the light conversation that surrounds them. However, when the opening music begins, it is nothing like what we have been conditioned to expect.

Rather than something in keeping with the kitsch tone we might have anticipated, the first song on the *Pulp Fiction* soundtrack is "Misirlou," by Dick Dale and His Del-Tones. It is a melody that invokes entirely different cues for the viewer than the images that have been presented. The rather skinny, comically enraged Honey Bunny is silenced in her screaming and stands immobile in the still frame as the surfer music cuts across, filling our minds with filmic cues connected with the Middle East, surfing, rock and roll, and stick-up movies. Tarantino himself described the music as somewhat contrary to the film's content:

"It sounds like rock and roll spaghetti western music."[33] This opening scene is an optimal example of how *Pulp Fiction* frequently disregards the previously upheld understanding of film soundtrack within the movie industry: that "music should be subordinated to the voice, remaining in the background and unheard."[34] Time and time again we find Tarantino allowing the music to dictate the image rather than vice versa. For instance, when the first scene fades, the music changes but the screen remains black. All we hear is "Jungle Boogie," by Kool and the Gang, and the next step could be anything.

At this point it is helpful to ask ourselves what we might have been expecting to happen next. In terms of aural cues, we have been promised excitement and fighting and the great American heist, some of the traditional movie interpretations of the feelings evoked by those previous sounds. Now we are offered a modern '70s pop song. Tarantino is alienating us from our expectations, leaving us more open for the fantastic aspects of this story that might follow, allowing us to suspend our disbelief or rationality. We might, in this state, believe anything Tarantino shows or tells us. We might be able to believe it because we are instinctively cut off from the prejudices of film-watching we have inherited.

These prejudices might be better understood within the metaphor of a language that we have learned. Sometimes language does not enlighten because the language itself does not possess the words for all aspects of life. And because these aspects cannot be given a place within canon language, they are discarded. Likewise, our instinctive film language does not let us make new connections or override our conditioned responses to sound and image. Tarantino's response is instead to direct his movies in an entirely different film language, alienating us from our learned responses.

[33] Jeff Dawson, *Quentin Tarantino: The Cinema of Cool* (New York: Applause Books, 1995), 154.
[34] Reay, 31.

Some of Tarantino's critics might say this is merely a trick, an example of Tarantino manipulating his audience's expectations in order to revolutionize music in film in such a way that engenders a positive rather than negative response. By giving us something so unlike what is familiar, the chances are higher that we might be so distracted from our former prejudices that we would be open to form new opinions. However, I suggest that these critics profoundly miss the possibilities of interpretation that are invoked when artistic alienation is optimized, sometimes with spiritual results.

Alison Milbank's essay "Apologetics and the Imagination: Making Strange" discusses some of the benefits of alienating oneself from something familiar in order to re-see it anew. She refers to the well-known anecdote about Charles Dickens (retold by the theologian and writer G.K. Chesterton), who upon seeing the sign for "COFFEE ROOM" backwards from the inside, read it as "MOOR EEFFOC" and found the word transformed.[35] Milbank suggests it is estranging moments like these that achieve the theological in art, and that they are needed if "we are to shock people into engagement with reality, so that they may appreciate the religious sense and we can begin to explain the Christian faith at all."[36]

This is what we shall see achieved in Tarantino's musical discord, and what we have already witnessed at the outset of the opening credits of *Pulp Fiction*. Artistically speaking, we are slightly unmanned by Tarantino's choices, first by his opening credits music and then by his decision to switch the music over a blank screen, so that the sound of "Jungle Boogie" is followed by the image. This slight dissonance of expectation allows us a potential MOOREEFFOC moment, the chance

---

[35] Alison Milbank, "Apologetics and the Imagination: Making Strange," *Imaginative Apologetics, Theology, Philosophy and the Catholic Tradition,* Andrew Davison, ed. (Norwich: SCM Press, 2011), 38.
[36] Ibid.

to re-engage with what has been presumed. The whole movie is about things the audience expects to see, but never does. We might consider how so much of the film's dialogue focuses on things that remain unseen in the film: Tony Rocky Horror's terrible "accident," or the death of Butch Koolidge's opposing boxer, or even the suspicious contents of Marsellus' briefcase. Tarantino is creating an interest in the off-screen moments, which only heightens our fascination with what is on-screen, but what is on-screen often only creates divergence from what we are hearing, or perhaps I should say what we are hearing only creates divergence from what we are seeing.

For instance, the musical choices leading into the opening scene after the prelude have left the audience in a state of confusion with regards to their expectations, as we have seen, but the scene between Vincent and Jules does little to auto-correct the viewer back to a level playing field. Rather than providing plot, the discussion between the two characters is the purest type of meaningless chat, banal conversation about popular culture that we would not expect to find in this moment. This increases the sense of alienation, and in such an alienating situation, the audience might begin to consider deeper meanings in the conversation. Why are they talking about cheeseburgers? Why was "Misirlou" chosen? The conversation, then, becomes far from meaningless, the music far from "background."

Some might have found it strange that I chose to begin this section with Vincent's observation on foot massages, but in the spirit of unveiling deeper meaning through alienating presentations, I believe we might find some of our meaning in Vincent's conclusions: Much like the seemingly small actions we choose in everyday life, we think these music choices don't mean something, but they do. As we move into our next section, we shall examine how this meaning can be perceived to be significant, not just in producing a thoughtful and challenging piece of cinema, but a potentially theological one as well.

The Sound of the Incarnation:
Accessing Holy Spaces through Sound

The Miracle you *witnessed. I witnessed a freak occurrence."*

—*Vincent Vega*

We should at least be open to the idea that art in its larger, more abstract form is capable of some kind of transcendent action. After all, our society happily embraces the idea that art is "moving" to the viewer, so why should that "movement" not be sacred in some way? However, it might be quite a step for some people to consider music to be naturally built for this type of transaction. It is all very well to say that Tarantino aligns his media in such a way in *Pulp Fiction* that allows for what we might call a mind-expanding alienation of subject, but it is another to say that all music can do this, or that it is music, specifically, that achieves this.

There is a significant chunk of theological writing dedicated to how art interacts with our perception of God, and many of these writings include musings on the importance of music. Richard Viladesau, author of *Theology and the Arts,* muses on the modern re-emergence of sacred music into popular cultural and suggests that "whatever we may make of it, it is, in any case a reminder of the intimate connections of music— from its very earliest and in its very highest moments, with religion."[37] His review of the historical development of this idea is helpful for observing how religion and music have intertwined, but also for illuminating how "music seems to have a spiritual dimension that goes beyond merely

---

[37] Richard Viladesau, "God and the Beautiful: Art As a Way to God," *Theology and the Arts* (New York: Paulist Press, 2000), 13.

sensual pleasure and that somehow reflects a deeper reality."[38] This is an idea inherent in some of the ways filmmakers use music. An example from *Pulp Fiction* is the shooting-up scene, which is a montage of drug-related images set to The Centurions' song "Bullwinkle Part II," which is a dark, lonely song presented without lyrics that draws the audience in beyond the image. The music, as we watch the heroin boil on the spoon and the needle forcibly perforate the skin, is not there to be background or filler noise. This is accentuated by the way the diegetic sounds are elegantly intertwined with the non-diegetic musical sounds; the metallic flick of the lighter is part of the sound experience, the music as present to the scene as that physical noise is. "Bullwinkle Part II" is there specifically to transport the audience, to make us feel like Vincent Vega as he cruises along in his car at night; in short it is transporting us to a different reality.

We could say it's not necessarily true that this is a theological experience—the fact that we believe we can almost feel the intoxication that Vincent feels when he shoots up only indicates that music and music in film can be emotionally manipulative. Viladesau demonstrates how this captivation of the imagination and senses is possible because of a layered association of human sounds and body movements, which in turn link to certain received emotional triggers, and asks the question: "Is musical experience merely the emotional *analogue* of sacred experience so that it works exclusively by association, or can music and art *in themselves* be an experience of the sacred?"[39] This is an interesting question in relation to *Pulp Fiction*, especially when we try to consider what exactly it is that makes a song necessarily sacred. We will explore this further by contrasting the two musical high points of the movie: Vincent's entrance to Mia's home to "Son of a Preacher Man," and Mia's accidental heroin overdose to "Girl, You'll Be a Woman Soon."

---

[38] Ibid., 37.
[39] Ibid., 40.

It is fascinating that the common vocabulary used to describe how music and scenes interact instinctively draws a dividing line between visual text and aural text. The action is set "to" the music, when in reality the two are not so easily separable. Let us consider the sentiments of Donnelly, who says, "The combination of music and the moving image is always more than the sum of its parts. It is never merely the vital aspects of the shots and the music; they become a totally different genus when unified."[40]

When searching for the theological in the music of *Pulp Fiction*, we should never presume to be isolationist and only draw conclusions that affect our perceptions of the soundtrack. The alienation of the familiar is only brought to fruition in the film as a whole, not merely in one part of its intense structure.

So what is then achieved when "Son of a Preacher Man," written by John Hurley and Ronnie Wilkins, is set to the slow, languid images of Uma Thurman cutting lines of coke, or the walking soles of her feet? This is a scene that we might visually consider to be quite sexual. In the same way we have been trained by the film industry to understand certain sounds to indicate certain plot developments (for example, a shock of loud music is called a "stinger," and we recognize it as an indicator of a frightful encounter, surprising occurrence, or something else that encourages us to produce adrenaline), the same can be said of certain shot choices. In this scene with Vincent and Mia, the preoccupation with close-up shots of sensual parts of the body (lips or naked feet) make the audience feel as if they are watching an intimate scene. The golden effect of the lighting on the mirrored surfaces, the yellow whiskey, and Mia's red lipstick are there to remind us of the lighting and visual tricks used in most film sex scenes. Does this then make "Son of a Preacher Man" a sexy song, and is it only then a sexy song by association?

---

[40] Donnelly, 2.

"Son of a Preacher Man" sung by Dusty Springfield certainly has some elements which lend themselves to a sexual interpretation. It is a love song of sorts, in which Dusty (or the narrator) reminisces about an earlier love who she courted and still considers being "the only man who could ever reach me." There is implied cultural sexuality in the tone of the subject, though several leaps of the listener's imagination are needed to reduce the song to a ballad purely concerning young sexual experience.

We could consider it an intentional choice to use the word "reach" to describe a sexual advance or awakening, especially in the context of the "preacher man," and maybe this is purely an ironic innuendo, but perhaps it is not. "Reach" is a religious word in an evangelical sense, as in 2 Corinthians 10:13–14, where Paul describes how the mission of the converted has been "to reach even to you" with the gospel they have been given.[41] It is particularly poignant when we also consider that Vincent Vega will not only provide much-needed friendship to Mia, but also, later in the film, he will save her life in an act of personal sacrifice. By deciding to save Mia rather than, say, running out of town, Vincent risks not only his reputation but his life. So how exactly should we consider this scene? There is a duality to the lyrics that is not defined by the tone of the song, and that perhaps defies definition entirely. The ambiguity presented in the combination of song and vision allows this piece of cinema to be more than simply "sexy."

Jeremy Begbie, a theologian who specializes in the interface between arts and theology, theorizes that this unique ability to evoke and retain duality of meaning makes music especially theological. He describes the way we actively hear music and how our ability to hear one note does not drown out our ability to hear a second one. What we hear, unlike other forms of art, is complete, and there is no form of internal competition or a space inside our hearing where one note is present and another is not.

---

[41] 2 Corinthians 10:13-14

"Unlike the patch of red on a canvas, it is in a sense, everywhere. Of course, I can identify the source of the note (the vibrating string), and its location ('it is over there'). But what I *hear* does not occupy a bonded space."[42]

Begbie wants to encourage listeners of music to consider how we assume we understand space. He suggests that, rather than something that is physical and can be filled or occupied, music implies a space "which is not the space of mutual exclusion, but space as relational, a space which allows for overlapping and interpenetration."[43] When we think about "Son of a Preacher Man," we might consider the space created by the sounds of the song as occupied by multiple interpretations. The tone of Dusty as she sings, which can be considered to be both sensual and spiritual, is not blocked out by what is created by the lyrics, which are both sexy and contemplative. When we think about the larger vision of the scene as a whole, we may seek to find an answer to what "type" of scene we are witnessing or even *what* we are witnessing, full stop. Begbie challenges us to consider the sounding of the chord, the vibrating strings in harmony with one another.

> It makes no sense to think of the strings in competition, or as simply "allowing" each other room to vibrate—the lower string enhances, brings to life the upper string, frees it to be itself, neither compromising its own integrity nor that of the upper string.[44]

This is a helpful analogy when we consider the idea of something being either theological or sexy, either religious or secular. The scene does not need to be considered one or the other, but can be considered to be both.

It is this type of consideration, the presentation of a scene that defies our previously upheld definitions, that allows us to be de-familiarized

---

[42] Jeremy Begbie, "Chapter 8: Through Music: Sound Mix." *Beholding the Glory: Incarnation through the Arts*, Jeremy Begbie, ed. (London: Darton Longman & Todd, 2000), 144.
[43] Ibid., 145.
[44] Ibid., 146.

from what we might have thought we had seen. But what do we gain from this de-familiarization? Begbie considers that by embracing the idea of a new type of space we are actually opening ourselves up to a new consideration of God and how he interacts with the world. The possibilities for reality are certainly broadened when we consider that multiple things might happen inside the same space, and our possibilities for understanding God and his incarnation are broadened. As Begbie says: "Why think of the humanity of Christ sitting awkwardly alongside the divine eternal Son (or competing?) within the one (visible) space?"[45] Our thinking can be literally freed, exceeding our previous conceptions of what is reasonable, allowing us to perceive human interaction with God not as compromised or invasive but as comparable with that divine communion between the Father and the Son.

In the same way, we can suggest that the "Girl, You'll be a Woman Soon," scene is partly indicative of this type of spatial interaction. It bears a similarity to the "Son of a Preacher Man" scene in that it also has a strange duality between the lyrics and the subject, diverting our expectations of an upcoming sex scene and replacing them with a bleak scene of overdose. However, a strong difference between the two is the way that music is both omnipresent and present in this scene. Although "Son of a Preacher Man" is a scene with a multiplicity of meaning that enables a broadening of the mind towards a theological understanding, it does not present both an in-time and out-of-time perception of music. This relates to how we might re-envision both space and God, as the music we experience in this scene is threefold: we hear the song as a piece of the soundtrack as a listener, but we also hear the song *within* the movie as it is playing on the radio, and in addition to that we hear the song as Uma Thurman sings it in her character. The three uses of the music allow us to experience what Begbie calls "the Sound of the

---

[45] Ibid., 147.

Incarnation," the sound of "an eternal lively resonance between Father and Son, mediated by the Spirit, into which we can be caught up."[46]

We should be careful not to steer too dangerously towards metaphorical comparisons with Trinitarian theology, for fear of becoming heavy-handed with our abstractions. This example from *Pulp Fiction* can, however, keep our vision suitably grounded; the song "Girl, You'll be a Woman Soon" is related to us through different experiences and media, but they are naturally cohesive and complementary as they drive the movie forward.

I return then to an earlier question that ties in with the quote preceding this section: what types of scenes have we witnessed, or more importantly, *what* have we witnessed? Much like Vincent, we always can choose not to see a miracle, or the MOOR EEFFOC in the window, but we *could* potentially have witnessed the artistic remodelling of our perception of God, moving him from an entity that pushes into our reality to a living being who experiences our experience within our space and reality.

Concluding Thoughts and Contemplating Ifs

All I'm doing is contemplating the Ifs.

—Marsellus

The important characteristic of music, and especially of film music, that we must always bear in mind is that it is perceived by musical scholars, theologians, and cinematic experts alike to be "ephemeral."[47] It is recognized as "celestial voices of film music,"[48] interacting with the audience in a somewhat supernatural way. After all, in our experience as film viewers we cannot be sure where it is coming from, or when it

---

[46] Ibid., 149.
[47] Donnelly, 9.
[48] Ibid.

will be coming. K.J. Donnelly calls it "The Spectre"[49] of cinema. Thus, there is always an element of mystery when it comes to the interpretation of music and therefore an element of choice, and to a certain extent we choose what we desire to hear or receive from the movie, just as we ultimately choose what image of God we live by. As Jules says to Vincent, "Look, you want to play the blind man, go walk with the shepherd, but me—my eyes are wide fucking open." We have considered music as a tool and then as proponent of the theological, and we have considered how Tarantino's work can act as an example of how a certain marriage of picture and sound may evoke the living reality of the true God. So perhaps not only our eyes will be open, but our ears will be too, as we not only look for God in the cinema but listen for him too.

The hearing ear and the seeing eye,
the Lord God has made them both.
—Proverbs 20:12

---

[49] Ibid.

ON *DEATH PROOF*: A DISCUSSION ABOUT THE ETHICS OF WATCHING AESTHETICALLY EXCELLENT BUT SUPER-VIOLENT MOVIES
(featuring a cameo by Quentin Tarantino)

Philip Tallon

INT Bar Evening

It's an Austin dive bar. There are all kind of patrons wandering around, as well as a film crew setting up lights and cameras.

Three guys are sitting at the bar, each having a beer. One is dressed in a black suit and tie, like a jewelry thief from *Reservoir Dogs*, one is dressed like a down-on-his-luck boxer a la *Pulp Fiction,* and one is dressed like the cowboy pastor from *Kill Bill, Vol. 2*. The THIEF is closest to the film crew. The PREACHER is closest to the door. The BOXER is right in between them. They are extras in a scene for the newest Quentin Tarantino film.

69

THIEF

(Looking around excitedly)

Hey, I think that's Samuel L. Jackson's stand-in right there. I hear he's going to be in this movie.

PREACHER

Samuel who?

THIEF

You know, Jules from *Pulp Fiction*. He's also in *Jackie Brown* and *Kill Bill*.

PREACHER

Oh. I didn't see those. I did see *one* Tarantino film. My son wanted to see it. It was the one with the crazy stuntman who kills girls with his car. Then he gets killed at the end.

THIEF

That's *Death Proof*. Tarantino says that's his worst film. But I loved it.

PREACHER

I didn't. That movie was boring at the start. Then gruesome. Then boring again. Then it got kind of interesting. But still can't recommend it.

BOXER

I saw it. It was interesting. Not sure what I make of it though.

THIEF

You guys think we'll see Tarantino here? I hope so.

PREACHER

Beats me. Don't even know what he looks like.

THIEF

Tarantino's in all his movies, pretty much. He does cameos like Hitchcock did. If you watch through all his movies you'll see him in most of them.

PREACHER

I'll pass. Don't care for his stuff. Now Hitchcock, that's a different story. There's a great director.

THIEF

So why are you even here?

PREACHER

I need the cash and background work is pretty easy. Plus, did you see that spread of pastries at craft services?

THIEF

I'm with you on the pastries, but why not watch Tarantino's films? The guy's almost like a new

Hitchcock. He makes great genre movies with style.
They're funny, and intense, and incredibly playful.

PREACHER

That's one of the things I didn't like about *Death Proof.*
The movie wanted you to laugh at all this awful stuff.
No thanks.

BOXER

(To the Thief)

That is an interesting feature of Tarantino's work, isn't
it? They mix humor and violence together into a bizarre
cocktail. It seems like it shouldn't work. But it does.

PREACHER

You're making me rethink even sticking around for the
shoot. Maybe it's better that I get out of here.

THIEF

No way! This is the opportunity of a lifetime. The
guy's not going to make movies forever. You can be
immortalized in cinema history here. Your grandkids
can watch this movie.

PREACHER

That's what I'm afraid of. Is this movie going to be
something that's bad for them to watch?

THIEF

Not if they're old enough, right?

PREACHER

I mean even after they're adults. I don't want anybody watching something that's going to hurt them.

THIEF

C'mon. It's just a movie. How can it hurt them?

PREACHER

Well, it could make them think that violence is funny. Or it could make them want to hurt other people.

BOXER

This raises a good question, Preacher. If movies could hurt people like you say, then maybe we shouldn't be part of this movie. But it looks like we've got some time to kill before shooting starts, so stick around and let's discuss it. If you win me over, I'll go too. You've said that maybe this movie could be harmful. If so, then maybe it's wrong to make it. In which case we'd be wrong to stay. So, what could prove that the movie is, in fact, harmful?

PREACHER

We'd all agree that movies can affect people, right? When *Bambi* came out deer hunting dropped remarkably, or so I've heard. Maybe violent movies make people more violent?

BOXER

So if the film has a bad effect then it's wrong to make it?

PREACHER

To put it a little simply, yeah. Or something like that.

BOXER

But does this apply in every case? The Beatles' *White Album* played a part in the Manson murders, but we don't blame The Beatles, do we?

THIEF

Exactly.

PREACHER

Of course not in those cases, but if there are big effects—if lots of people act violently after seeing a movie—you could show that it was wrong to make it.

BOXER

I'm not sure that violent movies do have that kind of problem. Studies don't show a consistent link between viewing violence and an increase in real-world violence. This has been studied a lot.[50]

PREACHER

I'm not convinced that violent movies don't affect people. Surely even the fact that they affect some

---

[50] Gordon Dahl and Stefano DellaVigna, "Does Movie Violence Increase Violent Crime?" *The Quarterly Journal of Economics* 124:2 (2009): 677-734.

people badly has to count against them, even if it's just unstable people that they affect.

BOXER

But none of us can be responsible for all bad consequences. If Henry Ford didn't make cars and Budweiser didn't make beer we wouldn't have drunk driving accidents. But there's an agent that brings those two things together to cause the bad effect. The sheer fact that they exist doesn't cause the drunken collisions.

PREACHER

Fair enough. People are responsible for what they do. I believe that. But surely there's something wrong with watching immoral entertainment, right?

THIEF

Nah. A movie's a movie. It's just an image on a screen. You're with me, Boxer?

BOXER

No. I agree with Preacher here, I think. It does seem like there can be something wrong with a movie, even though it's just a passive piece of art. So maybe we should be asking a different question. Maybe instead of looking at the effects of a movie, we should examine the work itself. The big issue might not be extrinsic. It could intrinsic.

THIEF and PREACHER (Together)

Huh?

BOXER

Maybe instead of looking to the effects, which seem hard to pin down, we should look at the thing itself. Uttering a false statement might not have any bad effects if no one believes you, but it could still be bad in itself. We could look at any statement and ask if it, in itself, has errors or moral problems.

PREACHER

I follow you.

BOXER

So the question then becomes, "How can we morally evaluate a work of art (like a movie) in itself? Can a movie just be morally defective whether or not it obviously hurts anyone?"

THIEF

I doubt it. A movie is a work of art. Works of art are aesthetic objects. What makes a movie good or bad is whether it works aesthetically. If it's good art, it's good. If it fails as a work of art it's bad art, but that doesn't mean it's wrong to make it. I've seen terrible drawings done by kids, but they aren't bad people for making bad art.[51]

---

[51] Aestheticism (or radical autonomism) is the view that aesthetic value is the supreme value, and hence that good art is self-justifying and immune from moral critique. This position has sometimes been held (more or less seriously). Oscar Wilde seems to defend a version of aestheticism in *The Picture of Dorian Gray*, writing, "There is no such

PREACHER

Oh, c'mon. We're not talking about poorly made art.
That's not what I'm worried about. I'm worried about
well-made art that carries bad ideas. The better made
it is, the worse a movie can be. More people see it and
like it. Then they watch it and re-watch it. It makes
the bad ideas sink in more. My father was in WWII,
and he talked about all these really well-made German
propaganda posters against the Jews. And there was
that movie called *Triumph of the Will* that was all
about how great Hitler was. Those were artistically
excellent works, but surely there's something wrong
with them. They weren't failures. They *worked*.[52]

THIEF

Hmm. That's a good point.

PREACHER

The power of a lot of artworks like movies is that
they tell stories and carry ideas. They make us think

thing as a moral or an immoral book," and "No artist has ethical sympathies" (Paris: Charles Carrington, 1905, v.). Philosophers sometimes defend more modest versions of aesthetic autonomism. J. C. Anderson and J. T. Dean, for instance, defend the view that an artwork will never be aesthetically better in virtue of its moral strengths, and will never be worse because of its moral defects...On a strict reading of moderate autonomism, one of its decisive claims is that defective moral understanding never counts against the aesthetic merit of a work. An artwork may invite an audience to entertain a defective moral perspective and this will not detract from its aesthetic value (Quoted in Noel Carroll, "Moderate Moralism," *British Journal of Aesthetics* 36: 3 [1996]). The most common version of "aestheticism" is simply the view that works of art exist somehow in a different realm from normal moral evaluation. Perhaps we could call this the "just a movie" defense.

[52] For a detailed discussion of this movie, consider Mary Devereaux's "Beauty and Evil: the case of Leni Riefensthal's *Triumph of the Will*," in Jerrold Levinson's edited volume, *Aesthetics and Ethics* (Cambridge: Cambridge University Press, 1998).

differently. That's one thing we like about them. Have you ever had a movie affect you in a good way?

THIEF

Sure. When I watch *Fight Club,* or *Lars and the Real Girl,* it makes me want to be less materialistic, or be more compassionate.

PREACHER

So if a movie can have good effects it can have bad effects. It's not "just a movie."

BOXER

Preacher's onto something. Artworks can inspire us or degrade us because they interact with what we believe about the world. They help us to *see* differently.

THIEF

Okay, but does that mean that anything that tells a different story from what we believe shouldn't be made? I think people have a right to tell those stories, even if I disagree. And sometimes what makes a work great is precisely that it challenges everything I've ever thought. This doesn't just go for art, but politics and philosophy too. People should express themselves. And how could I know if I disagree with somebody until I hear him? Are you saying that bad art should all be censored? Because then you'll be acting a little bit like Nazis too, won't you?

BOXER

Nobody's saying here that people can't express
themselves. We should all have the right to make art
or express ideas even if other folks object.

PREACHER

Within certain limits. You can't repaint the lights at an
intersection so that people get the wrong idea when to
stop and go.

BOXER

Okay, but you're talking about defacing public property
and breaking the law. Not exactly a fair comparison.

THIEF

Exactly. Movies are different, and they aren't
pretending to be real.

BOXER

But again, they do depend on things we believe about
the world. If we didn't have any sense of right and
wrong, how could we know who the villain is, and
who the hero is? Aristotle saw this as far back as
ancient Greece. For Aristotle, in order for there to be
tragic drama, we have to understand that the hero
doesn't fully deserve his suffering.[53] And if this is the

---

[53] In his *Poetics*, Aristotle writes: *It follows plainly, in the first place, that the change of fortune presented must not be the spectacle of a virtuous man brought from prosperity to adversity: for this moves neither pity nor fear; it merely shocks us. Nor, again, that of a*

case, then surely you could have someone misuse the
form of tragic drama to make a bad man's suffering
seem tragic, even when it's really not. If that happened,
then the playwright would be misleading the audience
using the artform, similar to the way the Nazis mislead
people about Hitler using movies. There's something
wrong with that, isn't there?

PREACHER

Preach on, Boxer.

BOXER

So I'm inclined to agree with Preacher. Surely there
can be *intrinsic* moral problems with a work of art.
And if so, maybe they shouldn't be censored, but we
could still say they're *bad* in some way.

THIEF

Perhaps.

*The Preacher shifts on his stool, looking like the issue is settled. He grabs
his cowboy hat.*

---

*bad man passing from adversity to prosperity: for nothing can be more alien to the spirit
of Tragedy; it possesses no single tragic quality; it neither satisfies the moral sense nor calls
forth pity or fear. Nor, again, should the downfall of the utter villain be exhibited. A plot
of this kind would, doubtless, satisfy the moral sense, but it would inspire neither pity nor
fear; for pity is aroused by unmerited misfortune, fear by the misfortune of a man like ourselves. Such an event, therefore, will be neither pitiful nor terrible. There remains, then, the
character between these two extremes—that of a man who is not eminently good and just,
yet whose misfortune is brought about not by vice or depravity, but by some error or frailty.*
(Aristotle, *Poetics*, trans. S. H. Butcher [London: Macmillan, 1895], 41-43.)

PREACHER

I'm gonna nab one more Danish from craft services before
I split. I love the pineapple filling, you know what I mean?

BOXER

Don't get up yet, Preacher. We're not done.

Preacher sets his hat down again, looking incredulous and a little grumpy.

BOXER

Let's reframe the question once again: "If there can be
ethical problems with a work of art—like portraying
a bad man as virtuous—what does this mean for the
overall value of a work of art?" Perhaps a work could
have some moral flaws but still be good on the whole.
Surely most works of art, which are made by humans
after all, have some small moral errors. Does this
mean that the presence of any moral flaws discount it
as a morally bad work?

PREACHER

If you only have a little bit of poison in a smoothie,
would you still drink it?

BOXER

Of course not. Unless I knew that the poison would
only hurt me a tiny bit. I eat fruits that have tiny bits of
pesticide on them, because I know I won't be hurt too
much. But maybe the better analogy is this: Do you ever

talk to people who you know aren't entirely trustworthy?

PREACHER

Sure.

BOXER

But how do you know they won't deceive you?

PREACHER

I don't. But I also don't make friends with them.[54]

BOXER

Fair enough. But there can still be value in dealing
with someone even if they aren't always 100 percent
on-the-level. Artworks could be like that. You could
find value in a movie even if you don't fully trust it.

PREACHER

But wouldn't that rule out that person from being a *good*
person? The question you were asking is if a morally
flawed work of art could be a good work. It's the same
thing. An untrustworthy person isn't a good person. A
morally flawed work of art isn't a good work of art.[55] If
people don't get a pass for their flaws, why should art?

---

[54] Wayne Booth, in *The Company We Keep*, proposes a framework for ethical criticism
that focuses on the notion that the implied authors of texts can be evaluated as "friends"
(or not), in whose company we should like to remain (or not). This is a helpful image,
but not quite as philosophically precise as we would like to develop in order to consistently evaluate the overall status of artworks.

[55] Moralism is the view that moral values override aesthetic values in evaluating artworks. Its strongest form was endorsed by Leo Tolstoy, while weaker forms continue
today. A more modest variety of moralism, ethicism, will be defended below.

BOXER

Touché. But a somewhat untrustworthy person could
still be a good person in other respects. They could
be brave, and strong, and good at their job. Would
you rather have a slightly untrustworthy mechanic
(who might overcharge you) fix your car, or a friend
who is bad at fixing cars but works for free? Artworks
aren't only, or even primarily, moral entities, they are
aesthetic entities. That's why we make them and enjoy
them. Couldn't an artwork be great in all sorts of
artistic ways, but still have some moral problems?

PREACHER

I suppose.

THIEF

Craftily played, Boxer! Hear, hear.

BOXER

I think so too. Consider this: imagine a gorgeous
painting that's beautifully rendered, large in scale, and
is stirring to look at. But it depicts a scene from history
or Greek mythology, say, that isn't entirely admirable.
Let's say it's the illicit impregnation of Danaë by Zeus,
who took the form of a golden rain. You object to
Zeus' bad behavior, but the painting doesn't condemn
it. Nevertheless, the painting is lovely to behold. Is this
a bad painting?[56]

---

[56] St Augustine discusses this example in his *Confessions,* Book I, Chapter 16.

PREACHER

It's bad morally.

BOXER

We'll assume it's bad morally in that one aspect. But on
the whole, there are lots of great-making features. You
could say it's a good painting, but it would be better if
its moral features were better. The immorality of the
scene in some way distances you from fully engaging
with the work. In this case the moral problems
become aesthetic problems.[57]

THIEF

Let's get back to talking about Tarantino.

BOXER

Very well. Take the case of *Death Proof,* which I know
you dislike, Preacher. The movie is made with clear skill

[57] Here (and elsewhere) I am leaning strongly on the work of Berys Gaut, especially his book *Art, Emotion, and Ethics* (Oxford: Oxford University Press, 2007). Gaut articulates a view he calls "ethicism" which seeks to avoid the mistakes of "autonomism" and "moralism." Ethicism refuses to segregate moral values from aesthetic ones in works of art where ethical considerations are relevant. Relevant positive ethical values increase the overall aesthetic value of a work, and relevant negative ethical values decrease the aesthetic value of the work. Here is Gaut's argument, formally expressed: A work's manifestation of an attitude is a matter of the work's prescribing certain responses toward the events described. If those responses are unmerited, because unethical, we have reason not to respond in the way prescribed. Our having reason not to respond in the way prescribed is a failure of the work. What responses the work prescribes is of aesthetic relevance. So the fact that we have reason not to respond in the way prescribed is an aesthetic failure of the work, that is to say, is an aesthetic defect. So a work's manifestation of ethically bad attitudes is an aesthetic defect in it. Mutatis mutandis, a parallel argument shows that a work's manifestation of ethically commendable attitudes is an aesthetic merit in it, since we have reason to adopt a prescribed response that is ethically commendable. So Ethicism is true. (Berys Gaut, "The Ethical Criticism of Art," in Jerrold Levinson [ed.], *Aesthetics and Ethics,* [Cambridge: Cambridge University Press, 1998], 195-6.)

and charm. It cleverly plays with the tropes of horror films, subverting audience expectations while still inhabiting the genre. Nevertheless, it allows us to take a certain delight in the bad behavior of the villain, which as we've said before, Aristotle might call a problem. The villain, Stuntman Mike, gleefully kills five women with his car. The car crash scene is stunning as it alternates between being gruesome and funny. We recoil in horror as we see the women all die from the collision, while still taking a certain sort of pleasure in the virtuosity of the editing. We're conflicted. There's also a complex, but playful, indictment of the audience, as a movie actor (the stuntman) uses his movie skills to kill women for his personal satisfaction (which of course is wrong), but the viewer is watching a movie actor carry out this stunt through his movie skills for our aesthetic satisfaction. Even though we are invited to reflect on our complicity, there does seem to be a real sense in which we are also invited to relish the violence of the scene. The movie is artistically masterful, but its morality seems shaky at best.

THIEF

Though we should note that Stuntman Mike isn't the hero. He's charming at the beginning, but later on in the movie is portrayed as evil and pathetic. Plus he loses in the end when he meets his match. The stuntwomen he tries to kill in the second half turn the tables on him and destroy him.

BOXER

Though even there, when the girls turn the tables, they seem to take vindictive pleasure in killing him. They're not exactly the noble heroes we might want from a great work of art. There do seem to be some potential moral problems. And a movie with moral problems is going to be less great than an equivalent film without those problems.

PREACHER

So you're saying that the flaws of the film don't completely take away from its value as a work of art?

BOXER

Exactly.

THIEF

But here's the issue I have. So what if there are some moral problems? It doesn't make the movie any less awesome!

BOXER

I disagree. In a movie with moral flaws, the very fact that we have to recoil and evaluate the morality of the movie is an artistic problem as well as a moral one. It separates us from our engagement with the characters. It keeps us from fully giving ourselves over to the story. Moral problems detract from the greatness of a work, even if they don't destroy its value completely. Whenever we are interacting with anything as complex as a movie, we bring our whole person to its appreciation. If there are moral problems then there are aesthetic problems. If categories like right and wrong are relevant in any way to the work of art, then those categories are relevant in our evaluation of the work. Clearly you can't watch a horror film without understanding things like the value of human life. That's part of the effect of the film, that the villain wrongly takes people's lives. If we can understand that, then it's appropriate to critique the movie as a whole for getting something wrong about the value of human life.

PREACHER

Okay, so does *Death Proof* make that mistake? Because it seems to me that it does. Could there be a Tarantino film that didn't make those mistakes?

BOXER

Hmm…

THIEF

Hey, wait, look who just walked in! It's the man! Tarantino himself.

TARANTINO walks behind the bar. He's talking to his Director of Photography.

TARANTINO

How long will that take to set up? Thirty minutes?
Cool. We'll shoot in thirty.

He spots the extras.

TARANTINO

Hey guys.[58]

THIEF

Quentin, help us settle this argument; we're just
talking about *Death Proof*.

TARANTINO

Hold on, let me finish this Danish. Have you guys
been to our crafty table? Best meal in town.

*He stuffs one last bite of Danish into his mouth and swallows it. Preacher
looks hungry.*

TARANTINO

Okay, hit me. I don't get many questions about *Death
Proof*.

THIEF

Okay, so, we're talking about the violence in your
movies, and whether that's good or bad.

---

[58] In the following section, I'll be making up some dialogue for Quentin Tarantino. Bits
of dialogue within quotation marks are taken directly from interviews and cited below.

PREACHER

Yeah, why's there so much violence in there?

TARANTINO

I do get *that* question a lot. Look, "I love violence in movies, and if you don't, it's like you don't like tap dancing, or slapstick, but that doesn't mean it shouldn't be shown. My mom doesn't like Abbot and Costello or Laurel and Hardy, but that doesn't mean they shouldn't have been making movies."[59] People ask me about that ear-cutting scene in *Reservoir Dogs.* Harvey, who produced the movie, wanted me to cut it out. I said, "[I]t's part of the movie, for people who appreciate the whole package...If violence is part of your palette, you have to be free to go where your heart takes you."[60]

PREACHER

But where's the justification for that? Are you making people get excited about seeing something that would be utterly horrible in real life?

TARANTINO

"Sure, I think the scene is pretty horrible. I didn't make it for yahoos to hoot and holler. It's supposed to be terrible."[61] You have to remember that "When I started to develop, for lack of a better word, my 'aesthetic,' I

[59] Gerald Peary, ed. *Quentin Tarantino: Interviews* (Jackson, MS: University Press of Mississippi, 1998), 32-33.
[60] Ibid., 29.
[61] Ibid.

loved exploitation movies. I loved in the '70s when
New World was cranking out their pure stuff, like
Jonathan Demme's *Caged Heat*. And all the Roger
Corman stuff, drive-in movies."[62]

THIEF

So the genre that you're working in is "exploitation."

TARANTINO

Right. A big part of the goal is to give the audience
an experience. I want people to go on a rise where
you shift back and forth between humor and horror.
"There are two kinds of violence. First, there's cartoon
violence like *Lethal Weapon*. There's nothing wrong
with that. I'm not ragging on that. But my kind of
violence is tougher, rougher, more disturbing. It gets
under your skin. Go to a video store, to the horror
section or the action-adventure section, nine out of
ten of the films you get there are going to be more
graphically violent than my movie, but I'm *trying* to
be disturbing. What's going on is happening to real
human beings. There are ramifications to it."[63] In that
scene in *Reservoir Dogs*, "I sucker-punched you...
You're supposed to laugh until I stop you laughing."[64]

THIEF

So do you think that part of the reason people object
to the violence in your movies is because you make it

---

[62] Ibid., 12.
[63] Ibid., 32-33.
[64] Ibid., 46.

more upsetting than other screen violence often is?

TARANTINO

Yeah, totally.

The Director of Photography comes back. He and Tarantino begin talking again.

TARANTINO

Gotta go, guys.

THIEF

That was incredible.

PREACHER

I'm still disturbed.

BOXER

Hmm. So it seems like part of what Tarantino was saying there is that the genre he's working in, exploitation, is already a morally ambiguous genre. Exploitation movies were always, from the outset, intended to be a bit morally askew. Their primary selling point was the inclusion of socially unacceptable content. Furthermore, the crime movies, horror movies, kung-fu movies, and blaxsploitation films (especially in the '60s and '70s) were often amoral in their treatment of human stories.

PREACHER

But that's a problem, right? That means that the whole genre he's working in is already morally corrupt in some way.

BOXER

Possibly. Though it also makes the genre less deceptive. It shows that there's a high level of coherence between what the artist is trying to accomplish, and what's he's actually doing. If the audience understands this, it helps us to engage appropriately with the film… We aren't supposed to feel like we're in safe hands. That his aesthetic is shaped by exploitation in some way suggests that you almost can't make a Tarantino film without it having morally ambiguous elements.

THIEF

That's one of the things I love about Tarantino; you feel like you never know how the story is going to unfold.

BOXER

Right. But it's interesting that in all of his films after *Reservoir Dogs*, the main characters all triumph over evil in the end. The wicked are punished and the good guys triumph.

PREACHER

But even given that, there are problems. We're often

chuckling and sympathizing with the bad guys, and the good guys are often somewhat corrupt themselves.

BOXER

True. In *Inglourious Basterds* it's hard to genuinely approve of the savagery of the American hit squad as they scalp, mutilate, and terrorize their enemies. Yet we are intended to empathize with their situation.

PREACHER

Even if he's just channeling exploitation tropes, maybe the whole genre is corrupt.

BOXER

Perhaps. Maybe part of Tarantino's whole aesthetic is that he's going to channel exploitation themes.

THIEF

You just can't make a Tarantino film without humor and violence. You can't make a Tarantino film that's perfectly morally centered. That's not what he does.

BOXER

And if this is a problem, it implies that all Tarantino films will somehow be lessened in value by their moral flaws. The question then that remains is, "Does the overall value of the artistry outweigh the moral flaws?"

PREACHER

Nope. Not for me. See y'all some other time.

Preacher takes his hat and leaves.

THIEF

Oh, absolutely. I'm staying. What about you, Boxer?

Boxer sits and thinks awhile.

FADE TO BLACK

THE OLD TESTAMENT AND *KILL BILL*: A DANGEROUS LIAISON?

Lawson G. Stone

Quentin Tarantino has become synonymous with cinematic violence. Not merely graphic or plentiful, a marked stylization of violence distinguishes these films. For this reason, some Christians find Tarantino's movies problematic or, in fact, abominable. This judgment, however, encounters obstacles. After all, the scriptures report violence. At times violence is reported in summary form, "Thus Joshua struck all the land...and all their kings. He left no survivor, but he utterly destroyed all who breathed, just as the LORD, the God of Israel, had commanded" (Joshua 10:40). While the statement itself points to great violence, it remains detached, even clinical. Just as we castigate Tarantino for violence in his stories, and violent storylines, Christianity's cultured detractors disparage "Old Testament violence" as though they were equivalent.

When I watch the *Kill Bill* movies, I am drawn irresistibly not to the book of Joshua, with its military actions, but to the book of Judges, which I have spent decades studying, writing about, and teaching. The cinematic story- and character-bound violence of *Kill Bill* comes closer to Judges than to other books. In this essay, I offer neither a systematic analysis nor a formal study of either the movie or the book of Judges, though I will draw on my own previous work on Judges.[65] I make no judgment on either book or movie, but rather flag the points where I see one evoking the other. In addition, no discussion of heroes, vengeance, and violence in western culture can ignore its other two monuments to skull-caving, body-cleaving violence, Homer's *Iliad* and the Anglo-Saxon poem *Beowulf*. Since I can't avoid making associations with these works, and have no actual methodological necessity for including them, I do so simply because they are fantastic stories that enrich our enjoyment of all such stories, *Kill Bill* included. I also can't finally say if these movies are not actually a very clever trap loaded with layers of ironic misdirection. I'm taking the story at face value and will present my impressions and connections as one steeped in the book of Judges and other stories of mind-numbingly fearsome, chaotic berserkers.

The Isolation of Violence

All movies featuring truly face-melting violence, especially when massive death tolls and impressive property damage are involved, provoke the same set of questions from some viewers about the surrounding environment. "Where are the police?" "Where are the bystanders?" "How can the Bride just walk away after slaughtering the Crazy 88 and demolishing a night club?" "How can the Bride fly on an airplane with a Hanzo Hatori katana?" In a hoplophobic culture where a school child

[65] For the book of Judges, see Lawson G. Stone, "Judges" in *Joshua, Judges, Ruth*, vol. 3 of *Cornerstone Biblical Commentary*, ed. Philip W. Comfort (Carol Stream: Tyndale, 2012), 185-494.

can get detention for pointing with his finger and saying "Bang!" how'd she get *that* cranium-cleaving cutlery on board a plane? In *Kill Bill*, the Bride and the Deadly Viper Assassination Squad (DiVAS) move freely and wreak their violent mayhem with impunity. The law officers that do appear serve as icons of impotence, stupidity, and not a little disdain for rural southerners. Additionally, not even wounds or medical impediments stop the hero. When the Bride awakens from a four-year coma in a dive of a hospital, neglected and subjected to repeated rape by her nurse-*cum*-pimp, she does have problems walking around, but otherwise manages to kill her rapist, escape from the hospital, steal his truck, and drive it away, all within an hour of awakening. Presumably in this universe, stolen trucks are not reported, license plates are not traced, and Uma Thurman driving a vehicle called the "Pussy Wagon" attracts not a flicker of attention in a normal middle-class suburban neighborhood. Yes, we see her struggle with non-responsive legs, but really... why not her arms too? Where are the inevitable bed-sores, the disorientation, all the normal things that happen to comatose patients getting four years of crappy care and sexual abuse? And then what about all the physical punishment endured by the Bride and other heroes like her in their combat? Other than being momentarily stunned or slowed down, the hailstorm of physical punishment hardly affects her. Much blood is shed, but little seems actually to be lost. How many roundhouse kicks to the face can one sustain and still possess perfect teeth, intact jawbones, socketed eyeballs (except for Elle Driver, of course) and functioning brain cells?

I know, *these are silly questions to ask of this genre.* The very modus of such material is precisely the hero's ability to be only sporadically touched by such "real-world" complications and inconveniences. The action-hero genre demands more than the normal suspension of disbelief expected in fiction. This type of story inhabits a universe we can term *liminal*. The liminal is the in-between world, the world between the empire and the new republic, with the revolution ongoing; the world between the frontier and statehood, between conquest and kingdom, between apocalypse and New Jerusalem, between darkness and dawn. Historically, liminal eras occur between the collapse of one long-running social order and the rise of a new order. The early Middle Ages in Europe and the "Old West" era in U.S. history were liminal times, as was the period depicted in Homer's *Iliad* and *Odyssey,* and the Old Testament books of Judges and 1 Samuel. Liminal eras tend to have conspicuous, common features, which I'll illustrate from the book of Judges.

Moving from the book of Joshua to the book of Judges is a passage between different worlds. The world of Joshua is one of coherence. This generation of Israelites, born in the wilderness, tutored by Moses in the book of Deuteronomy, functions as an almost apostolic generation, an exemplar of an obedient community. All the promises and demands of the covenant between God and Israel are in full view. Israel repeatedly acts "according to the law of Moses." In Joshua 5, the Israelites assert their unique identity as God's people by ensuring every male is circumcised—a curious and awkward way to begin a military campaign! They then celebrate the Passover, the foundational commemoration of the core event in Israel's history. That event, the crossing of the sea (Exodus 14-15), is reenacted by Joshua and the Israelites as they cross the miraculously dried Jordan River (Joshua 3-4). When an Israelite violates the prohibition on profiting from the conquest of Jericho, he is exposed and executed (Joshua 7-8). In the midst of the campaign, Joshua leads the Israelites to Mount Ebal where, in the very heart of Canaan, the blessings and curses of the Law of Moses are read aloud with all Israel affirming their allegiance. Naturally, the story unfolds also as one of steady victories as the Israelites serve more as a clean-up crew following the Divine Warrior. From Jericho (Joshua 6) to a sweep through the southern regions of the land (Joshua 9-10), culminating in a preemptive strike on a massive northern Canaanite coalition in which the mighty citadel of Hazor falls (Joshua 11), the Israelites "occupy" the Law and, simultaneously, occupy the land.

The book of Judges, however, comports a darker reality. The coherence of Joshua cracks, the covenant becomes tenuous, and a generation abandons its God, serving almost any other god except its own. Judges 2:10-17 speaks of this different generation, one that "did not know the Lord" and followed after the gods of Canaan: Baal, the storm and fertility god, and Ashtoreth, the Canaanite goddess. By Judges 10:6–10, the list of gods worshiped by Israel includes deities worshiped by every nation surrounding Israel: Syria, Sidon, Moab, Ammon, and Philistia. These were the very nations that oppressed Israel! They more readily serve the gods of their enemies than the Lord who had given them the Promised Land. God's anger burns, not against godless pagans, but against his own people, his un-godded, or even over-godded, people. With the center broken, the line cannot hold, and the peoples surrounding Israel, smelling the blood in the water, always ambitious to seize control of the strategically vital territory of Canaan, move in with a vengeance, laying Israel low. Six times in Judges, a despairing Israel shrieks out to God in agony, who, almost in violation of his own covenant, saves his people by raising up the heroes named in scripture as "judges."

Which brings us to our topic. The curious English term "judge," combined with the gauzy, hyper-pious sheen of sanctity we cast over the narrative, is a legacy of too many Vacation Bible School lessons given in bathrobes by youth-workers. We miss the reality of exactly who these judges were. In short, they were *beserkers* and *warlords*. They lived in a period of social meltdown. The year 1200 BC, nominally the year of transition into the "period of the judges," saw a level of political, social, and economic collapse in the eastern Mediterranean world so severe that Vanderbilt historian Robert Drews justly terms it "the catastrophe," commenting that "the end of the eastern Mediterranean Bronze Age, in the twelfth century BC, was one of history's most frightful turning points...[it] was arguably the worst disaster in ancient history, even more calamitous than the collapse of the western Roman Empire."[66] Another recent scholar, using the somewhat later year 1177 BC as his vantage point, characterized it as "The Year Civilization Collapsed."[67] The land of Canaan, the intersection of every major trade and military campaign route of the ancient world, a no-man's land claimed by all, owned by none, had already witnessed centuries of harsh rule under Egypt through the petty tyrants who ruled its cities and towns in Pharaoh's interests. An Israel that thought itself free from Egyptian tyranny when it left Egypt around 1275 BC entered Canaan forty years later only to find it gripped in the fist of...Pharaoh. The battles reported in Joshua center on destroying Egypt's command structure and breaking its stranglehold on Canaan, allowing Israel to settle the highlands in small, unwalled villages devoted to a mixture of farming and herding. Israel had just begun to expand down the slopes of the central highlands when, about 1207 BC, the empire, Egypt, struck back. The son of Rameses II, the pharaoh Merneptah, ravaged the land of Canaan and provided us with the first certain reference to Israel outside the Bible. In a famous monumental inscription, Merneptah declares, "Israel is laid waste, his seed is not." This would have been a devastating blow to the newly planted, eagerly expanding Israelite communities. Merneptah's strike probably corresponds with the catastrophic decline reported in Judges 1:1–3:6. The resulting loss of cultural and social momentum seen

[66] Robert Drews, *The End of the Bronze Age: Changes in Warfare and the Catastophe ca. 1200 B.C.* (Princeton: Princeton University Press, 1993), 3.
[67] Eric Cline, *1177 BC: The Year Civilization Collapsed* (Princeton: Princeton University Press, 2014).

in the book of Judges could well mirror the repercussions of Merneptah's near-fatal blow.[68]

So the book of Judges takes us into a dark, almost post-apocalyptic world of comprehensive, widespread cultural collapse, with the accompanying social chaos. Lacking any centralized government, its faith shattered and its solidarity fragmented, Israel found itself shipwrecked in a sea teeming with sharks: Moabites, Canaanites, Ammonites, Midianites, and ultimately, the Philistines, the most dangerous expeditionary military force the ancient Near East had ever seen—camped in view of the ridges occupied by the Israelites. The book of Judges immerses the reader in this epoch of tyrants, freedom fighters, criminals, heroes, assassins, gangsters, thugs, whores, and tricksters—exactly the kind of folks who populate Quentin Tarantino's movies. Seen in this context, we realize that the "judges" represent Israel's version of a familiar character: the lone warrior, the assassin, the warlord, not unlike the leaders of the tribal armies seen in Homer's *Iliad* or in Louis L'Amour's novels, people in some ways not unlike Tarantino's Bride.

So the apparent isolation of the events in *Kill Bill*, the book of Judges, or any other story of this type arises from the intentional placement of the narrative in liminal space and time. In the absence of rules, societal structures, or benevolent authorities, the focus falls squarely on the protagonists themselves, their quality, caliber, character, and, most of all, their deeds. The author of Judges, like Tarantino, "revels in the gusto of physical action and in the stylish ferocity of personal combat. He sees life lit by the fires of some central, ineradicable energy. The air seems to vibrate around the heroic personages, and the force of their being electrifies nature."[69]

---

[68] See Stone, "Judges," 204-206; For a review of the entire historical era, cf. "Israel's Appearance in Canaan," in *Ancient Israel's History: An Introduction to Issues and Sources,* ed. Bill T. Arnold and Richard S. Hess (Grand Rapids: Baker Academic, 2014) 127-164.
[69] George Steiner, "Homer and the Scholars," in *Homer: A Collection of Critical Essays,* ed. G. Steiner and R. Fagles (Englewood Cliffs, NJ: Prentice-Hall, 1962), 8.

The Focus on the Hero

A liminal universe, either in history or in art, throws the characters against a backdrop of burning cities, smoking fields, marauding vandals, and even the hostile forces of nature. Cruel injustices inflicted on vulnerable people go unpunished. Into this liminal, disordered, unstable universe comes one axial point of order: the hero. They have no help or support outside their wit, skill, strength, and courage and exceedingly fine and lethal weaponry.

In *Kill Bill*, we trace the story of the Bride through what emerges as a traditional vendetta tale. We learn (later, in Vol. 2) that at her own wedding rehearsal, the Bride and her party are attacked by assassins led by Bill, her erstwhile lover and employer. All in the wedding party are savagely killed, as is, seemingly, the Bride and her unborn child. But she survives, only to be sexually assaulted repeatedly while in a coma. All this we reconstruct, as the story is not told in chronological order but via flashbacks. Still, a story emerges of a brilliant and lethal killer who now must turn all her skills and passion upon avenging not only the death of her friends, and presumably herself, but also of her unborn child.

Hero stories are universal, and common features mark the genre. Using the book of Judges as a foil, heroic tales

> ...celebrate the exploits of an outstanding individual. No eulogizing of the ordinary here, no democracy of the mediocre. Physicality becomes the idiom of excellence. Whether handsome or ugly, heroes are never common...The storyteller relates the deeds of the heroes, invariably violent encounters, with delicious detail. Such gusto, such exaltation of the violent, scandalizes the domestic sensibility of later readers, ancient and modern. The tale master recounts the murder of Eglon by Ehud and of Sisera by Jael with gleeful energy, celebrating

the heroes' craftiness with humor, sometimes scatological or sexual. Likewise, his interest in the weaponry or implements of the heroes— Ehud's dagger, Jael's tent-peg, Gideon's torches—is an element of this savoring of every violent detail.

The sheer brutal joy of such passages confronts the reader sharply with a vision of life in which honor, valor, and a good death count for more than mere comfort or longevity. The hero functions not from some external "law" but rather from an internalized "code," more expressive of the clan and its right to vengeance than "the law" and its claims to justice. ...[70]

In such material it will not do to present, as the author of Joshua does, formulaic summaries not unlike Curly Bill Brocius' crack in *Tombstone*, "Well, I guess we win!" No, the heroic tale savors each shattering blow, each crash of blade, the crunch of bone. Homer set the standard, as in the account of Patroclus, disguised as Achilles, confronting Thestor in battle:

And next he went for Thestor, son of Enops,
Cowering, crouched in his fine polished chariot—
Crazed with fear, and the reins flew from his grip
Patroclus rising beside him stabbed his right jawbone
Ramming the spearhead square between his teeth so hard
He hooked him by that spearhead over the chariot rail
Hoisted, dragged the Trojan out as an angler perched
On a jutting rock ledge drags some fish from the sea
Some noble catch, with line and glittering bronze hook
So with the spear Patroclus gaffed him off his car
His mouth gaping round the glittering point
And flipped him down face first,

[70] Stone, 197-198.

Dead as he fell, his life breath blown away

—*Iliad*, 16.478-89[71]

The heroic narrator does not flinch from the violence, nor is it presented merely to shock. The graphic depiction of violence articulates a code or worldview that "...looks on life with those blank, unswerving eyes which stare out of the helmet slits on early Greek vases. His vision is terrifying in its sobriety, cold as the winter sun."[72]

A persistent feature of hero stories is the hidden elite status of the hero. All the great names of Homer's *Iliad* are nobility, holders of sprawling estates, leaders of their own personal armies—true warlords. Likewise, the Bride seems a sad victim of a brutal murder, medical neglect, and abuse. But in fact, she belongs to an elite group of trained assassins, the Deadly Viper Assassination Squad, most of whom are women, led by the ruthlessly lethal Bill. Tutored by the most prestigious instructor in the deathly arts, the aged and distractingly moustached Pai Mei, she learns his most jealously guarded secret strike: the "Five Point Palm Exploding Heart Technique." While the whole segment depicting the training of the Bride pokes good fun at the stereotypical "training of the hero" motif, in which the hero descends into despair and then rises to mastery, driven always by a relentless teacher who seems intent on the pupil's mastery or death, it still devotes a good chunk of time to this episode in the story. This elite training, parody aside, drives the plot. The weeks of frustration and agony learning the 2-inch power punch save the Bride when she is buried alive, and the FPPEHT figures in the story's climax.

The book of Judges likewise presents heroes who belong to a warrior elite, though the point is often obscured in modern translations. The judge Ehud is said to be "left-handed," but in fact, the Hebrew text reads

---

[71] Quoted from Homer, *The Iliad*, trans. Robert Fagles (New York: Penguin, 1990), 425-426.
[72] Steiner, 8.

"bound on his right hand." Evidence suggests this statement identifies him as part of a warrior elite, trained from childhood to be ambidextrous with all weapons. Gideon, initial hesitancy aside, is characterized as a "mighty man of valor," a descriptor applicable to ancient nobility and military elites. His enemies speak of his brothers as, *like Gideon himself,* possessing the look and bearing of a king. Jephthah is an outcast but the leader of a band of fighting men, and Samson is the elite of the elite, a Nazirite from birth, for his entire life consecrated to serving God as a spirit-embued berserker, continuously fighting those early Iron Age apex-predators, the Philistines. All these elite warriors have their trademark oddities as well as characteristic choices of tactics or weaponry. Ehud constructs his own sword, a type so novel in its ancient setting that the narrator lacks decent Hebrew words to describe it. Jael murders Sisera, mercenary commander of the Canaanite force, with a tent stake—of a size appropriate to a large bedouin-type tent—and a mallet equal to the task. She is no ordinary lady, but is "most blessed among women" for her deed. Moreover, instead of the stake in the temple, as most English translations suggest, the best evidence suggests she drove the stake through Sisera's open mouth, through his palate, severing his spinal column and staking him to the ground as he died a drawn out, miserable, paralyzed death by asphyxiation.[73] Gideon goes to battle with torches and pitchers and personally butchers the two kings of Midian; wild-haired Samson kills a lion with his bare hands, ravages the city of Ashkelon to settle a party bet, and pulverizes a whole detachment of Philistines with the jawbone of an ass. These contemporaries of Homer's heroes share with them a clear affinity. And the narrator shares Homer's gusto and relish in these details. Indeed, the poetic narration of Sisera's death ends, "So may all your enemies perish, Oh Yahweh, but

---

[73] For explanation, cf. *New International Dictionary of Old Testament Theology and Exegesis,* ed. Willem Van Gemeren (Grand Rapids: Zondervan, 1997) 2:915.

may those who love you rise like the sun in its strength!" (Judges 5:31). Cold as the winter sun, indeed.

The Bride's elite training culminates in her quest for the ultimate weapon, the last sword made by the legendary Hattori Hanzo after his retirement. Elite, almost magical status clings to these weapons. Ehud's sword is christened "The Word of God" in Judges 3. Gideon's pitchers and torches are headlined by the cry "Yahweh's Sword—and Gideons!" Interestingly, the weapon theme in the Anglo-Saxon *Beowulf* poem goes the other direction. Beowulf, when he fights Grendel, refuses sword and armor, judging it unfair to confront the unarmed demonic monster with blade and shield. Instead, after a long wrestling, Beowulf rips Grendel's arm off and flogs him mercilessly with it, driving Grendel into the deep forest to suffer his death agony.

The element of comedy is not alien to the portrayal of this elite status and armament. In Judges, Gideon is transformed from a hiding, hesitant shirker of his obligation to avenge his countrymen into "Yahweh's Sword" by overhearing a demoralized Midanite solder recount a dream in which a gigantic barley biscuit bounces into the Midianite camp and destroys it. This "Attack of the Killer Dinner Roll" draws a smile from the reader but begets a grim certainty in Gideon. Likewise, Ehud's murder of the Moabite king Eglon is laced with humor surrounding the spilling of Eglon's bowels after Ehud drives home the point of "God's Word." As Ehud escapes through the latrine access of Eglon's palace, the attendants stand outside the door, assuming the king is relieving himself.[74] In a single-verse cameo, a hero named Shamgar takes on a contingent of 600 Philistines, killing them all with nothing but an oxgoad. The humor surrounding these stories accentuates the utter competence, the "stylish ferocity" of the hero, as if we ever doubted the outcome.

---

[74] Stone, 237-247.

The First Kill: The Template

Heroic tales, when long and complex, typically give us a picture of the hero's style in an early episode that serves as an establishing shot for the story's concept. In the book of Judges, the story of Ehud (Judges 3:11-30) provides just such a narrative.[75] We see sinful Israel prostrate before an enemy, the nation of Moab, ruled by the terrifying, physically imposing king Eglon, whose name means "Bull Man." Young bulls in the ancient Near East were emblems of virility, potency, and physical strength. Likely, Eglon did not acquire this name at birth but earned it in the old-fashioned Iron Age manner, by his beefy bulk and by slashing people from skull to groin in very large numbers in battle. Eglon establishes his headquarters in the town of Jericho. For Old Testament readers, this is pregnant. Israel's possession of Canaan began with the miraculous fall of the city of Jericho. Joshua had cursed the town and anyone who lived in it afterward. So here's Eglon, occupying Jericho, a living mockery of Joshua's curse, defying Yahweh's miraculous victory. In addition, the marker of Eglon's headquarters is the site of Gilgal, which had formed the base camp for Joshua and the conquering Israelites. So this story is not simply the story of a clever killer offing a bulky bad-guy. By alluding to the book of Joshua, the Judges narrator signals that, in fact, the whole enterprise of Israel's life in Canaan is at stake. What began with victory at Gilgal and Jericho is now falling apart, starting at Gilgal and Jericho. Our story tells us there are more issues here than simply a cruel king and his demand for tribute. We see hints as well of what Israel really needs to do: Ehud "turns back from the idols at Gilgal" which form the "city limit" signs for Eglon's headquarters. Then "trespassing the idols at Gilgal"—again, passing the city-limit markers on the way out—seals Ehud's escape after gutting

[75] Cf. Lawson G. Stone, "Eglon's Belly and Ehud's Blade: A Reconsideration," in *Journal of Biblical Literature* 128/4 (2009) 649-663; "Judges," 237-247.

Eglon. Allusion to Gilgal also evokes the memory of Joshua 5, where Israel reaffirms its identity as God's covenant people through circumcision—a cutting—and Passover. These allusions call on the Israelite hearer or reader to break away from the idols they have served and recover their true identity (cf. 2:10-3:6, 3:11-12).

In many ways, the "desperate housewives" scene when the Bride kills Copperhead (aka Vernita Green, aka Jeannie Bell) serves as an orientation or establishing scene. Importantly, the killing of Copperhead is not chronologically the Bride's first killing. One name, O-Ren Ishii, is already crossed off the list, though we will not see that episode until later. By appearing first, the Copperhead scene gives us a self-contained episode of single combat. It juxtaposes the way of the elite assassin with the life of a middle class mother, the stylized and boundless violence of the hero over against the constraints of bourgeois civility. They stop in mid-fight to welcome Copperhead's daughter home, and then, as if wanting to return to some juicy gossip, nervously dismiss her so they can return to their mortal duel... after having coffee. The death of Copperhead combines a surprise weapon hidden in a box of cereal ("Kaboom") answered by an even more surprisingly ready Bride's thrown dagger, skewering her. Copperhead's death comes startlingly and abruptly, just as Ehud's blade flashes from his right thigh in his left hand, plunging into the abdomen of Eglon, a single devastating blow instantly incapacitating him and leaving him to die silently in his own feces. Both deaths feature a bystander witness. Eglon's attendants wait politely until they are compelled to enter the king's private chamber, finding him "fallen down dead" with the "Word of God" buried from blade to hilt in his belly, Ehud's grim calling card. Copperhead's young daughter sees her mother dead from the Bride's blade and likewise receives a message: "It was not my intention to do this in front of you. For that,

I'm sorry. But you can take my word for it, your mother had it coming. When you grow up, if you still feel raw about it, I'll be waiting." Like the Ehud story's intimation that this is only the beginning, we wonder if Copperhead's daughter will in fact decide to avenge her mother, a story arc not completed in the two volumes of *Kill Bill*, though rumors persist of plans for a "Volume 3" in which Vernita Green's daughter does, indeed, seek vengeance for her mother's death.

These establishing stories—Ehud in Judges, the Copperhead killing in *Kill Bill*—show us what we're in for. When the Bride says, "It's mercy, compassion, and forgiveness I lack, not rationality," we hear the perennial code of the hero. Forgiveness is a private privilege denied the hero, whose honor and rage are implacable forces that must spend themselves fully on the destruction of their adversaries. We tend to gloss over these early episodes, but they reward close re-viewing.

Revenge Versus the Reckoning

Which brings us to the theme of revenge, the essence of this story. We learn from *Kill Bill* that "When fortune smiles on something as violent and ugly as revenge, it seems proof like no other that not only does God exist, you're doing his will." When a single human hero is placed at the center of a narrative, the story of necessity turns around the motives and character of that hero. So the *Iliad* begins, "Rage— Goddess, sing the rage of Peleus' son Achilles, murderous, doomed... (1:1)"[76] A classic plot move is to begin the story with one motive driving the character, such as rage, honor, or vengeance. Homer begins with Achilles' rage at Agamemnon for stealing his hot captive servant girl, which, for a time, motivates the warrior's refusal to fight for his king. Likewise, the *Beowulf* poet articulates the central axiom of the hero:

---

[76] Homer, 77.

Wise sir, do not grieve. It is always better

To avenge dear ones than to indulge in mourning.

For every one of us, living in this world

Means waiting for our end. Let whoever can

Win glory before death. When a warrior is gone,

That will be his best and only bulwark.[77]

The great epic poets cannot leave things with mere personal revenge but ultimately must complicate the driving emotion and, in effect, transform or subvert it to something more significant. In the *Illiad*, Achilles' rage keeps him from the battlefield until Patroclus is killed, and then Achilles' rage turns to a passion to avenge the death of Patroclus, launching him as a one-man frenzy of bleeding death into the battle. The story derives its dramatic tension from the anger of its hero that only breaks when confronted with an even larger motivation, avenging the death of Patroclus. Achilles' rage is trumped by the demands of vengeance. Beowulf likewise kills the first monster, Grendel, as a show of his triumphant, young manhood. By the end of the story, the aged Beowulf goes to fight the dragon, quite certain he faces his own death, but equally certain that he must do so for the sake of his people and his own legacy, represented in the person of a young follower named Wiglaf, who bears the memory and honor of Beowulf into the future.[78] The vengeance theme appears also in the book of Judges, though in a different way. The story of Gideon unfolds as the account of an apparently hesitant hero slowly coming to accept his role as savior and leader of his people, until at the very end, when he has captured the two princes of Midian, Gideon asks, "How would you rank the two men you killed at

[77] Seamus Heaney, *Beowulf: A New Verse Translation* (New York: W. W. Norton, 2000), 97, ll. 1384-1389.

[78] J. R. R. Tolkien, "Beowulf: The Monsters and the Critics," in *Beowulf: A Verse Translation—Authoritative Text, Contexts, Criticism,* trans. Seamus Heaney, ed. Daniel Donoghue (New York: W. W. Norton, 2002), 103-130.

Tabor?" The two princes, apparently seeking survival through flattery, say, "They were just like you, both of royal mien." To which Gideon then replies, "They were my brothers, the sons of my mother. Had you let them live, I'd not kill you."[79] So here, delayed until the very end of the story, after many lines searching through Gideon's motivations and hesitations, the author unveils a key to the entire narrative: a vengeance Gideon should have already been pursuing, and which finally is satisfied only as Gideon becomes God's champion, the deliverer of Israel. The book of Judges also features revenge as a powerful force in the story of Samson. The narrative unfolds as a series of vengeance exchanges in which Samson declares he will avenge himself "just one more time" and then he will quit. The story escalates until he slaughters a Philistine host with the jawbone of an ass, and the text suggests that Samson then saw twenty years of uneventful leadership in Israel. But in Judges 16, Samson re-enters the Philistine culture, first with a prostitute, then with Delilah, culminating in his desecration, loss of sacred status, loss of strength, loss of his eyes, and imprisonment. In the final scene, Samson is the butt of Philistine comedy in their temple when he prays that God will avenge him, even of just one of his lost eyes. But now his vengeance is not a personal vendetta, however personally it might be expressed. Samson is in position to kill a multitude of Philistines and their leaders while also humiliating their god and destroying their holy place. His vengeance is personal but is now caught up in something much larger. Like Gideon, his revenge is caught up in a larger quest to see the world made right. As Doc Holiday said of Wyatt Earp in the movie *Tombstone*, "Oh, make no mistake. It's not revenge he's after; it's the *reckoning*." Revenge is getting even; the reckoning is making the world right again.

In keeping with the unfolding and transformation of the hero's motive, the Bride begins on what is a classical vengeance quest. She has her list,

[79] Author's translation.

and we see each name crossed off as they meet their doom. Of course, the targets are pursued beginning at the outside of the circle and moving toward the center, with the mastermind, in this case Bill, confronted last. This serves the story's drama. Let's face it: if this were Clint Eastwood's "anti-heroic" *Unforgiven,* the Bride would have just found Bill sitting half-drunk and hungover in an outhouse, kicked the door in, and "shot him all to hell," or, more elegantly, just located Bill and shot him with a silenced sniper rifle. But the escalating cunning and skill of each successive target of the Bride's vengeance allows us to see her prowess and perseverance, and also raise the possibility that as enemies become more capable, perhaps the Bride will be unequal to the task.

Like other heroes, the Bride's original motivation undergoes subversion and transformation. In the original two-volume format, the first volume ended with the discovery that the Bride's baby did not die when she was shot, but survived, and is being raised by none other than Bill. The Bride's motivation is completely transformed. Revenge never thinks of the future, only of redressing the past. But with a living daughter, Beatrix shapes a new future. She will still kill with gruesome, brain splattering brutality everyone who had anything to do with the massacre in Texas, but in addition, she will kill them so that she can take her daughter, raise her, and live unthreatened by the Viper organization. She kills to leave the life of an assassin and simply do what she pointedly prevents Copperhead from doing: live a normal life and raise her daughter. This is the quest portrayed in Volume 2.

The Reckoning?

The transformation of the hero's motivation from something merely personal, merely about avenging past wrongs, about getting even, into a battle for life, for the future, for normalcy, should have the effect of creating a space for the violence of the hero. The violence is not really justified or made right by the final outcome, whether it's peace for Israel, a future for the Scandinavian tribes (Beowulf), a new era for the Greeks, or a normal family life for a child. Still, the transformation of the motive, by elevating the outcome and moving the vision to the future—a future free of death and destruction—does reframe the violence and make it meaningful, if not fully justified.

The book of Judges explores this issue with a macabre twist. The final chapters portray a vengeance quest. A Levite seeking to restore his lover and bring her home spends the night in the town of Gibeah within the tribe of Benjamin, presumably safe under the umbrella of fellow Israelites' hospitality. But the night turns sinister as his lover is thrown to a mob and brutally raped all night, to death. The Levite loads her on his donkey, takes her home, and cuts the body into twelve pieces, sending one to each of the twelve tribes of Israel in a grim call to justice. In the battle that follows Benjamin's refusal to bring the rapists forward for justice, the tribe of Benjamin is nearly exterminated, throwing Israel into crisis. The men of Israel have sworn not to allow their daughters to marry any of the remaining Benjamites, since any of them might have been among the violent mob of rapists. As a result, the Israelites slaughter all of the men and married women in an isolated town of Jabesh-Gilead, which had not reported for battle and thus had not taken the oath. This unfortunate town's unmarried women become brides for the unworthy Benjamite survivors. Still needing women for the men of Benjamin, the Israelites allow the Benjamites to abduct women participating in a religious festival at Shiloh, compelling the girls to marry the honor-tainted men of Benjamin. The text then simply notes, "They all went each one to his inheritance," as though it's a happy ending.

But it's not. Can the Israelites, after this chain of horrors, simply go home and resume their lives, living in their cities rebuilt from the char and ash of holy war, enjoying their farms, and going about "normal" life? Did they ever think of the cost in slaughter and mayhem of their pastoral tranquility? Did a Benjamite man ever look across the kitchen fire at his wife, a daughter of Jabesh-Gilead, and wonder what genuine love in marriage would feel like? Even after life seems "back to normal," if the normalcy has come at the cost of righteousness and covenant love, everyone will be wearing a mask, with dead eyes peering through the eyeholes.

At the end of *Kill Bill*, when Beatrix goes away with her daughter, we are tempted to say yes, this was worth it. She has gained peace, a normal life for her child. But at what cost? Is simply vanishing into suburbia, to pick up where Vernita Green could not continue, really an ending that makes the blood-soaked vendetta meaningful? Beatrix, the Bride, has her revenge, but is it just possible that the reckoning still awaits?

SEEING RED:
THE SIGNIFICANCE OF BLOOD IN
TARANTINO'S OEUVRE OF VIOLENCE

Rebecca Ver Straten-McSparran

Introduction

Imagine a scene from a Tarantino film, any Tarantino film. Close your eyes for a moment and look around the scene. Whatever scene you visualized will almost surely include two things: a weapon—a sword, a gun, a knife, or a bat—and blood. If your scene includes only one of the two, it will be blood. The DVD covers of *Reservoir Dogs*, *Inglourious Basterds*, and *Django Unchained* are splashed and gashed with blood. Tarantino's film collection, *Tarantino XX*, includes eight Blu-rays, each with a different cover design in blood. And while the older, sleeker *Kill Bill* covers forego blood, the new pre-order combination of the two films, *Kill Bill: The Whole Bloody Affair*, has a sword-shaped gash of blood across the front and spine. I mention these items because they paint with blood an even larger picture of Tarantino's *oeuvre* than just our favorite spectacle moments in his films. Blood is clearly important to Quentin Tarantino.

If blood makes you queasy, you may wish to skip this chapter, but it's hard to imagine a Tarantino fan who is faint of heart. One of the holiest moments of my life was at the autopsy of one of my patients. I was a hospital chaplain, alone in the quiet room with the diener, the autopsy assistant who makes the initial cuts. To see the interior of the body—bones, spine, sinew, flesh, and muscle—is to be awed by its beauty. I too have been long fascinated by blood. In this chapter I suggest that the way Tarantino uses blood offers insight into the literal, mythic, and theological significance of blood.

Tarantino's love affair with pop culture and its integration in his films is well known. The pop culture icons of '70s bubblegum music or surf music, milkshakes, hamburgers, pulp fiction novels, film noir, stylized black suits and skinny ties are juxtaposed with the narrative or woven into the design to expose truth, Tarantino-style. He wants to change the world and wants to use pop culture icons as tools to do it, using them as lenses through which to see the way the world should be. He gets so much right—including pop culture's love of blood, revenge violence, and vigilante justice. He elevates blood to the status of pop culture icon, along with its accompanying violence. And Tarantino's ethos is soaked with it. His central aesthetic is blood.

An icon, as a symbol, offers windows of meaning into a culture, both present and past. Traditionally, the icon is a devotional painting used as a prayer tool. Christ or a saint is in the foreground, painted darker than the background, the opposite of normal perspective. The figure helps the person praying to focus meditatively, but the goal is to be drawn beyond the figure into the light behind: into God's light, God's presence. Consider then how a pop icon is defined. That favorite academic source, Wikipedia, offers a more insightful definition than most dictionaries:

> A pop icon is a celebrity, character, or object whose exposure in pop culture constitutes a defining characteristic of a given society or era…"Pop icon" status is distinguishable from other kinds of notoriety outside of popular culture, such as with historic figures.[80]

Pop culture icons include pin-up girls in the forties, bobby-soxers of the fifties, the flower children of the sixties, etc. Common to pop icon status is its ubiquity, that is, its presence everywhere, in many places at the same time, or allusions to it outside of its original celebrity status. While it may seem a simple object, it has the capacity to unfold meaning, to open up multiple levels of meaning.

"How can blood be a pop icon?" you ask. "It's been around as long as life!" Good question. Blood carries depth of meaning, symbol, and metaphor from ancient history to diverse, present day media and issues like television, racism, vampire obsession, and *Santeria*. In recent years blood has moved into unprecedented prominence in expressions ranging from the horrific to the humorous. From video games like *Mortal Kombat* (1992), *Resident Evil* (1996), *Carmageddon* (1995), *Manhunt* (2003), *God of War* (2006), *Mad World* (2009), and *Splatterhouse* (2010)[81], to blood drenched Japanese anime such as *Akira* (1988), *Evangelion* (1995), and *Elfen Lied* (2004), we see the popularization of the spectacle of blood.

Bloody scenes reached a new level of acceptability with the greatly publicized O.J. Simpson trial (1994-1995), and little was held back of the

---

[80] Wikipedia contributors, "Pop icon," *Wikipedia, The Free Encyclopedia*, http://en.wikipedia.org/w/index.php?title=Pop_icon&oldid=581717778 (accessed September 5, 2013).

[81] "Top 10 Bloodiest Games of All Time," *examiner.com*, June 23, 2011, http://www.examiner.com/article/top-10-bloodiest-games-of-all-time (accessed September 6, 2013).

gore of war during Desert Storm in Iraq. Popular TV shows like *True Blood*[82] and *Dexter*,[83] along with the popularity of vampire books, movies, TV shows, zombies, and bloody horror films, exemplify the extent to which blood is now embedded as pop icon. It is so popular that there are companies devoted to providing imitation blood: mail-order blood. They offer a wide range of color choices depending upon the need, like ordering paint colors or nail polishes, including designer colors.[84]

Tarantino makes fun with our pop icons turned into idols,[85] gleefully reveling in their excesses. *Kill Bill*'s spectacular and overwhelming Japanese fight scene shows professional killer Beatrix Kiddo (Uma Thurman) slashing and gashing her way through swinging Samurai swords, while severed body parts fly through the air, spurting fountains of blood. The scene threatened to give the film an NC-17 rating unless it was changed, so Tarantino, unwilling to lose a drop of blood, made the scene black and white, having the blood appear white on the black suits and black on Beatrix Kiddo's yellow bodysuit.[86]

Is the proliferation of blood popular simply because of the promise of "blood money": if it bleeds they will come? Has the scent of blood created a trail to an empty holy grail, bled of content? The movie trailer for *Inglourious Basterds* shows Brad Pitt doing what Tarantino loves best: talking. In a bland cobblestone courtyard Pitt is pitching his project to the

---

[82] The relationship between the blood of Christ and popular cultural and television shows has not gone unnoticed by Christian authors and theologians. One recent book focuses on vampires in popular culture and the show *True Blood*: John K. Bucher, Jr., *There is Power in the Blood: The Rising Vampire in Popular Culture* (USA: Gray Matter Books, 2011).

[83] Zach J. Hoag, *Nothing but the Blood: The Gospel According to Dexter* (Los Angeles: Gray Matter Books, 2012).

[84] Jad Abumrad and Robert Krulwich, Blood, podcast audio, WNYC Radiolab, NPR, July 31, 2013, http://www.radiolab.org/story/308403-blood (accessed August 15, 2013).

[85] Jayne Svenungsson, "Representing Pain in Film: A Phenomenological Approach to Gibson, Tarantino and Lynch," *Culture and Religion* 13, no. 1 (March 1, 2012): 69, *ATLA Religion Database with ATLASerials*, EBSCOhost (accessed September 1, 2013).

[86] "Tarantino Analysis," YouTube video, 13:09, posted by "Kenobil15," April 27, 2011, http://www.youtube.com /watch?v=vU9h4JPgu6Q

basterds, inspiring them with the requirement of scalps. Intercut with his speech are white stills smeared in blood with words like "exterminate," "activate," and "infiltrate" stamped into the blood. Is blood in fact an empty pop icon? Is it simply marketing a need for more and more intense entertainment? We live in a cultural environment where entertainment is so overblown that we demand a maximized experience. Our appetite for excitement and thrill is insatiable. As new heights of thrill are offered we are bored with the old normal. This state has a name: "anhedonia."

I think it is quite obvious that the above reasons for the popularity of blood are at least part of the truth. But I also believe there is a lot more at stake here, and that the pop icon blood, instead of being empty, offers windows into the meaning of blood, its mysterious magnetism, and why we are drawn to it. When we enjoy it as spectacle without content or history, we see it with limited understanding. Images of blood on the screen trigger ancient, primal resonances that rise from our collective subconscious and join our current appetite for gore.

Blood could appear to be merely the visual expression of violence. It refuses to let us forget the activity of violence and its ends. At first blush, blood in Tarantino's films seems to scream death and revenge, whether in *Reservoir Dogs, Kill Bill, Pulp Fiction, Inglourious Basterds,* or *Django Unchained.* I think Tarantino is smarter than this. His thinking is not that simple. While he has great fun with us in the scenes of endless blood, he turns on a dime to drive the sword of identity, empathy and truth into our hearts. What, then, is the deeper significance of blood, Tarantino-style?

Clearly, blood is that red fluid that is essential to life, circulating throughout the body's arteries, veins, and capillaries. It brings oxygen and nourishment to the body's tissues and removes from them carbon dioxide and waste. But the meaning of blood is paradoxical and complex. Is it primarily about life or is it about death?

Radically Bonded: Blood as Life

The function and significance of blood lies first in its capacity to sustain life. This is why there is "power in the blood." It is the life principle in humans and animals. The central OT scripture on blood states: "For the life of the creature is in the blood, and I have given it to you to make atonement ("at-one-ment") for yourselves on the altar; it is the blood that makes atonement for one's life" (Leviticus 17:11). Even in vegetables it is considered the life principle: "You drank the foaming blood of the grape" (Deuteronomy 32:14). The first mention of blood in the Bible is of God calling out to Cain, "Where is your brother Abel?" Cain offers the infamous reply, "I don't know. Am I my brother's keeper?" The Lord says, "What have you done? Listen! Your brother's blood cries out to me from the ground" (Genesis 4:9-10). Although Abel is dead, the focus is on his life, his blood crying out. The second mention of blood, Genesis 9:4-6, is God's blessing and covenant-making with Noah following the flood. The word used is not simply "blood," but "lifeblood." "You must not eat meat that has its lifeblood still in it. And for your lifeblood I will surely demand an accounting…for in the image of God has God made [human]kind." Blood is a gift; it is life itself. And it has something to do with being made in God's image.

Love is inseparable from blood as life. The most primal human-to-human relationship is the family, relationships born of blood. Almost nothing can equal the depths of the family bond. When a man and a woman give birth to a baby, their bloodline continues indefinitely. They have given life that will be traceable for a thousand generations. The instinct to love and protect one's offspring is the most primitive instinct of all. It is the most intimate, powerful, radical bond in the world.

If this is true, can we see echoes of this in Tarantino's films? As much blood as there is in *Kill Bill: Vol. 1* and *Kill Bill: Vol. 2*, the entire story springs from this radical, unbreakable bond of blood and love between parent and child. Tarantino understands the power of this bond. The story opens with the pregnant Bride (Uma Thurman) rehearsing for her wedding in the rundown, isolated Two Pines Wedding Chapel, purposely chosen so that no one would find her. The Deadly Viper Assassination Squad, from whom she is hiding, suddenly appear and massacre the entire wedding party, leaving her brutally assaulted and believed to be dead. Awakening from a coma four years later with no baby in sight, the Bride's rage propels her across the planet to avenge her child. She is not the only one, however, who has rejected a life of murder and violence to raise her child in freedom and out of harm's way. Another Deadly Viper Assassin, Vernita Green (Vivica A. Fox), finds a new life for her child in a quiet Pasadena bungalow. Yet the Bride/mother's rage finds her and destroys her attempt at peace by a violent, bloody death. Another mother plays a critical role in the story, only this time it is her daughter, O-Ren Ishii (Lucy Liu), who watches her mother's blood soak through the bed, dripping on her, in the famous animated sequence of *Kill Bill: Vol. 1*. She becomes the most enraged, bitter, and powerful of all the Assassins, caught in the loop of forever avenging her parents' death. Last, and tying up the stories of both *Kill Bill: Vol. 1* and *Kill Bill: Vol. 2*, the Bride discovers her daughter safe, sound, and loved, with her own father, Bill. And Bill's eyes, in his last moments of life, killed by mother-love, offer the Bride the lightest hint of understanding and forgiveness.[87] Love born of the blood bond of parent and child is the ultimate and most radical bond of all.

Powerful blood bonds connect clan, tribe, and race. Identity, love, protection, and trust are built within these bonds, and throughout history, maintaining their purity is central to their strength. They are

---

[87] The element of forgiveness was first suggested in a journal article that can no longer be located.

the deep code of life.

Surprisingly, the consistent anthropological evidence in ancient and primitive cultures supports Leviticus 17:11, pointing to blood being representative of life, not death. Giving of blood is considered the giving of life, receiving blood as receiving life, and sharing of blood as the sharing of life.[88]

One of the most famous Tarantino scenes is the final scene in *Reservoir Dogs*, the confession. Blood slowly oozes out of Mr. Orange, the undercover cop who has been shot in the stomach. In an ever-increasing pool it circles around him on the cold warehouse floor while arguments, torture, fights, and death surround him. Joe Cabot (Tierney), the boss and father figure, states that Mr. Orange is a cop, and points his gun to shoot him. Mr. White, for whom something profound has happened in caring for Mr. Orange, transfers his faithfulness from his father figure, Joe, to his new found "son," and kills Joe in a Mexican standoff. Mortally wounded, he painfully drags himself over to Mr. Orange, his own blood mixing with Mr. Orange's as he passes through the huge pool of blood to cradle Mr. Orange's head and stroke him, as a father to a son. For all of his coolness and professionalism, Mr. White suddenly recognizes in those last minutes in the warehouse something missing, something found. It is far greater and deeper than criminals turned family. It is the bond of father and son made one through sacrifice and shared blood. Loved unto death, humbled and horrified by the tragic results of his lying, a newly born father-son bond gone wild, Mr. Orange can do nothing but call out the anonymous Mr. White by his own, family-given name, Larry, and then divulge the truth of his own duplicity: he is the cop. The failure of the heist and all of the deaths are a result of his lie. Mr. White discovers a betrayal of love that has gripped him, perhaps for the

---

[88] H. Clay Trumbull, *The Blood Covenant: A Primitive Rite and Its Bearing on Scripture* (New York: C. Scribner's Sons, 1885), 299.

first time, at a deeper, more primal level than he could imagine, the self-sacrificing love of a father for his son. While his blood pools and is made one with Mr. Orange's blood, he throws his head back and howls with the anguished grief of the deceived father. In an interview with Graham Fuller, Tarantino says about this scene:

> I'm not trying to preach any morals or get any kind of message across, but for all the wildness that happens in my movies, I think that they usually lead to a moral conclusion. For example, I find what passes between Mr. White and Mr. Orange at the end of *Reservoir Dogs* very moving and profound in its morality and interaction.[89]

The most ancient blood rite is the blood covenant, a shared covenant that is considered the most sacred and lasting covenant of all. It involves the inter-commingling of two people's blood either by tasting or inter-transfusion. From Egypt's ancient Book of the Dead to the poetic myths of the Norse, from the Mayan culture to Assyria, ancient Greece to China and Native American culture, this rite has been practiced for thousands of years. It binds one person to another so closely that marriage between two with whom the covenant exists is considered incest. In Arabia, this blood binding makes brothers closer than those who were nursed at the same breast, or even closer than those of common descent.[90]

Ancient history and literature count the heart, or blood fountain, as the symbol and substance of life. The gift of the blood as life is understood as the gift of the very nature of its original owner. As it transfers from one organism to another in both classic stories and in medical practice, it carries with it a revitalizing or re-creating power. In both Egypt and ancient Mexico, legends are told in which the world was

[89] Gerald Peary, ed., *Quentin Tarantino: Interviews* (Jackson: University Press of Mississippi, 1998), 61.
[90] Trumbull, 10-12.

destroyed completely. The gods mingled human blood with other blood (in Egypt, mandrakes' blood) and poured it out on the earth. Its flow revived the earth.[91]

In ancient religions over all the world, blood-giving was understood as life-giving. "Life-giving was love-showing. Love-showing was heart-yearning after union in love and in life and in blood and in being."[92]

Radically Divided: Blood as Death

Tarantino wouldn't be a successful filmmaker if he focused on the life-giving aspects of blood. His is a cinema of excess, of blood, violence, and death. It's not a stretch to say that hardly anyone has even noticed the life-giving aspects of his films. When a random Tarantino scene arises in my mind, it's invariably one of the following: the Bride killing the Crazy 88 fighters, O-Ren's death scene in the snow, or Django in the bloodied, silent vestibule. If the first word of blood is life and it radically bonds human life together, why do we have such fun with it and glory in its gore and violence? Is death the last word of blood? Are we "stuck in the middle" of the violence, as the song famously says in *Reservoir Dogs'* ear-slicing scene, and can't get out? Why is it so fascinating? Why, in fact, are we so mesmerized that we cannot leave it, or even move?

Tarantino distinguishes between two kinds of violence: cartoon violence and a deeply disturbing kind of realistic violence.[93] Cartoon violence is spectacle violence. Blood flows in outrageous proportions and revenge is full, sweet, and complete, whether there are 88 Samurais, a plantation home vestibule filled with dead white men, or a theater full of Nazis. The blood sprayed or splattered everywhere is an odd,

[91] Ibid., 110-112.
[92] Ibid., 96.
[93] Peary, 33.

unblood-like bright red, almost cartoonish in color and in action. In Tarantino's directorial hands it is a dance, performance art, so that we cannot turn away, cannot keep from feeling glee. We are riveted, caught in its fascination. When the last head, or arm, or body falls silent, we are relieved. There is a sense of catharsis, and it feels like there will be peace again through the redemptive violence that has taken place. A "problem" is solved, whether it is Deadly Viper Assassin Vernita Green (Vivica A. Fox), O-Ren Ishii (Lucy Liu), Mr. Candie, or Stephen. Resolution is found.

In spite of the feeling of catharsis and even humor in this over-the-top violence, the real truth is clear if we reflect on it at all after the film is over. The violence is a cycle and it will come back again. In *Kill Bill: Vol. 1*, the Bride tells Vernita Green's young daughter that someday she (the daughter) will seek revenge for her mother's murder. O-Ren Ishii's violence and brutality is initiated by watching her parents' brutal murder. The ends of violence are clear, and in most cases Tarantino makes sure we get it: revenge incites revenge. It does not initiate peace.

Django Unchained's dazzling showdown presents an imaginative story distant from reality. It is closest, however, to the true Nat Turner story of leading a short-lived rebellion of slaves against their plantation owners. Within two days the rebels were caught, although Turner wasn't found for about two months. Between fifty-five to sixty-five whites were killed in the rebellion, but most reports list between two hundred to three hundred blacks killed in retribution, some free and some entirely unaware of the circumstances.[94] When the oppressed rise up against the powerful, the powerful crush them with greater bloodshed, greater vengeance. Should the oppressed win, history shows that too often they

---

94 Christine Gibson, "Nat Turner, Lightning Rod," American Heritage Magazine, November 11, 2005, http://web.archive.org/web/20090406063535/http://www.american-heritage.com/articles/web/20051111-nat-turner -slavery-rebellion-virginia-civil-war-thomas-r-gray-abolitionist.shtml (accessed October 20, 2013).

in turn simply become the oppressor, as evidenced in backlashes in Detroit, Soweto, Egypt, and Tunisia.[95]

The second kind of violence, according to Tarantino, is:

> tougher, rougher, more disturbing. It gets under your skin. Go to a video store, to the horror section or the action-adventure section, nine out of ten of the films you get there are going to be more graphically violent than my movie (Reservoir Dogs), but I'm trying to be disturbing. What's going on is happening to real human beings. There are ramifications to it.[96]

Mr. Orange's long, slow suffering from his gunshot wound mirrors this second kind of violence. Being shot in the stomach is the most painful place a person can get shot. When the bullet enters the stomach wall, acidic juices from the stomach are discharged into the body, causing unimaginable pain until the body becomes numb from it. During filming, the process is overseen by a medic to

---

[95] Rowan Williams, *Wrestling with Angels,* ed. Mike Higgins (London: SCM Press, 2007), 171-172. Williams summarizes Rollo Mays' landmark work, *Power and Innocence: A Search for the Sources of Violence,* in which he connects violence with powerlessness, an aggression that is first toward the self, since that self feels it has no worth because it has no power. May says that violence is an irrational assertion and a creation of power out of nothing. Williams shows that the violence of oppressed communities, particularly in wealthy nations (Detroit, Soweto) is usually turned against the welfare agencies or community workers, that is, the community itself instead of against its enemies. The danger of the oppressed becoming the oppressor, common in less affluent nations, is central to Paulo Freire's important study *The Pedagogy of the Oppressed: 30th Anniversary Edition* (New York: Bloomsbury, 2000). He says, "[Dehumanization of the oppressed] is a distortion of being more fully human, sooner or later being less human leads the oppressed to struggle against those who made them so. In order for this struggle to have meaning, the oppressed must not, in seeking to regain their humanity, become in turn oppressors of the oppressors, but rather restorers of the humanity of both" (44). Friere's study is cited in relation to the backlash in Tunisia and Egypt (http://blogs.independent.co.uk/2011/10/26/why-paulo-freires-pedagogy-of-the-oppressed-is-just-as-relevant-today-as-ever/), and it is difficult to miss in the violence with the Islamic State of Iraq (ISIS).
[96] Peary, 33.

ensure that it is graphic and entirely realistic in terms of the amount of blood released before death comes and the time it takes to die. It is disturbing by design. "It shows violence as it would really be—blood-soaked, panicky, inglorious, and slow."[97] The horrific and nauseating tearing apart of the runaway Mandingo slave by dogs in *Django Unchained* mirrors the disturbing truth of what happened to slaves. Tarantino wants us to be drawn into its horrific truth, to experience these people as real human beings. He wants us to have empathy for them. The blood doesn't spurt or spray in bright red fountains. It is experienced as the real blood of a victim. Blood as pop icon unfolds into more meaning than expected at first drop.

The two kinds of violence articulated by Tarantino are surprisingly similar to the groundbreaking work of René Girard (b. 1923), a significant French philosopher of social science and anthropology who recently retired from Stanford University. Girard believes that in every person there resides a desire to imitate others. This desire to imitate goes so deep that it is part of the very structure of each human being. He calls this "mimetic desire" (think of mime, mimic, imitate). This imitative desire is the source of all conflict. We desire an object because someone else desires it. Conflict arises over the object, but soon the object is forgotten and the conflict is between persons, which Girard calls mimetic rivalry. A structural feature in humanity, equated with mirror neurons by some neuroscientists, mimetic desire springs to communal life not just in mimetic rivalry, but also in the fascination that arises from watching violence (mimetic fascination). During war or uprisings, for example, people are glued to their television screens, relishing every image of bloodshed and violence. A certain glitter in the eyes is almost apparent when people are mesmerized while watching a physical fight or a bloody video game.[98]

[97] Ibid., 47.
[98] Gil Bailie, *Violence Unveiled: Humanity at the Crossroad,* (New York: The Crossroads Publishing Company, 1997), 80.

When one person or side "wins," the violence ends, and for the winner, the evil is purged. Catharsis brings a sense of peace. Lifeblood has been shed to preserve life. But it is a false peace, for the vengeance of one sows the seed of revenge against the victim. The cycle begins again. Tarantino does not let us forget this. The violence reaches deep into the structure of each human in mimetic desire and has radically divided the even deeper union of humanity's family: its blood.

Girard shows that since the beginning of time the cycle of revenge has been minimized and temporarily subdued by offering an innocent victim as scapegoat and sacrifice. At predictable times the ritual is repeated and effectively resolves the violence. This has occurred throughout history in all cultures and is evident in biblical history. While in most archaic cultures the victim is human, in biblical history the scapegoat and atonement sacrifice literally are goats. Leviticus 16:8-10 says:

> [Aaron] is to cast lots for the two goats—one for the LORD and the other for the scapegoat. Aaron shall bring the goat whose lot falls to the LORD and sacrifice it for a sin offering. But the goat chosen by lot as the scapegoat shall be presented alive before the LORD to be used for making atonement by sending it into the wilderness as a scapegoat.

While developing his theory, Girard saw suddenly that a decisive turning point occurred at the historical time that Christ was crucified on the cross. At that precise moment something fundamental altered, or shifted, in the universe. For the first time the suffering victim was not nameless and faceless, which was crucial in archaic cultures. Instead, the identity of the victim was recognizable, and with recognition came empathy. Empathy for the victim caused sacrifice and scapegoating to become less and less effective in silencing the call to violence. Girard recognized that Christ's death and sacrifice broke the bonds of something deep and structural within humans: mimetic desire, the root of conflict and violence. Consequently, the time between sacrifice and empathy for the victim became increasingly shorter until the ritual was no longer effective at managing violence. Identification of the victim and the empathy that followed opened a new way to peace. This insight moved Girard so deeply that he became a Christian. The impact of his theory of mimetic desire and scapegoating has influenced fields such as anthropology and social theory, entirely outside the bounds of Christianity. Arenas as diverse as economics, literature, and neuroscience also apply his understanding of violence.

A Fragile Peace

Insightfully, Tarantino purposefully employs both kinds of violence toward his ends. He exploits mimetic rivalry and fascination, with riveting, over-the-top cathartic violence and swaths of blood flowing, but in a blink confronts us with intimate, provocative, and brutal violence, evoking empathy for the victim as if to say, this too is us: we are implicated. He illustrates the confusion between a.) the spectacle of violence and revenge that historically results in sacrifice to subdue the violence, and b.) intimate, painful, disturbing empathy with the victim. Empathy for the victim is the post-Crucifixion/Resurrection hint that the possibility of the end of violence exists every time it is experienced, and that there is a way of peace opened through empathy. But unbelieving culture is blind to this, or stops short of accepting it.

Unlike Rene Girard, who sees that Christ broke the bonds of violence, Tarantino's empathy for the victim resolves nothing.

How blood is used in Tarantino's films reveals his vision of violence. Blood for Tarantino is not simple. It is not an empty pop icon, the symbol of the passion or consumerism of an era. Each film explores different facets of the meaning of blood. The blood of revenge in *Reservoir Dogs* is self-destructive, evil, and annihilates everyone in its path. The blood of revenge in *Kill Bill* is an unending cycle of blood and violence. At the same time, the bond of family blood, the deepest blood covenant, is exalted and defended by Tarantino in *Kill Bill,* as is the blood of the family of race in *Inglourious Basterds* and *Django Unchained.* Although radically divided through bloodshed, the yearning for peace through the shedding of blood has its heart prints all over Tarantino's work. Forgiveness and reconciliation through bloodshed are even evident in the closing moments of *Kill Bill,* when a knowing, almost tender and forgiving look passes between Bill and the Bride. In the end, however, the peace made in Tarantino's work is only a temporary peace, a fragile peace signed in blood. The resurrection it offers is a resurrection of violence once again. It is doomed to repeat itself. But it is the best we can come up with without Christ's blood, shed to end the cycle of violence and to bring a lasting peace, and Tarantino has captured this difficult but poetic struggle and unfolded its meaning and its ends in the icon of the blood he presents.

The End of Death

Blood is a visual reminder of our violences. It doesn't allow us to idealize violence for long or to keep it abstract, separate from life experience. And ultimately, if the life is in the blood as history and theology have appeared to maintain, if blood really does have effective power, and if the most primitive blood rite is the blood covenant, which is always a giving of life by giving one's own blood, a sharing of blood, it is a deeper word than sacrifice. It seals something with permanence. It can never be broken. Sacrifice is a ritual that must happen again and again. By his blood shed in covenant to us, Christ ends the blood system, unlocking the grip that coveting, desire, and rivalry have held over us since the beginning of time.

Earlier I stated that the first words of blood are life and love, and that the most radical bond of blood is the family. While bleeding on the cross for our sin and deeply rooted violence, Christ does something that forever seals his blood as life: he gives birth to the first entirely spiritual and eternal family born of his life-giving blood: "When Jesus saw his mother there, and the disciple whom he loved standing nearby, he said to her, 'Woman, here is your son,' and to the disciple, 'Here is your mother.' From that time on the disciple took her into his home" (John 19:26-27). Down through the ages until now, all who will may participate in this spiritual family through the radical bond of Christ's reconciling blood that brings peace.

> For God was pleased...through him to reconcile to himself all things, whether things on earth or things in heaven, by making peace through his blood, shed on the cross. Once you were alienated from God and were enemies in your minds because of your evil behavior. But now he has reconciled you by Christ's physical body through death to present you holy in his sight, without blemish and free from accusation.
>
> —Colossians 1:19-22 (NIV)

We celebrate this union and the life that is in his blood by the sharing of it in the Lord's Supper with Eucharist, which is Latin for "thanksgiving."

Communion celebrates the end of sacrifice and beginning of the eternal at-one-ment and life that we may have through Christ's blood.

The mind-haunting image of Mr. White holding Mr. Orange, who is dying in his own blood, echoes an image that has endured over centuries and cultures: Mary cradling Jesus in his death, named "The Pietà." Pietà literally means compassion, or pity. It may be one of the most powerful images of empathy for the victim ever—the mother holding her dead son. The meanings of this icon have unfolded over the centuries as double-bound empathy for the victim: Christ has given his life for Mary and all the victims of sin, that is, all humanity, and she has reached out in compassion, pity, and love to her son and Savior. Christ's blood as icon unfolds for us a multiplicity of meanings—of life everlasting, of peace and reconciliation, of love and compassion, of forgiveness, of rebirth, the chance to become new all over again.

The Pietà Tarantino-style begins in compassion and an unfolding love so poignant that it wrings confession out of the lips of the dying Mr. Orange. Tarantino even goes so far as to open up the space for reconciliation, peace, compassion, forgiveness, love, and even life through blood sharing and empathy for the victim. But the response is radically different: in the last dying act of his savior he is shot to death. But Mr. White chooses the way of death, and we the audience have to sit in the shock of that final choice. It's as if Tarantino is shining the spotlight on himself as well as us. We have choices and their consequences are weighty.

Our Present Blindness

Our thirst for blood runs deep. In centuries past, experiments were performed at various times by scientists and doctors to show that giving the blood of a person or animal to another would change their very nature: blood could transform a violent man into a docile sheep. No obvious change has ever resulted. However, a recent Radiolab podcast,[99] dedicated entirely to the topic of blood, discusses experiments that show a remarkable change when the blood of a young rat is injected into an older rat. The rat begins to act younger. Its memory and activity increase. The brain neurons change and take on the appearance of younger neurons. When the blood of a baby is pumped into an old heart, the heart begins to decrease in size, like a younger, healthier heart. It is believed that the cause is certain proteins. Although there is a long way to go in such research (looking for 1-600 proteins out of 100,000) the surprising conclusion is that the key to youth and life is in the blood.

As pop culture icon unfolds into ancient icon, blood has supreme significance in human culture. Presumed to be vacuous and gory, blood instead holds clues to the mystery of life in the universe, to the end of violence, and, through the shed blood of Jesus Christ, to life eternal. It is, perhaps, the key to an inclusive gospel that reaches into the deep, multifaceted structures of human culture and human hearts to make peace with God. While Tarantino may not see the full significance of blood and the multiple layers of life it brings, he draws us into a complex experience of blood. And in doing this he does not hinder, but urges us to enter deep, interior meanings of the pop culture icon blood.

---

[99] Abumrad and Krulwich.

JACKIE BROWN'S FOUR LOVES: AN EXPLORATION OF THE CHARACTERS AND RELATIONSHIPS OF *JACKIE BROWN* THROUGH C. S. LEWIS' *THE FOUR LOVES*

Ben Avery

Introduction

Jackie Brown might not seem to fit in Quentin Tarantino's filmography. Coming at a time when many in Hollywood were trying to be Tarantino (if it makes money, copy it!), Quentin Tarantino himself seemed to go the opposite direction.

Based on Elmore Leonard's *Rum Punch*, *Jackie Brown* is still trademark Tarantino. It tells the story of a flight attendant (Jackie Brown) who is bringing money into the country for gun dealer Ordell Robbie, but when another of Ordell's partners in crime tells the law too much, Jackie is picked up. Now she finds herself caught between the murderous Ordell and the lawmen who want to take him down, but she has a plan. With bail bondsman Max Cherry helping her, she has figured out how to give Ordell to the law, take Ordell's money in the process, and walk away to a new life.

Perhaps *Jackie Brown* is not as quotable as some of his other movies, but it still retains Tarantino's smooth and artificially realistic dialogue. Lacking the on-screen blood and violence of his previous two films and cutting out violent scenes from the source material altogether, *Jackie Brown* still creates tension and shock value when violence does occur. And while it does not feature the over the top cool or quirky characters found in *Pulp Fiction* or *Reservoir Dogs*, it is full of strong performances by actors who are clearly enjoying their job and turning in strong, funny, and emotional work.

Everything that makes a Tarantino movie great is here; it's just dialed back to bring the story Tarantino wants into focus. "I wasn't trying to top *Pulp Fiction* with *Jackie Brown*. I wanted to go underneath it and make a more modest character study movie," Tarantino said in a 2003 interview. "So, if you were waiting for *Pulp Fiction* part two, you were going to be disappointed."[100] In focusing on the characters and the quiet moments of their stories, Tarantino made a movie that put the people and their relationships ahead of the tension that would normally come from a crime thriller.

This focus on characters results in a two-and-a-half-hour movie with quiet and thoughtful character moments, deliberate and tense action, sudden explosions of violence, and then a return to the quiet character moments.

A brilliant and emotional exchange between Samuel L. Jackson's Ordell Robbie and Robert De Niro's Louis Gara near the end of the movie is one such example. They argue. They stop to think. They accuse. They both realize their relationship has changed and there is no turning back. Everyone— Ordell, Louis, and the audience—knows there is now only one way for things

[100] Jeff Otto, "An Interview with Quentin Tarantino," *IGN*, October 10, 2003, http://www. ign.com/articles/2003/10/10/an-interview-with-quentin-tarantino (accessed August 5, 2014).

to play out. And everyone—Ordell, Louis, and the audience—is waiting for it to happen. It's inevitable, but it is directed and acted and written (much of the power of this scene comes directly from the novel) in a way that it's not the suspense in the plot that holds tension, it's the suspense of what will happen to the characters.

These drawn out, silent moments force the viewer to enter the heads of the characters to figure out what they are thinking, which makes the characters more real. And these real characters, these empathetic characters, play off each other as circumstances and choices and consequences cause relationships to change and deepen and fall apart.

Looking at the relationships, *Jackie Brown* becomes a movie that is a more believable romance/love story than so many others that Hollywood churns out. But it is also a movie about friendship and other relationships.[101]

Another examination of relational themes is found in the pages of Christian apologist C. S. Lewis' book *The Four Loves*, a collection of radio talks he gave in the late 1950s, compiled and published as a book in 1960. In *The Four Loves* Lewis defines four Greek words that describe different types of love and gives them a practical, relatively modern[102] context, while also commenting on the Christian application of these definitions.

The book uses C. S. Lewis' usual blend of wit, everyday practicality, and theological understanding to create definitions that are eloquent and understandable to both the layperson and the scholar. It is also a blend of his different non-fiction works. Like some of his academic

---

[101] In looking at the relationships of *Jackie Brown*, there is one aspect that looms large but that will not be explored here. The exploration of the themes of race and race relations is beyond the scope of this essay, but it is worth noting that Tarantino uses *Jackie Brown* as a vehicle to look into those themes. Casting Pam Grier was a conscious decision. In the book, the character is Jackie Burke, a white woman, and changing her race intentionally changes the core of many of her relationships on that level. For example, her romance with Max Cherry becomes an interracial romance, but it is the more general and generic relationships between the characters that will be examined here.

[102] Relative in that, although these ideas were presented some sixty years ago, they are not by any means confined to his time or place.

works, it is a word study; like his theological works, it expresses practical and deep spiritual meaning.

The Four Loves is the lens that will be used here to dissect and examine the various relationships in *Jackie Brown*.

Affection

> *Baby love, my baby love*
> *I need you, oh how I need you*
>
> —"Baby Love" by Holland-Dozier-Holland,
> performed by The Supremes

The Greek word for Lewis' first love is *storge* ("two syllables and the g is 'hard'"[103]), which he defines as "Affection." Lewis goes on to define Affection as a "warm comfortableness" and "satisfaction of being together." He explains,

> Almost anyone can become an object of Affection; the ugly, the stupid, even the exasperating…it ignores the barriers of age, sex, class and education. It can exist between a clever young man from the university and an old nurse, though their minds inhabit different worlds. It ignores even the barriers of species. We see it not only between dog and man but, more surprisingly, between dog and cat.[104]

Affection almost seems to be the only positive emotion Ordell Robbie can afford to give to anyone. Ordell is easily identifiable as the antagonist of the movie, but when he is with people he likes, or people he wants something from (which may be the only reason he likes anyone in the first place), he is likeable. We are introduced to his character soon after we follow Jackie Brown during her long tracking shots through the airport to her job. In fact, we spend so much time with him after those opening credits with Jackie that it's almost easy to forget this is her movie, not his.

---

[103] C. S. Lewis, *The Four Loves* (1960, repr. New York: Harcourt, Brace, 1991), 31.
[104] Ibid., 32.

Ordell's first scene presents us with three different relationships: Ordell's blonde-haired surfer girl and live-in girlfriend (or at least, she was a girlfriend at one time), Melanie Ralston, played by Bridget Fonda; Louis Gara, Ordell's partner in crime who has just gotten out of jail and who Ordell seems to be spending a lot of time trying to impress with his tales of being a black market gun dealer; and Beaumont, known only by one name to Ordell—and he's not even sure if it's the first or last name—but who is also connected to Ordell through crime.

Passing through these relationships, we see a wide range of Ordell's reactions. With Louis, Ordell laughs a bit too loudly, showing off his knowledge of guns and exploits in crime, crimes that took place while Louis was in jail and Ordell was not. When the phone rings, Ordell interacts with Melanie, ordering her to get the phone even though she says what they both know: it will be for him. But he orders her to do it anyway, with scorn in his voice and a threatening scowl on his face. He barks orders at her like she's a dog, and she's not afraid to snap back, even as she acquiesces. As he tries to keep up the façade while interacting with Louis, his frustration boils under the surface, but not for long. The third relationship is introduced with a second phone call. Beaumont is calling from jail, asking for Ordell's help, and the anger and frustration from another go-round with Melanie turn quickly to annoyance with (and perhaps concern for?) Beaumont.

Louis and Ordell's relationship will be explored more with another of the loves. The Affection, the *storge* love, is illustrated the most by Ordell and Melanie. It can actually be seen in Ordell's relationships with all of *Jackie Brown*'s primary female characters. With Simone and Sheronda, Ordell's affection is evident. He likes them. They amuse him. He likes having them around. Jackie Brown, perhaps, held a similar place in his life at one time in the past. And so did Melanie.

But of all the women not named Jackie Brown, Melanie is the one with the most screen time. She is the one Ordell actually lives with. Their past is vague. She's been around for years, and Louis knew her from the old days running with Ordell. There was a romance with someone in Japan since then, but for whatever reason she is back with Ordell.[105]

At the moment in time in which *Jackie Brown* opens, Ordell and Melanie are accustomed to each other. They inhabit the same physical space, but relationally could not be farther away from each other. In fact, they really seem to reflect the other side of Affection, a darker side that Lewis warns against. The assumption could be made that Ordell and Melanie are unhappy because they do not have Affection for one another. C. S. Lewis actually addresses similar situations in *The Four Loves*, asking, "Are all the unhappy (homes) unhappy because Affection is absent?" His answer: "I believe not. It can be present, causing the unhappiness. Nearly all the characteristics of this love are ambivalent. They work for ill as well as for good. By itself, left simply to follow its own bent, it can darken and degrade human life."[106]

"Dark" and "degrading" are two very apt descriptions of Ordell and Melanie's lives. The opening scene is uncomfortable, with its long shots of characters who are not speaking but are simply staring at each other or avoiding eye contact. Making it even more uncomfortable is Louis, sitting between the two roommates, bothered by the abusive back and forth but unwilling to address it.

Ordell's treatment of Melanie, and hers of him, is certainly born from their constant presence and familiarity. Melanie could leave, but she is comfortable; Ordell could kick her out (her name is on the apartment buzzer, but he rules the roost), but she's his. And that is another level of Ordell's relationship with her (and Sheronda and Simone, too, to an extent). They are possessions or, at least, objects. Ordell does not treat them like people but

[105] This backstory is touched on in the novel and in Leonard's earlier novel, 1978's *The Switch*. But the novel is not the movie, and the movie does not give that information.
[106] Lewis, 62.

like things, toys or tools to be passed around and moved from one place to another. He has more interest in guns and money, and the women in his life (including Jackie Brown) are merely means to an end.

Melanie's death at Louis' hands is no more than an inconvenience to Ordell. He does not mourn her; she is merely a lost thing. Or perhaps Melanie is more like a pet: a small, sharp-voiced dog, always underfoot, sometimes annoying, sometimes leaving a mess, but also there and willing when she is needed to fetch something.

Meanwhile, Jackie is a mule, transporting money into the country for Ordell. There is a loyalty of some sort in play for Ordell and these women, but that loyalty lasts only as long as it doesn't have any personal cost. Again, Lewis, in describing the dark underside of Affection, gives what could be a description of Ordell: "Selfish or neurotic people can twist anything, even love, into some sort of misery or exploitation."[107]

This brings up the other relationship we were introduced to in this first scene: Beaumont. At first, it almost seems there is something genuine between the two of them, but that cannot last long. Beaumont is the character that, unintentionally and off screen, sets everything in motion when he gets caught with a gun and jailed. Before his bond is posted, he tells the authorities enough to put them on Jackie Brown's (and because of that, Ordell's) trail.

This brings out Ordell's true colors, which have been hinted at but not fully revealed. Here is where Ordell uses every tool at his disposal for self-preservation: money, used to pay Beaumont's bail; the façade of a friendship, given support by the bail and used to help convince Beaumont to do something he would never do otherwise—climb into a man's trunk; temptation, finally luring Beaumont into the trunk, and his death, with the promise of a trip to a chicken and waffles shack; and then the final tool, a gun, used to shoot Beaumont in the trunk of the car.

[107] Ibid., 53.

In another hypothetical essay about spiritual elements in Quentin Tarantino's movies, it would be easy to compare Ordell to Satan (and in contrast, Max Cherry to Christ). And the comparison is apt. He uses temptation, lies, and intimidation to dominate, subdue, or destroy whatever or whoever has the misfortune to end up in his path. He is, perhaps, one of Tarantino's greatest villains. His scene in Jackie's place, when he turns the lights off over and over, shrouding Jackie and himself in darkness, is particularly chilling.

His primary characteristic is selfishness; his primary motivation is self-preservation. Everything he does ultimately serves those two ends. And so he murders, and he attempts murder. His faux friendship with Beaumont lasts only until it threatens Ordell's freedom. He stops trying to murder Jackie Brown only when his manhood is on the line.

But while Ordell casts his shadow over everyone in the movie, this is still Jackie Brown's movie, and not all relationships are so negative and self-serving. Jackie Brown's relationship with Max Cherry, which will be explored a bit later, starts with positive affection.

And then there is ATF agent Ray Nicolette (Michael Keaton), one of the genuinely good people Jackie Brown comes into contact with, who wants to help Jackie, although he is more interested in taking down Ordell and upholding the law. Jackie uses his own morality against him later on, but their relationship is purer than most in this story. Their relationship works because, as Lewis describes a positive *storge*-driven relationship, "there is common sense and give and take and 'decency.' "[108]

Ray actually shows some kindness to Jackie, extending it to her even though he knows she cannot or will not accept it, because he is asking her to help bring down Ordell. But he treats her fairly, even as the two of them are working toward their own goals: her goal, to stay alive and get away from Ordell; his goal, to bust Ordell. Their goals rely on each other, thus the give

---

[108] Ibid., 54.

and take.

This goodwill and affection is harmed, though, when Jackie has to lie to him about the money she has taken from Ordell. He knows she's lying, and she knows that he knows. But Ordell is still at large and needs to be taken down, so they still must work together. This common goal is almost enough to make Ray and Jackie friends.

Almost.

Friendship

I got one more thing I'd like to yell about right now
Hey brother, there's a better way out

—"Across 110ᵗʰ Street" by Bobby Womack

"When either Affection or Eros is one's theme, one finds a prepared audience. The importance and beauty of both have been stressed and almost exaggerated again and again…But very few modern people think Friendship a love of comparable value or even a love at all," C. S. Lewis says in the opening paragraph to the Friendship chapter.[109] Lewis spends a lot of time defining Friendship and contrasting it with companionship, in that it arises from companionship, but also transcends it. In Lewis' definition, Friendship comes from shared views or interests or religion or activity, but "…few value it because few experience it."[110]

Perhaps the second strongest relationship in *Jackie Brown* is the friendship shared by Louis and Ordell. Separated for six or so years, they pick up where they left off before Louis went to jail. The bond of their friendship is again warned against by C. S. Lewis:

Friendship, I have said, is born at the moment when one man says
to another "What! You too? I thought that no one but myself…"

[109] Ibid., 57.
[110] Ibid., 58.

But the common taste or vision or point of view which is thus discovered need not always be a nice one. From such a moment art, or philosophy, or an advance in religion or morals might well take their rise; but why not also torture, cannibalism, or human sacrifice?[111]

This is Ordell and Louis. Together they are criminals. They have the same view about murder. After Louis admits to killing Melanie, Ordell replies, "If you had to do it, you had to do it, brother."[112] They share drinks, they share laughs, they share a past, they share Melanie. Ordell takes the lead in the relationship, to be sure. He reveals his own murder of Beaumont to Louis only to demonstrate his dominance. But it is a friendship that they share.

Until the friendship goes sour. It is not the actual murder of Melanie that breaks down their relationship. Rather, the foundation of that relationship, a relationship based on violence and lies and crime, crumbles when it looks to Ordell as if Louis' story about killing Melanie could be a lie.

This scene is difficult to watch, particularly because Ordell and Louis have a stable friendship when they first drive away in the van, but slowly, as Ordell tries to piece everything together, their friendship begins to unravel. It is brilliant filmmaking, letting the audience think with Ordell. Roger Ebert's review of the movie starts with a reference to the scene:

I like the moment when the veins pop out on Ordell's forehead. It's a quiet moment in the front seat of a van, he's sitting there next to Louis, he's just heard that he's lost his retirement fund of $500,000, and he's thinking hard. Quentin Tarantino lets him think. Just holds the shot, nothing happening.[113]

But so much happens in that scene, so much of it happening in the faces

[111] Ibid., 78-79.
[112] *Jackie Brown*, dir. Quentin Tarantino, by Quentin Tarantino (Alliance Atlantis, 1997).
[113] Roger Ebert, "Jackie Brown," *RogerEbert.com*, December 24, 1997, http://www.rog-erebert.com/reviews/Jackie-brown-1997 (accessed August 4, 2014).

of the characters, not in the words.

Until this point, Louis is safe with Ordell. Ordell has shown him Beaumont's body, and Louis has accepted that that would be his fate if he ever crossed Ordell, and both Louis and Ordell are secure in the knowledge that it will never happen. Now? Jackie Brown has hatched a plot that costs Ordell everything. She has his money, and he is confused. Louis has no good answers, so Ordell asks the obvious question: did Louis and Melanie concoct the story that Louis killed her as a way to make off with half a million dollars?

De Niro proves to be a master of his craft here, as Louis goes from indignation to masculine bluster to helplessness. As soon as the question is out of Ordell's mouth, it cannot go back in. "Aw, fuck you for asking me that," Louis says. "Fuck you, brother. How could you fucking ask me that?"[114] The turmoil and fear on his face after that tell us everything. This friendship is over.

And so is his life.

The scene continues, though. They figure out that Jackie has the money, and the tension slowly goes away. We're relieved. Louis is relieved. Until Louis reveals that he saw Max Cherry and didn't think anything of it. Ordell is not the forgiving type, and this is unforgivable. The gunshot we are expecting somehow still manages to come unexpectedly.

As C. S. Lewis says, very few people experience friendship, and the same is true in *Jackie Brown*. Probably the only other example of the principles of Friendship comes from someone who starts the movie with no friends: Max Cherry, the bail bondsman Ordell visits to get Beaumont, and later Jackie Brown, out of jail.

While Ordell seems to know and have connections to many different people, Max Cherry brings almost no one into the narrative. Almost every relationship he has is strictly professional. His closest possible friendship is with Winston, but even that is only shown in a photograph and in a few job-related interactions.

---

[114] *Jackie Brown*

Max is alone and lonely, and Robert Forster plays him with thoughtfulness and melancholy. It is not a sad life, but it does not seem to be fulfilling.

His relationship with Jackie Brown, however, becomes something close to friendship. It starts as affection, as Max listens to what Jackie has to say and actually cares about her. They have almost nothing in common, but conversations about cigarettes and music and aging and Jackie's problems with the law and Ordell bring them closer. More than with agent Ray Nicollete, Jackie is able to trust Max, and Max trusts Jackie enough to get caught up in her scheme to betray Ordell and make off with his money.

Not only do they trust each other, but also theirs is the only relationship without deceit. Together, they deceive others around them, but never each other.

Lewis says, "When the two people...are of different sexes, the friendship which arises between them will very easily pass—may pass in the first half hour—into erotic love."[115] For Max anyway, that's just about the right running time.

But this section is not about Eros. The next section is.

Eros

I loved the girl with the golden hair
And the Tennessee Stud loves the Tennessee Mare

—"Tennessee Stud" by Johnny Cash

Jackie and Max share a kiss. Two kisses, actually, both of them heartfelt and awkward. It happens at the end of the movie, just as Jackie is preparing to leave. She has Ordell's money. The law has Ordell. She is free to go. Jackie has the chance to escape Ordell's shadow, finally.

But it means leaving Max behind. The previous two and a half hours have been spent watching these two get to know each other while they work

---

[115] Lewis, 67.

together to help Jackie make this escape. It's not a Hollywood romance, but it is a love story.

The love is Eros, a love that is not mere sexual desire. "Sexual desire, without Eros, wants *it*, the *thing in itself*; Eros wants the Beloved," Lewis says. "The *thing* is a sensory pleasure; that is, an event occurring within one's own body."[116]

Eros is what causes sexual desire to transcend the selfishness of a physical pleasure. Max Cherry and Jackie Brown's relationship stands in stark contrast to Ordell's relationship with women. There is no trace of Eros in these other relationships, although the physical pleasure of sex is hinted at. Louis and Melanie, too, share the pleasure of sexuality without any Eros in their relationship. Sex is something to do, a physical relationship removed from whatever Affection or (possibly) Friendship they may have shared.

On the other side of the coin, Max Cherry, tired and lonely, gets pulled into Jackie's story and finds himself enamored with "the Beloved." Unlike Ordell, who seems to keep Melanie around for sensual pleasure (if not for himself, for his guests), Max is interested in the person of Jackie Brown. He cares what will happen to her. He wants to help her.

And he absolutely is attracted to her. This is evident from their first meeting, when he goes to pick her up. The scene is played out with the flourish of a Hollywood cliché. He sees her coming down the walkway from the prison to the gate. Cut to his reaction shot. There is a physical

attraction. And that may be the first thing that interests him about her, but there is also a sense of protectiveness as he learns her story.

Not that she needs protecting. She is a capable woman, and while her arrest and Ordell's suspicion just might be the worst thing that could possibly happen to her, she sees the opportunity in it, and she's the one who comes up with the plans. She's the one who steps into the lions'

116 Ibid., 94.

dens on both sides of the law.

What makes it a tragic love story is that, like all the other relationships (except the professional relationships of Ray Nicolette and Mark Dargus, and Max Cherry and Winston), at the end it is pulled apart. Max is fifty-six years old and has a comfortable life. Jackie needs to leave the country. They do not belong in each other's worlds.

They each start the film alone, and they end the film alone. Max enters the film alone in his office and he exits the film alone in his office. Jackie starts the movie alone, with "Across 110th Street" playing on the soundtrack, as a flight attendant heading to Cabo San Lucas, where she will bring Ordell's money back into the country. She exits the movie alone, listening to "Across 110th Street" on the radio, driving to the airport where she will take Ordell's money out of the country.

The end result is tragic, but that sharing of Eros love, and their awkward goodbye kiss, is the culmination of a relationship that has changed their lives. Max, the lonely recluse who lives to run a business, has something else to live for, for a time. Jackie, who has been used so often, by Ordell at least, finds someone who cares without asking for anything in return.

But there is one more aspect to Max and Jackie's relationship.

Charity

La la la la la la la la la means I love you
—"La-La (Means I Love You)" by Thom Bell & William Hart,
performed by the Delfonics

Lewis doesn't use the word Agape in *The Four Loves*, but it is the Greek label he applies in one of his letters. "*Charity* means love," he writes. "It is called Agape in the New Testament to distinguish it from Eros (sexual love), Storge (family affection) and Philia (friendship). So there are 4 kinds of love…but Agape is the best because it is the kind God has for us and is good in all circumstances."[117]

Charity is a dangerous love, not for its negative sides (unlike the other loves, there is not much negative to be said about Charity), but because it is a love that invites pain. "To love at all is to be vulnerable," Lewis says. "Love anything, and your heart will certainly be wrung and possibly be broken. If you want to make sure of keeping it intact, you must give your heart to no one, not even to an animal."[118]

Agape, like Storge, is a love that loves the unlovable and the undeserving, but while Storge's Affection could come merely from familiarity, the Charity of Agape comes from purity. It is the ultimate gift, something holy God gives to unholy man. Humans are able to give Agape love to other humans, but only as a pale imitation of the love God offers.

"Divine Love is Gift-love," Lewis writes. "The Father gives all He is and has to the Son. The Son gives himself back to the Father, and gives Himself to the world, and for the world to the Father, and thus gives the world (in Himself) back to the Father too."[119] God, the inventor of all the loves, gives Agape love to humans, who, on recognizing this love and what it means, must also recognize their own unworthiness.

So where is Agape love in *Jackie Brown*? Well, it's not there—not intentionally—but there is a metaphorical interpretation of Max and Jackie's romance that does, actually, resemble Agape.

In the hypothetical "other essay that could be written" mentioned previously, Ordell Robbie's devilishness is evident in his character's actions, motivations, and tactics. He tempts people to their doom. He prowls like a hungry lion, seeking to consume and destroy. (Indeed, for Act Three, Ordell lets his hair down and it resembles a lion's mane.)

---

[117] C. S. Lewis, *Letters of C. S. Lewis*, ed. W. H. Lewis, (1966; repr., New York: Harcourt, Brace, 1993), 255.
[118] Lewis, *The Four Loves*, 121.
[119] Ibid., 1.

Max Cherry would be the metaphorical Christ-figure, with Jackie caught in between Ordell and Max, belonging to Ordell while Max tries to save her from Ordell's satanic grip. It's not a perfect metaphor (is there such a thing?), but the elements are there.

It's in taking a metaphorical look at Max Cherry's actions in *Jackie Brown* that a glimpse of Agape love emerges. Max genuinely cares for Jackie, and his first action in the film is to pay the price for her bail, to set her free. After that, the illegality of their actions aside, Max does everything he can to help Jackie, putting himself in harm's way and advising her professionally.

On Jackie's side of the relationship, she sees only her imperfections. When Max visits Jackie the morning after they meet, she begins asking him about how he feels about getting old, allowing some vulnerability in front of him, and he tells her with a smile, "You know, I can't really feel too sorry for you in this department."[120] She pours out her heart about her aging body, her job, her fears, and her value. It's her future, or lack of it, that scares her more than Ordell.

So Max goes above and beyond his job as bail bondsman, appointing himself as her helper and protector, whether she deserves it or not. Her plan involves stealing from a killer and lying to two branches of law enforcement, but Max is selflessly willing to put himself on the line for her.

In the end, she chooses to leave him behind, after he sacrifices for her, risks his own life and livelihood for her, and gives her nearly all the spoils (which he could have taken for himself). Granted, he is helping her break the law, which as mentioned before, contributes to the imperfection of this metaphor for Christ's love.

Looking at the events in the Jackie/Max relationship, a tragic element of the Christ/humankind relationship is portrayed: Jackie needs help, Max sacrifices to help her, and Jackie chooses to leave him. Jackie

---

[120] *Jackie Brown*

knows she owes him so much, but only offers him more of the money he gave back to her; he refuses, only taking the cut he deems rightful and fair under his business standards. He knows she must leave; she asks him to come with her, knowing he will stay. Jackie leaves, not to return, with only the promise of some postcards.

In movies, this kind of ending is unusual. In life, this is a tragedy with eternal repercussions. Agape love is not always returned in kind. Christ's love and sacrifice are denied by some, mocked by some, and refused by some. Like Jackie driving away from someone who truly loves her, humans run away from God. Like Max Cherry watching her go with sadness etched into his face, Christ allows humanity to exercise its free will.

Conclusion

The theological writings of an Oxford don might not be the first place to look when exploring themes in a Tarantino movie, but within the pages of his book, Lewis actually gives a reason for doing so. He explains why he uses examples from his own pop culture, so to speak, although for him it is the written word and not the silver screen. "I am driven to literary examples because you, the reader, and I do not live in the same neighborhood; if we did, there would unfortunately be no difficulty about replacing them with examples from real life."[121] And so too with using our own pop culture to discuss spiritual ideas and themes.

Obviously, Quentin Tarantino did not set out to make a film adaptation of C. S. Lewis' *The Four Loves*, and while exploration of these loves is unintentional, it is not coincidental. Both Lewis and Tarantino are members of the human race who create works of art for other members of the human race.

---

[121] Lewis, *The Four Loves*, 39.

Art reflects life, and there are some things in life that are universally experienced, love being the most universal. Tarantino explores other primal story themes in his movies, but the intimacy of the filmmaking and singular focus on characters and relationships make *Jackie Brown* a tale that may not be a morality play, but one that certainly has a number of moral ideas in play.

I LIKE THE WAY YOU DIE: RETRIBUTION, RESTORATION, AND REWRITTEN HISTORY IN *DJANGO UNCHAINED* AND *INGLOURIOUS BASTERDS*

Josh Corman

The path of the righteous man is beset on all sides by the iniquities of the selfish and the tyranny of evil men. Blessed is he who, in the name of charity and good will, shepherds the weak through the valley of darkness, for he is truly his brother's keeper and the finder of lost children. And I will strike down upon thee with great vengeance and furious anger those who would attempt to poison and destroy my brothers. And you will know my name is the Lord when I lay my vengeance upon thee.

—Ezekiel 25:17 (Standard Tarantino Version)

I n a book about Quentin Tarantino and theology, it's hard to imagine that the director's most famous reference to scripture (invented scripture, sure, but still)—and possibly his most famous lines, period—won't show up a few times. I apologize for the potential redundancy. But read those words again. Or better yet, cue up on YouTube the clip of Samuel L. Jackson's Jules Winnfield delivering them with a still-chilling malice.

Those four sentences do about as good a job as any others you're likely to find of summing up Quentin Tarantino's approach to filmmaking, from screenplay to editing bay. Notice the dynamic of the righteous man (or, as in *Kill Bill* and *Death Proof*, woman) and the evil people terrorizing the path out of the valley of darkness. Who are the righteous, if not Tarantino's heroes? His Jules, his Butch, his Beatrix, Aldo, King, and Django? And who are these evil men, if not his Zed, his Bill, his Landa, and Calvin Candie? This is all familiar stuff, of course— heroes and villains, good and evil, the fight of the righteous in the face of the wicked.

But notice also the third element in Tarantino's scriptural vision. Notice the vengeful Lord, blessing the shepherd of the weak and striking down in anger the selfish and the tyrannical. It is in that role—the role, of course, of the Almighty—that we find Mr. Tarantino. As the writer and director of his films (and with notably little studio interference), Tarantino is their god.

If we accept the notion of Tarantino as a kind of celluloid deity, acting out his will upon all of Quentin-dom, then it's only fair for us to conduct a simple theological inquest to determine what kind of god we're dealing with. We might start by asking what matters to Tarantino as a creator. (The casual observer may likely say violence, profanity, and stylistic homage, but these are merely the means by which Tarantino effects his more substantial thematic goals.) The answer we find when we look to the eight feature films he has directed is simple, even if the exploration of it will be slightly more complex: justice.

Yes, justice matters to QT. In so many of his stories, we find the put-upon hero, the righteous[122] person, seeking to put to rights some injustice that has been acted out upon him or her. For the purposes of this essay, I intend to focus on this dynamic primarily as it is found in *Inglourious Basterds* (2009) and *Django Unchained* (2012), because although the motif of justice populates Tarantino's entire filmography, in these two films, the director takes the unusual step of literally rewriting history in its name. They mark a departure from the simple presentation of a character (take Uma Thurman's Beatrix Kiddo) who seeks retribution for cruel treatment, and signal a new approach that sees Tarantino remaking history as a means of redemption, of administering a version of justice that those who encountered these events in real life—including God—failed to administer.

Tarantino's newly favored extra-historical approach seems to recognize openly our need (or at the very least our potent desire) for a savior, some entity who can account for the world's evils, engage them, and rectify them. We will examine the ways in which Tarantino's most recent films display this recognition and how the director positions himself as the required Messiah, as well as how the particularly gruesome form of retributive justice showcased in both *Basterds* and *Django* fails to meet the standard of restorative justice exemplified by Christ.

Section II

Quentin Tarantino's films respond to injustice in deeply satisfactory ways that feel almost innate to our beings. It is easy, as the bullets fly (or swords slash, or fires rage), to feel that the cause of justice is being advanced. In H.L. Mencken's seminal essay "On the Penalty of Death,"

---

[122] Admittedly, "righteous" is a relative term in the Tarantino-verse (as is "justice," for that matter). As we will see, Tarantino's definitions of certain concepts may frequently clash with those more widely adopted by society-at-large and certainly by the Bible.

the famed American journalist calls this "balancing out" *catharsis.*[123] Seeing others punished for the crimes they commit against us fulfills a deep-seated need within our beings, he claims.

Tarantino's films have walked in lock-step with this view of human nature from the very beginning. In *Reservoir Dogs*, we see Mr. Orange risk his cover to blow away the maniacal Mr. Blonde as he threatens to burn a police officer to death. In *Pulp Fiction*, Butch takes down that sword and heads back into Zed's hellish basement. *Kill Bill*...well, that one kind of speaks for itself, no?

But these films are not too far out of step with what we see from directors of all stripes, at least in terms of vengeance and justice. The tendency to equate revenge with justice is not exactly rare subject matter in Hollywood. Oscar winners like *Unforgiven, Braveheart, Gladiator*, and *The Departed* are teeming with wronged protagonists seeking blood payment for what's been taken from them. What *is* rare, what sets Tarantino apart, is the expansion of his vision, his messianic takeover of history itself, his broadening of the scope of his films to address massive historical atrocities in *Inglourious Basterds* and *Django Unchained*. Simply put, Tarantino does the only thing a feature film-maker can do when faced with so much inhumanity and atrocity: he plays God.

Consider Tarantino's remarks from the 2012 *Django Unchained* press tour, when he was questioned repeatedly about how making a spaghetti-western revenge flick like *Django* might potentially undermine American slavery's grave reality: "We all intellectually 'know' the brutality and inhumanity of slavery, but after you do the research it's no longer intellectual anymore, no longer just historical record—you feel it in your bones. It makes you angry and want to do something."[124]

---

[123] H. L. Mencken, "On the Penalty of Death," in *Prejudices: Fifth Series* (Octagon Books: 1976). (It's worth noting that the seriousness of Mencken's essay is in question, as many view the piece as satire. But even if Mencken is mocking the "katharsis" argument, that argument is both real enough and deeply held by enough people to warrant its place as one of Mencken's targets.)

[124] From Tarantino's address to the British Academy of Film and Television Arts, 2012.

By choosing to tell stories set during two of the most massive, historically visible incidences of evil in history—the Jewish Holocaust and American slavery—Tarantino uses his films to rewrite history so that the bad guys get what's coming to them, at the hands of those whom they've oppressed and tortured, no less. In this way, the historical backgrounds *Inglourious Basterds* and *Django Unchained* lend to those films provide much more than simply recognizable contexts or ready-made narrative markers. What they provide is a chance for Tarantino to deal more substantively with the problems of evil and injustice than he ever had before.

And make no mistake, both of those films take evil and injustice very seriously, in spite of their stylistic flourish and often cartoonish violence. Each film's principal villain represents the vile attitudes and actions that, when spread across a culture, allowed the grave evils of the Holocaust and American slavery to occur. Col. Hans Landa, *Inglourious Basterds'* "Jew Hunter," seems to act not simply out of a misguided sense of duty to his nation, but out of the deep-seated predatory sense of racial superiority that coursed through Nazi ideology.[125] Similarly, *Django Unchained's* Calvin Candie displays a vicious disregard for the humanity of slaves. Of course, the mere act of keeping slaves shows enormous disregard for their humanity to begin with, but Candie is especially brutal in this regard. This is evident in his propagation of mandingo fighting and his self-justifying, literally skull-crushing monologue about the weak, servile nature of black people.

Both *Inglourious Basterds* and *Django Unchained* detail revenge missions carried out against oppressive, monstrous institutional evils represented by a few particularly heinous individuals. Both feature protagonists who have themselves been personally wronged (Shosanna

---

[125] In fact, Landa condescendingly shares many of these views in the film's very first scene.

and Django, respectively) or are representatives of the unjustly treated, as with The Basterds[126] and King Schultz. And, most importantly, both films offer the same moral response to evil: great vengeance and furious anger. The Basterds and Shosanna converge bloodily upon Hitler and his minions in the small French theater, Django lays waste to the denizens of Candieland, and the audience cheers.

Retribution is the template for justice in the Tarantino-verse. And we shouldn't be surprised. This is the answer to the question I posed earlier: what kind of deity is Tarantino? A vengeful one, to be sure.

But a potentially more important question must be answered as well: *Why?* Why has Tarantino elected to use his films to rewrite history and seek (his or any version of) justice for the subjects of those films?

The answer, I would argue, speaks to a need felt by a great many people, a need thoroughly addressed by the Christian worldview: the need for a savior, someone who can put to rights, in an ultimate way, the world's wrongs.

Tarantino's expression of this need starts with the lines he draws so clearly in the sand in both *Inglourious Basterds* and *Django Unchained*. Hans Landa and Calvin Candie are *evil*. The acts they perpetrate are inarguably *wrong*. In fact, they are representative of much larger social and historical evils thoroughly rejected by Tarantino as morally impermissible. This rejection is the first step on Tarantino's messianic path. As Greg Ganssle, Philosopher of Religion and Senior Fellow at Yale University's Rivendell Institute, writes: "When we call something bad we are expressing, at the very least, a rejection of that thing. We aim either to avoid the situation or to change it. We want to stop things from

---

[126] The titular Basterds are a group of Jewish-American soldiers whose only directive is to intimidate the Third Reich by killing (as viciously and creatively as they can manage) Nazis across Europe.

being bad or evil."[127]

Think about these words in relation to the response Tarantino provides to evil and injustice via *Inglourious Basterds* and *Django Unchained*. The "Bear Jew" saunters from his cave, baseball bat in hand. Shosanna piles her flammable film stock as high as it will go and watches the Nazis take their seats. Aldo Raine leaves Hans Landa with a helpful physical reminder of his inhumanity. King Schultz collects his bounties with a wry smile. Django leaves Candieland a smoldering, bloody ruin.

These films engage with historical evil through art in a way that rejects and reconstructs injustice so that what is bad is thoroughly defeated and what is good is enabled to flourish. Quentin Tarantino clearly offers a moral response to injustice in line with Ganssle's thinking; he wants "to stop things from being bad or evil." Film is his only recourse for accomplishing this goal, and he has pursued it hammer and tongs with his recent works.

As Tarantino stated in his BAFTA address, once he felt the depth and breadth of the evil and injustice of history, he could not help but be moved to a desire to "do something" about it. This impulse carries important theological weight. As Ganssle notes, rejecting what we view as morally untenable hints at a state of existence where goodness represents a kind of default setting. In such a state, he argues, the presence of a good God makes some sense.[128] So by simply representing immoral action as corrupting in its effects, Tarantino acknowledges some kind of moral construct built into the way we see the world. This stands, to some degree or another, with the Christian view of an initial state of good corrupted by sin, and the need for restoration.

C. S. Lewis, in a chapter of his book *The Problem of Pain* titled "The

---

[127] Gregory E. Ganssle, "Evil as Evidence for Christianity," in *God and Evil: The Case for God in a World Filled with Pain,* ed. Chad Meister and James Dew (Downers Grove: InterVarsity Press, 2012).
[128] Ibid.

Fall of Man," offers some insight into, among other things, humanity's sinful lapse and God's role in restoring the world as we know it to the goodness He intended for it from the beginning. Says Lewis, "The world is a dance in which good, descending from God, is disturbed by evil arising from [his] creatures, and the resulting conflict is resolved by God's own assumption of the suffering nature which evil produces."

Meanwhile, noted theologian and writer N. T. Wright explains the impulse for justice (which Tarantino clearly feels) as a natural part of "our Western philosophical tradition" which

> inclines us to expect—and indeed to ask for—... an answer to the question, What can God say about evil? We want an explanation. We want to know what evil really is, why it's there in the first place (or at least in the second place), why it's been allowed to continue, and how long this will go on.[129]

Both statements may provide perspective into Tarantino's confrontation of evil and justice. *Inglourious Basterds* and *Django Unchained* represent Tarantino's awareness of the need for redemption, but they also suggest that he is unwilling to wait for answers to Wright's questions. He wants to answer them himself. He has not only rejected evil (and in so doing implied an alternative where moral good is the default setting) but has taken the further bold step of "doing something," as it were, to rectify some of the most glaring wrongs in history.

Dare we suggest it? Enter QT the messiah, cool theme music blaring and both guns blazing!

Section III

Every messiah needs a method, and Tarantino's, as is clear from

---

[129] N. T. Wright, *Evil and the Justice of God* (Downers Grove: InterVarsity Press, 2006), 44.

even a glancing examination, is violent, retributive justice. In this section, I hope to compare this methodology with a profoundly different view of redemption and justice to be found in the pages of Scripture. My scriptural focus will turn to two of the Bible's most interesting and high-profile responses to injustice: the respective stories of Job and the Prodigal Son, both of which provide us ample insights into the often gaping divide between humankind's and God's senses of justice.

Let's start with Job, the prototypical man done wrong. In Job 9: 21-25, after Job has cursed the day of his birth[130] and claimed that his misery outweighs the sand of the seas,[131] he calls himself blameless and complains that God "destroys both the blameless and the wicked" and "mocks the despair of the innocent." The book's tenth chapter continues in this vein. Job paints God as an inconsistent bully, stalking Job for the pleasure of displaying power against him.

What permeates these verses is Job's sweeping sense of injustice, and Job rejects the degrading quality of his life as deeply unfair, as many of us will when we feel that injustice has been visited upon us. This reaction is more than understandable. Recall that Mencken speaks of *katharsis*, Ganssle of a desire to reject that which we see as wrong while longing for right to be restored.

But Job and Tarantino share more than simply a rejection of injustice as they see it. Critically, both turn in their own ways to God to seek a response. Job eventually addresses God directly, while the direction of *Basterds* and *Django* suggests, as we noted before, a dissatisfaction from Tarantino's perspective with the way God has allowed history to unfold. We see in Job and Tarantino typically human reactions, driven by frustration, anger, and impatience. But what we also see is a longing for things to be put right, a prayer that evil and

---

[130] Job 3:3-10 (NIV)
[131] Job 6:1-3 (NIV)

injustice will be addressed. Christianity's answer to this prayer is the Messiah, in the person of Jesus, though the way He addresses injustice may not be consistent with what we (or Job or Tarantino) desire in our most confused, reactionary moments.

So then how does God want us to respond to injustice, if not with Job's embittered questions or Tarantino's thirst for revenge? One of the Bible's clearest answers to that question comes in the story of the Prodigal Son, who foolishly "[squanders] his wealth in wild living"[132] before returning in shame to his home. The lost son's older brother fumes at his father's decision to welcome his errant brother back into the fold with affection and celebration.[133]

The older brother's reaction is in keeping with what we might expect after reading about Job's response to injustice. The older brother is indignant because his brother receives mercy, rather than retribution, from his father, who kills the fattened calf, throws a party, and joyfully notes that his lost son has been found.[134]

The older son echoes Job's frustration by rejecting what he perceives as a lack of justice. It simply isn't fair that he, who has mindfully tended his family's land and remained faithful and obedient to his father, should be, in his reading of the situation, cast aside for his disrespectful, miscreant brother. He presents a clear case and demands justification from his father. But famously, the father reassures his eldest of his love, then keeps on celebrating. And in that celebration, in the welcoming of his younger son's return with open arms, a different kind of justice is exercised, a justice built on restoration rather than on retribution. This other justice replaces punitive exclusion with restorative love and allows the son, the source of wrongdoing in this instance, to be reconciled to

---

[132] Luke 15:13 (NIV)
[133] Luke 15:28-31 (NIV)
[134] Luke 15:32 (NIV)

those he has wronged.[135]

Obviously, there is a clear discrepancy between this kind of mercy-soaked justice and the blood-soaked variety preferred by Tarantino and his arbiters. As New Testament scholar Christopher D. Marshall notes in his book *Compassionate Justice*,[136] the father has been cruelly wronged by his son, and yet he never abandons hope that their relationship might be restored. When he sees his son, Marshall writes, "He is overcome with emotion. He is stirred into action, *not by the dictates of strict justice* but by a compassionate craving to see his debilitated son restored to well-being and their relationship renewed" [emphasis mine].

In contrast, Django and Aldo Raine's crew operate firmly within the confines of what we might call "strict justice." And while the weight of the historical transgressions that Tarantino uses them to tackle far exceeds that of the much smaller personal failings referenced in the Prodigal Son story, the spirit driving the issue of the biblical path to justice is, when boiled all the way down, the same. These characters and their stories satisfy handily the knee-jerk human desire for a justice that amounts to little more than an eye for an eye, the justice that the older brother would have carried out. And satisfying it is. Watching Hitler, Goebbels, and Hans Landa—men representative of the holocaust's horrors—face retribution at the hands of those whom they have, directly or by proxy, terrorized and tortured scratches an unbecoming itch, and the same is of course true of Calvin Candie's and Stephen's brutal ends. As Django himself says to one of his "deserving" targets, "I like the way you die, boy." And some part of us, perhaps not so deeply buried as we might

---

[135] Christopher D. Marshall, *Compassionate Justice: An Interdisciplinary Dialogue with Two Gospel Parables on Law, Crime, and Restorative Justice* (Eugene: Cascade Books, 2012), 219.

[136] Marshall's book focuses primarily upon the stories of the Good Samaritan and the Prodigal Son, and how they might be used as lenses through which to approach the criminal justice system in a more restorative manner, but its discussions of justice are appropriate here.

wish, likes it too.

But as the parable of the Prodigal Son should show us, this satisfaction is ultimately limited and certainly not Christian. Jesus illustrates to us through this parable the arc of God's redemptive intentions for the human race. As Marshall claims, "... the father's forgiveness was without reserve. The boy deserves reprimand and punishment. At the very least, he merited a long period of probation to demonstrate the genuineness of his reform. Instead the father moves with lightning speed and in a flood of symbolic gestures to restore him to full belonging."[137]

Clearly, Christ's picture of justice looks demonstrably different from Tarantino's. The parable of the Prodigal Son highlights the divide between our instinctual, primal response to injustice—marked by bitterness, anger, and self-pity—and Jesus' response—marked by forgiveness and the hope of reconciliation. Marshall, again:

> The sheer magnanimity of the father's response is intended, we have seen, to characterize the restoring love of God—a God who is also filled with compassion at the distressed state of his children and who longs to heal, forgive and restore them (Ps. 103:6-18). But Jesus' intention in portraying God this way, and Luke's intention in locating the parable where he does in chapter 15, is not merely to say something about God; it is also to say something about the people of God. It is intended to furnish a viable model for how believers are to treat those whom the wider community judges to be treacherous offenders worthy only of punishment."[138]

Let's take that last sentence and carry it over into our discussion about *Inglourious Basterds* and *Django Unchained*. Don't Nazis and Slavers rest firmly in the category of "those whom the wider community

---

[137] Marshall
[138] Ibid.

judges to be treacherous offenders worthy only of punishment"? Of course they do. But part of the parable's larger message is that Christ and his followers are not meant to be part of the "wider community," and they are meant, as instruments of God's love, to seek justice that restores and reconciles aggressors and victims alike.

The phrase "easier said than done" has perhaps never been more appropriately applied. This kind of grace is not extended, nor accepted, cheaply. When the father accepts his son's repentance (a vital ingredient in the stew of restorative justice, it must be said, and one that is utterly lacking on the part of Tarantino's antagonists) and offers his forgiveness, he invites the anger and mockery of the older son and the community around them, who seem to view his mercy as a weakness of which the younger son is taking advantage.[139] But John 10:17-18 shows us the lead Christ set, and which the prodigal son's father follows: "(17) The reason my Father loves me is that I lay down my life—only to take it up again. (18) No one takes it from me, but I lay it down of my own accord. I have authority to lay it down and authority to take it up again. This command I received from my Father" (NIV).

Christ willingly laid down his life and accepted the burden of sin. With that choice, He also accepted ridicule and added bloody violence to the bargain. Indeed, the crucifixion itself highlights a telling contrast between the justice of Tarantino's films and the justice of the Gospels: the blood flows in opposite directions. For Tarantino (as we've mentioned) violence carried out *by* the oppressed sets his world aright. In the Gospels, violence and death committed *unto* Christ is the means by which God's extension of grace is exercised. As seminal theologian

---

[139] It's worth noting that the Basterds offer one Nazi officer the opportunity to repent (assuming, of course, that Lt. Raine is being truthful while speaking with his captive) by giving up the position of his men. He does not, and is promptly executed by "The Bear Jew." It's also worth noting that Lt. Raine seems pleased at the officer's lack of cooperation, as it affords the Basterds a front row seat as Ted Williams' stand-in steps to "the plate."

Dietrich Bonhoeffer notes in his book *The Cost of Discipleship*, "…
[grace] is costly because it cost God the life of his Son: 'Ye were bought
at a price', and what has cost God much cannot be cheap for us. Above
all, it is grace because God did not reckon his Son too dear a price to pay
for our life, but delivered him up for us." The prodigal son and his father
accept the cost of their reunion and rejoice in the celebration that awaits
on the other side of their painful transaction.

Tarantino's films, however, stand with the older son. The victims
of those films have been wronged terribly. They have been brutalized,
tortured, murdered, and made to live their day-to-day existences under
the constant shadow of fear for themselves, their families, and anyone
who dares to stand with them against oppression. As earlier noted, the
Hans Landas and Calvin Candies of the world make the younger son in
the parable look like a member of the Little Rascals up to some harmless
mischief. And when we see their misdeeds and remember the real-life
misdeeds of those they are meant to represent, it is easy for us to stand
with the older son as well. After all, these men are cruel and violent and
their actions reflect those qualities. Unlike the younger son, they are
unrepentant—even gleeful—in their attitudes and actions. Their lack of
repentance is no small matter. 2 Corinthians 7:10 tells us that sorrow
leads to repentance, which leads to salvation. 2 Timothy 2:25 notes that
repentance leads to knowledge and truth. It's nearly impossible to argue
that the Landas and Candies of the world deserve salvation if repentance
is one of its necessary components, since they show none.[140]

And yet.

Through the parable of the Prodigal Son, Jesus seems to command
us to stand, looking out at the road, waiting for the moment of these

---

[140] Of course, as their creator, Tarantino intentionally refuses to build any repentance
into these characters, which makes his narrative of retribution that much easier to swal-
low. However, Landa's and Candie's attitudes surely reflect, at the very least, the broader
attitudes of many in history for whom they act as ideological stand-ins.

men's return, their moment of humility and repentance, so that we can extend the reconciliation, restoration, and reintegration available through God's forgiveness and, indeed, God's Justice. If that moment never comes, then on their own heads be it (literally, in Tarantino's world), but what's clear is that retribution is not to be our first response, that the Christian narrative represented in this story is the narrative of we, the undeserving children of God, to whom the gift of grace has been extended, despite our failures.

Does QT Get it ALL Wrong?

It would be easy, in light of the Prodigal Son's story, to view every scalp Aldo Raine's men collect and every bullet Django fires as another step away from Christianity's most fully realized definition of justice and the answer to evil.

I would argue, though, that Tarantino deserves a little grace of his own. After all, his rejection of evil is thorough and clear, as is his desire to bring justice to situations that any rational observer would categorize as brutally unjust.

Inglourious Basterds and *Django Unchained* are monuments to this desire (and perhaps the desires of those who have suffered from the injustices chronicled in both films). Even if we contend (and I do) that his methods stray too far from biblical insight on the subject of justice to be acceptable in a Christian sense, it is difficult to fault Tarantino for asking what I would imagine almost all of us have at some time or another: Why were these great injustices allowed to take place, and what has God done or is He planning to do about them?

It seems obvious that Tarantino has had neither question answered for him to any degree of satisfaction, hence the creation of his avenging heroes set loose on the problems of the Holocaust and American slavery.

As in the Christian narrative, Tarantino's plan involves the intercession of someone equipped to put the situation to rights. Unlike that narrative, however, retribution, rather than restoration, is the tool that will see justice done. Tarantino recognizes the desire for a messiah, for one who, like us, rejects evil and injustice and aims (no pun intended) to set things to rights, even if, as a messiah, he operates about as differently from Christ as can be imagined.

N. T. Wright argues that, for Christians, the Bible (not always to our total satisfaction, he admits) offers the template for how that setting to rights is meant to happen. He writes, "[The Old Testament] isn't designed primarily to provide information, to satisfy the inquiring mind. It's written to *tell the story of what God has done, is doing and will do about evil*" [italics mine]. That story moves toward its most vital moment with Jesus on the cross and the promise of a world made new through the work of his death. Wright later observes, importantly, that this promise must be carefully understood.

> It is not enough to say that God will eventually make a new world in which there will be no more pain and crying; that does scant justice to all the evil that has gone before. We cannot get to the full solution to the problem of evil by mere progress, as though, provided the final generation was happy, the misery of all previous generations could be overlooked or even justified... No, all theories of atonement adequate to the task must include both a backward look (seeing the guilt, sin and shame of all previous generations heaped up on the cross) and a forward dimension, the promise that what God accomplished on Calvary will be fully and finally implemented.

God's justice is mysterious, and to our minds it often feels slow in arriving. But it is transformative. It actually reshapes the relationship between those who suffer and those who cause that suffering in a way that may be awkward or even painful in the offing, but which can restore all parties to the state in which God intended them to exist.[141]

It can be tempting to push against this justice, to exercise our own vision of the world, as Tarantino does, and declare that the putting back together of the world should look differently than it does. Wright warns against this. "Which bit of dry, clean ground are we standing on that we should pronounce the matter with such certainty?" he asks.[142] As we have seen in the stories of Job and the Prodigal Son, our knee-jerk pronouncements about justice could often use more than a little polishing.

This, I think, is at the core of Tarantino's rewritten histories. They indicate an impatience and frustration with God that many of us no doubt relate to. But true justice, restorative justice that offers hope and a true solution to the problem of evil, cannot be achieved by taking aim with our guns, even when we feel the evils of history in our bones and want, like Quentin Tarantino, to pull the triggers.

---

[141] Christopher Marshall, in *Compassionate Justice*, explores this concept and its relationship to the American legal system in great depth.
[142] Wright, 59.

NO LAUGHING MATTER:
TARANTINO AND
THE THEOLOGY OF HUMOR

Kevin Kinghorn

We read in Proverbs that "a merry heart doeth good like a medicine."[143] And yet, in keeping with the way God's gifts can be misused, we also recognize that laughter is sometimes ill-advised, ill-mannered, or at least ill-timed. We judge some attempts at humor to be inappropriate, indecent, and indefensible. The writer of Ecclesiastes tells us that there is "a time to laugh"—quickly followed by the reminder that there is "a time to mourn."[144]

So humor can be a kind of God-ordained medicine for us. It can also serve to undermine God's plans and purposes for us. Where do we draw the line? When someone tells a joke or shares a funny story, how would we determine whether it was a godly or a sinful use of humor?

---

[143] Proverbs 17:22
[144] Ecclesiastes 3:4

The films of Quentin Tarantino provide us with a large and very useful set of examples as we explore a theology of humor. A common element of Tarantino's films is that they are heavily reliant on humor—from the carnival-type scenes in *From Dusk Till Dawn* to the continuous, bubbling-below-the-surface humor throughout *Inglourious Basterds*. At the same time, Tarantino's films are notoriously violent, raising the potential objection that humor really can't find a proper context within these films.

God's Purposes for Humor

As a first step in distinguishing godly versus sinful uses of humor, we need to clarify the reasons God gave humans the capacity to appreciate and use humor. This task requires us to make certain working assumptions about the reasons God gives us *any* of the gifts and abilities we have. The following paragraph is my own best attempt to summarize the historic Christian consensus about God's reasons for creating us and giving us abilities.

God created us so that we might participate in the ongoing life—that is, the ongoing loving relationships—that exists within the Trinity. Our ultimate fulfillment as creatures in the image of God is to participate in the kinds of loving, interdependent, self-giving relationships enjoyed from eternity by the Father, Son, and Holy Spirit. As part of God's plan to draw us into these kinds of relationships with himself and with others, God has given us various gifts and abilities, including the capacity for humor. Accordingly, a use of humor that promotes the kinds of relationships that mirror the relationships within the Trinity will be a godly use of humor. Any use of humor that works *against* such self-giving, harmonious relationships will be contrary to the will of God.

With this working assumption about God's purposes for humor, we can now explore some of the specific ways in which humor can promote godly relationships. Four ways are especially important. I do not want to argue that these four avenues exhaust the ways in which humor can contribute to godly relationships, but these four ways do seem particularly noteworthy. In the following few sections, we will use examples from Tarantino's films to illustrate these four uses of humor, along with observing how these uses of humor, when perverted, serve to work against godly relationships.

OK, This Is Awkward!

A scene in *Pulp Fiction* has Vincent Vega reluctantly agreeing to take out the wife of his boss, Marsellus Wallace. Vincent and Mia sit across the table at a 1950s-style diner, trying to think of things to say.

Mia: Don't you hate that?
Vincent: Hate what?
Mia: Uncomfortable silences. Why do we feel it's necessary to yack about bullshit in order to be comfortable?
Vincent: I don't know. That's a good question.

As relational creatures, we can sometimes feel at ease with others; and sometimes we can feel *ill* at ease with others. It would perhaps be interesting to try to list all the reasons we can feel uneasy or uncomfortable around others. But whatever the reasons, the phenomenon of social awkwardness is something we all experience as very real. And of course this awkwardness works against the kinds of harmonious relationships through which we flourish as creatures in God's image.

One way to relieve social awkwardness is to draw attention, in a humorous way, to the source of the awkwardness. Typically, if we simply try to ignore an awkward situation, the tension only builds. It becomes the elephant in the room no one dares talk about. But by drawing attention to it and laughing about it, the tension is diffused. Mia uses just this strategy in the scene above. Instead of trying to ignore the uncomfortable silence with Vincent, she draws attention to it. She even adds, "Well, I'll tell you what: I'll go to the bathroom and powder my nose, while you sit here and think of something to say." By humorously making a "big deal" of the awkward silence, she paradoxically reduces the awkward silence to a playful, small deal. Humor has played its positive role of fostering a harmonious relationship.

Awkward situations also arise when various social expectations aren't met: when we say the wrong thing, eat with the wrong fork, or arrive at a social function either overdressed or underdressed. In *Pulp Fiction*, Vincent finds himself in yet another awkward situation when his gun goes off on a morning car ride (poor Marvin), necessitating an impromptu change of clothes for Vincent and his partner, Jules, at their friend Jimmie's house. With their new outfits of old tee-shirts and swim trunks, they will be uncomfortably underdressed for the rest of the morning.

Winston Wolf doesn't ignore the awkwardness of their situation. Upon seeing Vincent and Jules in their new clothes, he comments: "Perfect. Perfect. We couldn't have planned this better. You guys look like...what do they look like, Jimmie?" It's unclear to me whether Wolf is inviting humor in an attempt to *diffuse* the awkwardness of the situation or to *increase* it. If it's the latter, then the positive potential for humor will have become perverted. Instead of *relieving* awkwardness and aiding harmonious interaction, humor would be used with the intention of highlighting the cause of awkwardness and making it an even bigger deal.

What *does* seem clear is that Jimmie's response to Mr. Wolf's question involves an obviously negative use of humor. His response is to say, "Dorks. They look like a couple of dorks." By emphasizing just how awkward their outfits should make Vincent and Jules feel, Jimmie is clearly not concerned with making them feel better. He's not attempting to diffuse and move past the awkward situation. He's highlighting just how awkward the situation is.

We've seen the first positive role that humor can play. It serves to diffuse awkward situations and foster in their places harmonious interactions. But just as humor can play this first, positive role, it can also be perverted to have the opposite effect of fostering self-consciousness and alienation. This same general pattern emerges when we turn to our second divinely appointed role for humor.

The Path of Humility

The Christian scriptures repeatedly emphasize the importance of humility.[145] Humility is of course especially essential when it comes to our relationship with God, given God's role as our creator who invites us to relate to him as lord. Still, humility is important within any relationship. We have all experienced how bragging, competitiveness, and one-upmanship can cause others to be ill at ease and drive wedges between friends. Humility keeps such attitudes in check, allowing for healthy relationships where all parties feel encouraged and not threatened. Humorous self-deprecation is one avenue through which we can express humility to others. However, just as humor can play this positive role in fostering smooth relationships, the opposite effect can occur when we pervert this positive role and use humor to reduce and denigrate *others*.

Both this positive and negative use of humor can be found in various places within Tarantino's films. In one particularly humanizing scene in

---

[145] As a sampling, consider: "Do nothing out of selfish ambition or vain conceit. Rather, in humility value others above yourselves" (Philippians 2: 3); "God opposes the proud, but gives grace to the humble" (James 4:6); "Those who exalt themselves will be humbled, and those who humble themselves will be exalted" (Matthew 23:12).

Inglourious Basterds, the German soldier Frederick Zoller attempts to woo the young, French cinema owner Emmanuelle Mimieux as various German soldiers fawn over him and beg for his autograph. Emmanuelle is surprised: "You're not just a German soldier. Are you somebody's son?" Frederick tries to deflect attention, playfully responding, "Most German soldiers are somebody's son." When it becomes clear that Frederick is a war hero, he reluctantly explains that he is a sniper who killed 250 enemy soldiers over a three-day period. He sheepishly recounts how Goebbels himself made an upcoming movie, *Nation's Pride*, about the event and drafted Frederick to play himself in the film. Emmanuelle can hardly believe her ears: "*Nation's Pride* is about you? *Nation's Pride* is starring you?" Frederick again turns to humor in an attempt to downplay his achievements: "I know, comical, huh?"

What Frederick is trying to avoid is a situation where Emmanuelle thinks a meaningful relationship with him will not be possible on account of their dissimilar social standings, so he uses self-deprecating humor to protect the kind of equal footing needed for a healthy relationship between peers. (Emmanuelle has deeper reasons for despising any German soldier, but Frederick is not aware of these reasons.) Solely with regards to his attempt to use humor in this instance, he is using it as a way of expressing humility—which of course is the second positive role that humor can play.

Inglourious Basterds also contains scenes where deprecating humor is used in the *negative* way of ensuring that equal footing is *not* achieved. During a scene in a basement bar, three members of the Basterds are impersonating German officers and meeting at a table with movie star and double-agent Bridget von Hammersmark. A German soldier, Sgt. Wilhelm, is also in the bar with friends celebrating his son's upcoming first birthday. He asks Bridget for an autograph to give to his son, Max. He then overextends his welcome by asking, "So, Frau von Hammersmark, what brings you to France?" Archie Hicox of the Nazi-hunting Basterds, still impersonating a German officer and wanting privacy for his table meeting, bellows,

> None of your business, Sergeant! You might not have worn out your welcome with the fraulein, with your drunken boorish behavior, but you have worn out your welcome with me! Might I remind you, sergeant, you're an enlisted man. This is an officer's table. I suggest you stop pestering the fraulein and rejoin your table!

A startled and somewhat confused Sgt. Wilhelm takes a step back and notes that Hicox has an unusual accent, asking where he is from. Another member of the Basterds, Hugo Stiglitz, screams at the sergeant, "You must be either drunk or mad to speak to a superior officer with such impertinence!" Stiglitz then shouts at the sergeant's companions, "I suggest you take hold of your friend, or he'll spend Max's first birthday in jail for public drunkenness!"

The reprimands have their desired effects, and Sgt. Wilhelm's friends quickly bring him back to their own table. What has happened is that the (pseudo) German officers have minimized the social role of Sgt. Wilhelm, elevating themselves by comparison. This is accomplished by making Sgt. Wilhelm an object of ridicule, a laughingstock for everyone in the room to see. The Basterds here are repeating a pattern that playground children already understand. When we derisively poke fun at someone, we inhibit that person's ability to participate in a circle of friendship built on dignity and encouragement. Instead of using humor to foster our own humility, inviting others into our circle of friendship, the use of humor is perverted and healthy friendships are impeded. (Of course, in our movie example, the Basterds' decision to use derisive humor can probably be forgiven, as they had good reason for wanting their circle to remain isolated and exclusionary!)

An interesting example of our second use of humor occurs at the end of *Kill Bill: Vol. 2*. Beatrix Kiddo is struggling with mixed emotions after injuring her mentor and tormentor, Bill. With Bill's demise now imminent, she confesses through tears that perhaps she's a bad person. Bill responds, "No, you're not a bad person. You're a terrific person. You're my favorite person. But every once in a while you can be a real cunt." What's interesting about this example is that Bill's final remark comes in the form of a put down; and perhaps there's at least a small part of Bill that is still sparring with Beatrix. But his main motivation clearly is not to belittle her. He is instead trying, in a humorous and sarcastic way, to elevate her in comparison to himself. (After all, he's just referred to himself as a "murdering bastard.") And so this example seems to be a positive use of self-deprecating humor, even while the example is perhaps slightly mixed with a negative use of humor as well.

A Balm to Ease Our Pain

Aside from using humor to elevate Beatrix, Bill's use of humor in our last example also eases Beatrix's pain. It allows her to laugh in the midst of her tears, which introduces a third positive use of humor. Humor can be a wonderful relief from both physical and psychological pain. Even in the midst of trying circumstances, humor can give us moments of genuine reprieve. Indeed, we sometimes talk about a person "forgetting she is in pain" as she is distracted by a funny incident.

Generic action movies are replete with examples of using humor in this positive way of relieving pain. Frequently, one of a team of thieves will be mortally wounded during an attempted robbery. While traveling in a getaway car, another thief will try to comfort him by making him laugh: "Soon you'll be sipping margaritas on a sandy beach!" Whenever that line pops up in a movie, you can be pretty sure that the wounded thief is going to bleed out within the next twenty seconds.

This use of humor can be found within Tarantino's films, although the dialogue is usually subtler than an overused line about margaritas. In *Pulp Fiction*, Vince and Mia share a harrowing evening centered on a drug-induced emergency. At the end of the evening, a shaken Vince says goodnight to Mia, adding, "If you'll excuse me, I gotta go home and have a heart attack." Mia takes the opportunity to ask if he'd like to hear the corny joke she had earlier been too embarrassed to tell. She then tells her "ketchup" joke to Vince, which is her attempt to use humor to ease the psychological trauma he's experiencing. Vince doesn't manage to laugh, but the joke does make him smile.

Just as humor can serve this positive role of relieving pain, the use of humor can once again be perverted and lead to the opposite effect. In *Kill Bill: Vol. 2*, Elle positions a black mamba to strike Budd in the face. After Budd is bitten and writhing on the floor, Elle sits nonchalantly on a chair and reads from a notepad.

In Africa, the saying goes, in the bush, an elephant can kill you, a leopard can kill you, and a black mamba can kill you. But only with the mamba—and this has been true in Africa since the dawn of time—is death sure, hence its handle: death incarnate.

Elle looks up from her notepad and asks Budd, "Pretty cool, huh?" She finds her place in the notepad and says to him, "Now you should listen to this, cause this concerns you." She continues reading. "The amount of venom that can be delivered from a single bite can be gargantuan." Looking up again, she remarks, "You know, I've always liked that word 'gargantuan,' and I so rarely have an opportunity to use it in a sentence."

Elle's use of humor is an attempt to rub salt in Budd's wounds. She's adding psychological torment to the intense physical pain Budd is already experiencing. If ever there were an example of perverting our third use of humor in order to *increase*—rather than ease—another person's pain, this is it.

There's a Time and a Place for Laughter…But Is This It?

The fourth and final positive use of humor I want to consider involves the way we order our priorities. For any community to function as God intends, it must prioritize certain goals above others. We find in the Christian scriptures, for example, a much heavier emphasis on societal, structural injustice than on fashion appropriateness. Accordingly, a church has lost the plot if it exhibits more concern about the length and color of its choir robes than about the wages and working conditions of the poor who have little social voice. From the Christian perspective, any community whose priorities and values don't align with those of God will inevitably fall victim to antipathy, resentment, and other destructive dynamics.

Humor is one way for a community to regulate its priorities and prevent molehills from becoming mountains. We commonly make references to "laughing off" or "making light" of some minor issue, thereby preventing it from becoming a major issue. Even though two people may recognize that a point of tension exists between them, a humorous response to the issue can be a way of agreeing that the issue should not amount to any serious threat to their relationship.

Instead of illustrating these points using scenes within Tarantino's movies, I'd like to ask whether Tarantino himself, in using humor within his movies, is rightly prioritizing issues. Some viewers of Tarantino's movies may feel that his use of humor is inappropriate, if not obscene.

Does the juxtaposition of violence and humor within Tarantino's movies mean that he is unduly *de*-prioritizing the issue of violence itself? Of course, if the issue is merely one of taste, then there is no moral issue at stake. But we sometimes hear the deeper objection that Tarantino's use of humor de-sensitizes us to violence, that it leads us to overlook its terribly destructive effects. The issue here is one of prioritizing, dismissively making light of something that communities should instead keep highlighted.

We all recognize that there are occasions of seriousness and solemnity, where flippancy is clearly inappropriate. A well-known "out of bounds" topic for comics is the recently deceased. If we were to hear someone responding to a death announcement with a frivolous joke, we would rightly denounce this response. We would judge that the deceased person's life wasn't being appropriately valued and that the person was being dishonored. Even in *Kill Bill: Vol. 2*, Beatrix's nemesis, Elle, expresses indignation when she thinks that a great warrior like Beatrix has met her demise "at the hands of a bushwhacking scrub" like Budd.

This same kind of appreciation for the value of human life lies behind the objection that the humorous tenor of Tarantino's films is inappropriate, given that their context is so often the violent demise of people. For example, there's the comic element in the prolonged maiming and killing of the Crazy 88s in *Kill Bill: Vol. 1*, or in *Inglourious Basterds* the humorous revelry as the group awaits the Bear Jew's arrival with his executioner's baseball bat. In *Reservoir Dogs* we find ourselves suppressing laugher at Vic Vega "speaking into the ear" of the captive cop, recognizing that the horrific scene is certainly no laughing matter. We find ourselves smiling in *Pulp Fiction* at Butch's surveying of potential weapons in the pawn shop, even as we remain mindful that the scene he is trying to stop is as ghastly as they come. Do these (and many other) scenes in Tarantino's movies have the effect of acclimatizing us to violence and making it more palatable to us, despite the fact that our hearts truly should break when any of God's creatures are harmed?

A defender of Tarantino might suggest that we could approach this issue of priorities from a different angle. Perhaps, it might be suggested, in the light of eternity we really shouldn't prioritize *any* earthly event. The writer of Ecclesiastes declared, "I have seen all the things that are done under the sun; all of them are meaningless, a chasing after the wind."[146] Perhaps Tarantino's juxtaposition of humor and violence can be viewed as a useful reminder that we should never take any event in this temporary, earthly life too seriously. After all, from the Christian perspective we should never think that this world is our home. Instead, like the great characters of faith described in Hebrews 11, our eyes should remain fixed on "a better country—a heavenly one."[147] However, the mere fact that you even picked up this book suggests that you find these issues worth engaging on an intellectual level at the very least, and possibly even on a moral level.

I do not want to suggest that the issue of prioritization is the *only* issue on which we should reflect in assessing Tarantino's use of violence. To make such an all-things-considered assessment, we will want to reflect on broader issues about the purpose of art. Is there some goal toward which art *should* lead us? Should it point us to some objectively good value that exists beyond what we see in a painting or in a movie?[148] Or does art serve its purpose when it challenges our thinking and evokes emotions in us, irrespective of the moral direction in which we

[146] Ecclesiastes 1:14

[147] Hebrews 11:16

[148] For a defense of the beauty of art being grounded in objective values, see Roger Scruton, *Beauty: A Very Short Introduction* (Oxford: Oxford University Press, 2011). For arguments that our assessments of art should not involve *moral* judgments, but only aesthetic ones, see Richard Posner, "Against Ethical Criticism," in *Philosophy and Literature*, vol. 21: 1997; and "Against Ethical Criticism: Part II," *Philosophy and Literature*, vol. 22(2): 1998.

are led? Perhaps the very juxtaposition of violence and humor that I have currently placed under scrutiny is meant as an artistic ploy, not to trivialize violence, but to make us experience it in unexpected ways, and to encourage introspection as we consider our own reaction to seeing it portrayed so irreverently. Such broader issues lay beyond the scope of this essay, though the issues again become quite important in making an all-things-considered assessment of the appropriateness of Tarantino's juxtaposition of violence and humor.

My point has been that *part* of our assessment of Tarantino's use of violence should include a theological look at how it helps shape the list of our priorities. Is it our primary, sinful tendency to take temporary and finite things too seriously and allow them to play roles that only an eternal and infinite God should play?[149] If so, then perhaps Tarantino's use of humor serves as a useful reminder not to take any aspect of our fleeting, earthly existence too seriously. On the other hand, is our greater tendency instead to be apathetic toward the trials and suffering of others? If so, then perhaps Tarantino's use of humor does tend, unhelpfully, to acclimatize us to others' suffering, making them more palatable to us.

Finding myself ambivalent on these questions, I leave it up to the reader to form his or her own view. Whatever one's view on this matter, though, I again note that making an all-things-considered judgment about Tarantino's use of violence would not only need to consider the theology of humor, but more broadly consider the theology and philosophy of art.

---

[149] The term used throughout the Christian scriptures to describe this scenario is of course *idolatry*. For a nuanced discussion of idolatry see Robert M. Adams, *Finite and Infinite Goods* (Oxford: Oxford University Press, 1999), ch. 8.

Conclusion

To recap our discussion, we have linked the theology of humor with God's purpose of fostering human communities that reflect the loving relationships within the Trinity. God's gift of laughter can advance this community formation in at least four ways. It can help us move past awkward situations; it can serve as a way to express humility; it can ease pain we all experience; and it can help us prioritize our concerns. We have also seen that each of these positive uses of humor can be perverted. In such cases, humor serves the role of *undermining* the kind of community God intends for us.

The various positive—and negative—uses of humor are amply illustrated within Tarantino's movies. As for Tarantino himself and his set of priorities? Well, you can be the judge. His movies are really violent. They're also at times really funny. At the very least, given the uplifting nature of laughter itself, I don't think anything that makes me laugh can be wholly bad.

LOVE AND MEXICAN STANDOFFS: THE TRUTH IN *TRUE ROMANCE*

Jeff Green

Introduction

Unlike every other work in this anthology, this article does not center on a film or films that Quentin Tarantino directed. Rather, this article is centered on the film *True Romance* (henceforth "*TR*"), of which Tarantino was only the writer. However, it is an important part of his oeuvre, and the interactions between director Tony Scott and Quentin reveal much about how romance is portrayed in popular culture. In particular, the differing artistic intuitions that Scott and Tarantino held over how to end the film point to a false dilemma with regards to what romance is. (A false dilemma is a situation where only two options are presented but in fact there are actually more than two options.)[150]

---

[150] To be fair, neither artist portrays the two options as being exhaustive, so they are not dilemma mongers themselves. But I think both the fairy tale and tragic view of romance are represented often enough in contemporary culture, and to the exclusion of other views, to be the two horns of a false dilemma.

TR begins to call into question what romance and what the nature of true love are immediately, even in its opening title and early scenes. It then seeks to undermine various popular motifs in romance novels and romantic comedy, and it is largely successful. Finally, the Mexican standoff at the end of the film provides an opportunity for *TR* to become a fairy tale or a tragedy. Both Scott's and Tarantino's preferred endings would reflect only part of the story, and I believe that this dilemma is representative of a common misunderstanding of what love is. Put another way, either decision would fundamentally misrepresent the nature of love and romance despite the strong artistic reasons for each. In love, it is tempting to think of a relationship as a narrative, *the* great story of our lives. Conversely, I'm going to argue here that love, and marriage specifically, is not the story of our lives but rather a story of the relationship between Christ and his bride, the Church, albeit from a new angle. When seen from this point of view, traditional Christian views on marriage and sex can be more charitably articulated. By portraying romance in the context of a theological purpose we can move closer to an understanding of what true romance is.

What is love?[151]

Love is something people need and can give. It hurts[152] and heals. It is in constant use in typical human interaction. It is hard to understate its importance, especially in theology. After all, God is love.[153] Thus,

---

[151] At this point, the reader could, for their enjoyment, play 1993's "What is Love?" by Haddaway and perhaps even indulge in the music video of the song with its vampire theme—an interesting choice given that the song predates the recent popularity of the undead.

[152] If the previous musical suggestion was not to the reader's taste, then one might try the Everly Brothers' "Love Hurts" of 1960. To my knowledge, neither monster nor vampire makes an appearance in the performance of this song.

[153] "The one who does not love does not know God, for God is love," 1 John 4:8. (Except when noted otherwise, all verses are from the New American Standard Bible translation.)

increasing our understanding of love will increase our understanding of God and ourselves. So, what is love?

There is a cluster of questions we can ask about the word "love," all at the risk of complication, because the word "love" can refer to many different things. For example, we could inquire about what different emotions or relationships "love" refers to. We could ask metaphysical questions, such as *Is the relationship of love necessarily symmetrical?* (The answer to that question, as many of us know from experience, is no.) We could ask psychological, theological, and ethical questions, and this is all just for starters, but a full exploration of what love is would take much more than this article can facilitate. Thus, I want to narrow our focus to the quest for the nature of an ideal romantic relationship (and marriage, in particular). I say ideal, because this paper is more philosophical than sociological. I want to look beyond our actual relationships since they are necessarily flawed and in process of striving toward our vision of perfection. Rather, I want to think about what romantic relationships should be, and film is a great place to explore that idea.

Film is an incredibly powerful and expressive medium. As one of my colleagues has suggested, it is the literature of our age. Love stories, be they romantic comedies, supernatural romances, or heart wrenching tragedies, make up a large part of what we watch. In these stories, we can see the competing claims about what romance should be, what should be celebrated and what should be rejected. *TR* is especially intriguing because in it we see how artistic decisions shape a story, and it offers two different ideals for romantic relationships.

One might wonder how we can explore anything normative or ideal through film. The short answer is that art makes arguments. That is not to say that art is merely in the business of expressing arguments or that we can reduce a piece of art to an argument. Rather, I say this to point out that one of the things art does is express a worldview; it makes claims about the world. By looking at *TR* carefully we can piece together arguments about the nature of love and romance. These arguments may or may not be held by the creators of the piece; indeed, they may not be making a deliberate argument at all. The creators' beliefs and declarations are very important in understanding a particular piece, but they do not in and of themselves determine the meaning of a piece; artists, like the rest of us, can misspeak or be confused about what they are saying. To explore this particular point further would take us into deep water in aesthetics. I mention this issue here only to give some insight into how I approach the films and so that we are careful not to ascribe a particular set of beliefs to either Scott or Tarantino. This essay is not an attempt at mind reading.

Love Is Not a Romantic Comedy

> *I would never have guessed that true romance and Detroit would*
> *go together.*
>
> —Alabama Whitman, in *True Romance*

TR is like every other Tarantino film in that, among other things, it is about pop culture entertainment and other films in particular.[154] *Pulp Fiction,* for example, is replete with pop culture references such as those on display in the Jack Rabbit Slim's scene. *Jackie Brown* is an ode to Blaxploitation cinema, and both volumes of *Kill Bill* are heavy with references to East Asian cinema. In *TR* we see a critique of romantic ideals in films and romantic comedies in particular.

This critique is perhaps most relevant in the beginning of *TR*. The first scene involving Clarence Worley, played by Christian Slater, sets up the viewer in a more or less traditional way. The lovable loser protagonist, socially awkward and focused on genre works of pop culture (such as

---

[154] John McAteer, a contributor to this volume, is the first person I remember telling me this, but since then I've noticed it is a widely held position.

kung fu movies and comic books), fails to find a date on his birthday. However, we will see that the film does not stay within the traditional script for romantic comedies. The opening dialogue begins with a common lament heard by film characters: a cry to be someone different, someone with greater abilities. In this case Clarence wishes to be Elvis Presley, to possess Elvis' self-confidence and cool. Such aspirations are desirable in a character. We too want to be more than we are, and having the character voice his own insecurities and aspirations helps the audience identify and root for the character's success. If Clarence can find his inner Elvis, perhaps we can too.

Almost immediately, the film pivots as Clarence's words break the audience's building empathy for the character. He goes one step further in his identification with Elvis and enthusiastically speculates that if he were to have intercourse with a male, he would have intercourse with Elvis. This counterfactual is problematic for the romantic movie male because it undermines the masculinity he needs to fit into the expected genre trope. While romantic comedies are not homophobic or anti-homosexual, they do tend to have characters who are not sexually ambiguous and who give the audience cues as to what role they play in the romance. If a gay character does appear, it is often as a character who, by virtue of his sexual orientation, is not a threat to the ultimate goals of the two main characters and their love story. See, for example, the character of George Downes in *My Best Friend's Wedding*. In *TR*, the main male character goes beyond a loveable loser and instead almost disqualifies himself for the role in the first place.

Another signal that the film is attempting to undermine traditional romantic comedies is in the title itself. With the title "True Romance," the film claims to be somehow more accurate, pure, or ideal than other romance works (be they romantic comedies or romance comics). One is tempted to ask whether there is such a thing as a false romance. The film title implies that there is, and that true romance can be found in the narrative of the film. This attitude towards pop culture is refreshing in a Tarantino work. For example, in *Django Unchained* or the *Kill Bill* films, I can't help but feel that perhaps Tarantino loves his source material too much. With little or no subversion of the genre he is referencing, Tarantino's knowledge of film risks making his films self-indulgent.

Scenic pictures of Detroit in winter follow the opening title of *TR.* Streets lay covered in the salty, dirty mush of snow that has been driven over countless times. Homeless persons crowd around a trashcan, burning trash for warmth. A cop car appears and the boxy gray buildings of industrial Detroit serve as the backdrop. As credits appear on the screen, these images are contrasted with music that conjures up sunny Caribbean resorts and joyful times.

Detroit is not the ideal setting for a romantic comedy. Part of what makes a romantic comedy fun to watch is that it occurs in an idealized setting where people hope to find love. This need not be a natural paradise (though that is not uncommon), but if it is an urban setting, it needs to be the *right* urban setting. New York, for example, is a common setting and not just because of filming logistics. Making a successful life in New York, and specifically Manhattan, is one of the common aspirational stories we tell ourselves (on the small screen, for example, *Friends, Sex and the City,* and most recently, *Girls*). Even when a story is not set in New York, it only works if it allows our characters to thrive in a dense metropolitan area that is both financially and culturally rich. Sunbelt metro areas possess some of those characteristics but lack the density and downtown living experience. For a variety of reasons, encounters on I-285 (the highway loop around Atlanta, named "the Perimeter") are not part of our romantic ideal in the way meetings of fate on the Chicago "L" are. The recent romantic comedy *The Vow* succeeds in Chicago because it is appropriately connected to a hopeful aesthetic. The characters in that film have a life straight from Urban Outfitters. They have the lives the audience dreams of. The main female character, for example, has to decide between becoming a successful edgy artist or a successful lawyer at a top-notch urban law school. In a typical romance, the audience can fall in love with everything about the characters, including their setting.

In *TR*, the story is not in the recent Detroit of Eminem or confident Chrysler car ads. It is not Detroit as a phoenix rising. It is the Detroit of the Rust Belt, a place where dreams go to die. In this way, *TR* does not allow its setting to serve as a foreshadowing of the eventual happy ending. The setting itself is not romantic, so the romantic energy will have to come from a deeper, more complicated tale. Interestingly, even when the characters leave Detroit for sunny California and Hollywood, their hopefulness about their geographical change is not justified. California is not a safe haven or a paradise, and the trouble they are fleeing in Detroit finds them in their California dream.

Finally, the circumstances of Alabama's and Clarence's meeting undermine the traditional romantic comedy narrative. The characters appear to meet by happenstance, which is a key ingredient in many romances. There is something undeniably appealing about the fabled chance encounter. Chance encounters are magical because they can happen to any of us at any time. Even more amazing for Clarence, his chance encounter seems to bring him not to just any girl, but a girl who shares his love of kung fu movies. When Clarence brings Alabama to his place of work and his apartment, neither of which are impressive from the perspective of the audience, she does not scoff but is instead impressed. They end the night sharing a comic book romance and making love in the light of the candles of the Elvis shrine.

It's not long before there is trouble in paradise, and the film gives us a twist that would not work in a romantic comedy. The chance encounter turns out to be a fraud. It is revealed that Alabama is a prostitute and that she was hired by Clarence's boss to accompany and sleep with Clarence on his birthday because the boss took pity on him. This plot turn is problematic because the chemistry the characters shared is called into question.

Granted, romantic comedies, such as *Pretty Woman,* can feature prostitution and imperfect circumstances upon meeting. However, as Alabama and Clarence continue to bond under the light of the billboard, we can see that the plot of *TR* will be very different. The story of *TR* is not the romantic story of falling in love. Many romantic comedies end with a wedding after a lengthy series of misadventures and courtship. The bulk of *TR*, on the other hand, is about what happens to two people after they are married (Alabama and Clarence get married in the eighteenth minute of the film, which runs just over two hours). This focus on the challenges faced by the couple while they are in love undermines romantic comedies because it makes their mutual love the *problem,* not the *solution,* to their characters' situation. *TR* is not a story of two characters overcoming their fear of commitment. After all, they are "all in," as Alabama says. *TR* questions the cost of such a commitment and whether or not such a love can really conquer all.

Love is an "All In" Relationship

In the Bible we find a similar calling to an "all in" relationship, not just between two romantic partners, but between ourselves and God. The Bible is consistent in its story about God and his relationship to his people. In both the Old and New Testament, the Bible portrays that relationship as somehow akin to the relationship between a man and a woman in marriage. Importantly, marriage is modeled after the relationship between God and his people; it is not just a case of authors taking a human institution and finding in it a useful metaphor. As theologian Wayne Grudem writes, "The union between husband and wife is not temporary but lifelong (Mal. 2:14-16; Rom. 7:2), and it is not trivial but it is a profound relationship created by God in order to picture the relationship between Christ and his church" (Eph. 5:23-32).[155]

In the Old Testament we can find many examples of prophets drawing the connection between marriage and God's relationship to his people. In an extended passage in Ezekiel 16, we find Israel first being portrayed as an abandoned child and then as an adulteress. A similar comparison is found in Hosea, whose prophecy begins, "When the LORD first spoke through Hosea, the LORD said to Hosea, "Go, take to yourself a wife of harlotry and have children of harlotry; for the land commits flagrant harlotry, forsaking the LORD."[156]

It is not just in the prophets that we find the relationship between a man and a wife compared to God and his people. At the end of Genesis 2, an account is given of the creation of Eve from Adam's rib. Victor Hamilton, a well-regarded scholar of the Old Testament, translates Genesis 2:24 as, "Therefore a man forsakes his father and mother and clings to his wife, and they become one flesh."[157] He writes:

> Perhaps the most crucial element in this verse is the verbs it uses; *forsakes* and *clings*. The verb *forsake* frequently describes Israel's rejection of her covenant relationship with Yahweh...By contrast the verb *cling* often designates the maintenance of the covenant relationship....Already Scripture has sounded the note that marriage

---

[155] Wayne Grudem, *Systematic Theology* (Grand Rapids, Michigan: Zondervan Publishing House, 1994), 455.
[156] Hosea 1:2
[157] Victor P. Hamilton, *The Book of Genesis Chapters 1-17,* The New International Commentary on the Old Testament (Grand Rapids, Michigan: William B. Eerdmans Publishing Co., 1990), 177.

is a covenant rather than an ad-hoc, makeshift arrangement.[158]

Similar passages can be found throughout the Old Testament. The relationship between a husband and a wife is such that it is enough like the relationship between God and Israel that diverse authors across many different time periods compared the two, not in passing or with a light touch, but in lengthy sections with explicit comparison. Marriage reflects the story of a God and his people, and either can be used to illuminate the other.

The mutual illumination should not be mistaken for equal importance or ontological parity between the two relationships. As we've seen, Grudem goes so far as to suggest that one of the purposes of marriage is to shed light on the relationship between Christ and the Church. If he is right, marriage is evangelistic, in that it is one of the ways in which we share the good news about Jesus' death and resurrection in our lives. In obeying God and living in a marriage that represents the relationship between Christ and the Church, we can help others see and understand what God has done for us. I find this particularly compelling, because marriage is hard work. In difficult times in the relationship, it is, I think, comforting to know that marriage is grounded in theological truth.

A marriage can be evangelistic by each partner displaying a patient and long-suffering attitude to their spouse's faults. As sinners, Christ loved us and died for us.[159] In forgiving each other's sins, the couple mirrors Christ's love for the Church. The marriage is not based on the particular circumstances that day or week but is instead based on the choice made by each person to love the other. Such a choice is not easy,

---

[158] Ibid., 180-81.

[159] See Romans 5:6-8, "For while we were still helpless, at the right time Christ died for the ungodly. For one will hardly die for a righteous man; though perhaps for the good man someone would dare even to die. But God demonstrates His own love toward us, in that while we were yet sinners, Christ died for us."

and forgiveness can be difficult when we are called to forgive not just once or twice but essentially an infinite number of times.[160] This "all in" attitude is not an act of stubbornness but an act of love we show to others that is only possible when we rely on God to help us be more like Christ.

Is Love a Fairy Tale or Tragedy?

After a brief celebration of their marriage, Clarence and Alabama immediately face the problem of recovering her personal belongings and putting an end to her relationship with her former pimp, Drexel. (Again, note the contrast with *Pretty Woman*). Clarence, in an effort to solve the problem, ends up accidentally coming into possession of a large amount of stolen cocaine. So now the picture changes: Clarence and Alabama are in love, *and rich*, as long as they can sell the drugs. The subsequent series of adventures serves to further highlight the contrast of this film with other romances. The fight scenes are as brutal, creative, and detail-oriented as any other project associated with Tarantino. The violence, language, and harsh interrogations give the movie a completely different texture than any typical romance. Perhaps one could see the movie as the inspiration for a completely new genre, that of the romantic crime thriller—the grittiness even puts it beyond the less commonly talked about romantic dramas or other typical romance films.

The action comes to a climax in the hotel suite of Hollywood producer and potential drug buyer Lee Donowitz. In this scene we find a common trope in Tarantino's films: the Mexican standoff. A Mexican standoff occurs when three or more parties point their guns at one another but don't immediately shoot. Such scenes, regardless of their realism, create maximum drama in the story, as they produce the prospect of an imminent resolution of the plot but offer no clue as

---
[160] See Matthew 18:21-35.

to how the plot will resolve. Everyone could die, some could die, no one could die; the combinations are limited only to the creativity of the storyteller. The *TR* Mexican standoff consists of a standoff between law enforcement, the mob, and Donowitz's personal bodyguards. Clarence's party, which includes Alabama, is caught in the middle, while Clarence himself is in the bathroom receiving advice from a hallucinated Elvis.

The shooting begins when Donowitz throws coffee on his traitorous associate, actor Elliot Blitzer. Clarence enters the room and is quickly shot by a cop. It is here that director Tony Scott faces a choice: should Clarence live or should he die? How would the love story of Alabama and Clarence end?

Tarantino intended to have Clarence die from his gunshot wound, but Scott wanted to produce an ending in which Clarence lived. There was some dispute over this, and according to Tarantino's retelling of the events,[161] Tarantino persuaded Scott to shoot both endings, though Scott's preference ultimately prevailed. Tarantino characterized the choice between having Clarence live or die as the choice between a fairy tale and a tragedy.[162] Scott described feeling emotionally cheated by the ending in which Clarence dies and how he desired to "play out the romance" of the characters' lives getting better.[163]

The film gives us two ways to frame the challenges that Clarence and Alabama face. Tarantino's version presents a situation in which love does not conquer all and where love ultimately ends in heartbreak. We cannot have it all. The tragedy of love is that despite our deep commitment to one another, we are eventually at the whim of forces outside of our control. Sometimes things just don't work out. In Scott's

---

[161] See Tarantino's commentary on the alternative ending in *True Romance—Director's Cut*, dir. Tony Scott (Lionsgate Miramax, 2012), Blu-ray. This cut is one of ten discs included in *Tarantino XX: 8-Film Collection*, dirs. Quentin Tarantino and Tony Scott (Lionsgate Miramax, 2012), Blu-ray.

[162] Ibid.

[163] Ibid. See Scott's commentary on the alternative ending.

version, we eventually do come to the beach foretold by the soundtrack. Clarence and Alabama not only end up on the beach, rich, but they have a young son as well. The ending is a fairy tale, as it portrays love triumphing over all the odds to deliver the characters to a fabled ending.

This choice between a tragedy and a fairy tale is one that we are constantly presented with in media. We desire a clean ending, even if it is sad. Both of these choices play to an all or nothing mindset that is easy to understand but is ultimately mistaken. I think we are drawn to such stories because of our misunderstanding of romance. Often, we think of romantic relationship in utilitarian terms—about what the relationship is contributing to our lives. Given that relationships are not always pleasant or easy, we want to know if love is worth the pain, if it will ultimately conquer all.

It is, sadly, no surprise to me that only slightly over half of first marriages survive for twenty years[164] or that many more people are choosing to cohabitate and put off marriage.[165] Based on many people's experiences it seems that love cannot conquer all, and some would think it naïve to bet on something that seems so unreliable and impermanent. This is a mistake grounded in our understanding of what marriage and romance are. Remember, it is not in this world that we find the ideal of romance but in the spiritual world and in the relationship between Christ and the Church.

Love is the Story of Christ and the Church

Marriage is a relationship with purpose; it is, among other things,

---

[164] "Looking at 20 years, the probability that the first marriages of women and men will survive was 52% for women and 56% for men in 2006-2010" (page 7 of Copen CE, Daniels K, Vespa J, Mosher WD, "First Marriages in the United States: Data from the 2006-2010 National Survey of Family Growth," National Health Statistics Reports; no 49 (Hyattsville, MD: National Center for Health Statistics, 2012), PDF File, http://www.cdc.gov/nchs/data/nhsr/nhsr049.pdf.

[165] Ibid., 2, "Cohabitation has increasingly become the first coresidential union formed among young adults in the United States…"

an opportunity to mirror Christ's love for the Church. This gives a great joy to the relationship. It is not an internally focused relationship that finds meaning and inspiration in the limits of our frail being. Rather, marriage always has a majestic context and a reason for existing. Words, for example, have a tendency to lose their meaning when you say them over and over again. Similarly, I think some relationships tend to lose their meaning to us over time as well. In some relationships there comes a day when a husband or wife sees a marriage without a *raison d'être*. Even in those times, though, we can model God's faithfulness and the eternal relationship between Christ and the Church. We can take it upon ourselves to find the permanency of the marriage, not in the temporariness of worldly things or feelings, but in God's love for us.

I think Grudem is right and that part of marriage's purpose is to point beyond itself to Christ's relationship to his people. It is not only in the Old Testament that we find evidence for this claim. F. F. Bruce, a noted New Testament Scholar, translates Ephesians 5:22-33 as follows:

22. Wives, (be subject) to your own husbands as to the Lord,

23. for a husband is head of his wife, as also Christ is head of the church, being himself savior of the body.

24. But as the church is subject to Christ, so also let wives be to their husbands in everything.

25. Husbands, love your wives, as also Christ loved the church and gave himself up for it,

26. in order to sanctify it, purifying it by the washing of water with (the) word,

27. in order to present the church to himself invested with glory, free from spot, wrinkle or anything of the sort, but holy and blameless.

28. So indeed husbands ought to love their own wives as their own bodies. He who loves his own wife loves himself.

29. No one ever hated his own flesh but nourishes and cherishes it, as Christ does the church,

30. for we are members of his body.

31. "This is why a man will leave his father and mother and be joined to his wife, and the two will become one flesh."

32. This mystery is a deep one: I am quoting it in reference to Christ and to the church.

33. But as for you, individually, let each man love his own wife as he loves himself, and let the wife reverence her husband.[166]

This passage, like in the ones we saw before, reinforces the claim that throughout Scripture is a consistent comparison between the two relationships. Further, this comparison is beyond the superficial, it calls upon husbands and wives to model their relationship on that of Christ and his church.

Love and Heaven

Perhaps the reader feels that I am too hard on *TR* and fairy tales. After all, isn't there something wonderful about the ending in the film? Note that the ending is not just the escape to paradise, as if Clarence and Alabama were on a hedonistic voyage. Rather, the ending is family centered, the new family delighting in one another and in their safety. The paradise pictured isn't important as a destination in and of itself but is instead a symbol for the successful relationships that the characters have built. Neither Clarence nor Alabama has a strong, supportive family when the movie begins. The quick glimpse we're given of the relationship between Clarence and his dad is evidence that while there is a deep reservoir of love between father and son, they are not close.

---

[166] F. F. Bruce, *The Epistles to the Colossians, to Philemon, and to the Ephesians,* The New International Commentary on the New Testament (Grand Rapids, Michigan: William B. Eerdmans Publishing Co., 1984), 382-3.

In addition, given the events of the film, Clarence does not have the opportunity to reinvigorate or repair that relationship. Tellingly, the ending centers around Clarence's and Alabama's son, not on scuba diving, deep sea fishing, or some other typical beach-vacation activity. Elvis, the son, is emphasized not only because his name is discussed but because he is a sudden and important addition to the story. That suggests to me that the island setting is there to help the viewers understand that Clarence and Alabama have found the paradise of love between members of their family, not some shallow holiday fantasy vacation. Without marriage pointing to something bigger than itself, we are likely to be disappointed and not find ultimate happiness in it. Therefore, it's possible that the ending offers an unrealistic vision of what marriage can deliver. Our ultimate happiness is not to be found in our relationships with one another but in our relationship with God.

Note the quotation of Genesis 2:24 in Ephesians 5:31. The apostle Paul, the author of Ephesians, notes that there is a mystery here—a mystery that explains why marrying is so binding, indeed why any sexual relationship (see 1 Corinthians 6:16) brings with it so much gravity and connection. It is a mystery that is now explained by Christ and his death and resurrection. As Bruce writes:

> Gen. 2:24…is taken to convey a deeper, hidden meaning, a "mystery" which could not be understood until Christ, who loved his people from eternity, gave himself up for them in the fullness of time…The formation of Eve to be Adam's companion is seen to prefigure the creation of the church to be the bride of Christ.[167]

I find this interpretation compelling and would add that it helps us understand what may be a puzzling adage in the Gospels. Jesus makes the following claim in responding to the Sadducees and their questions

---

[167] Ibid., 394-5.

regarding the resurrection of the dead: "For when they rise from the dead, they neither marry nor are given in marriage, but are like angels in heaven."[168] One might puzzle and even be distressed about this, wondering why marriage, one of the more important and significant relationships we could have, would not continue. Why is it only "till death do us part" that wedding vows last? I suspect that it is because on the New Earth, marriage is no longer needed. One of marriage's chief purposes is to point to the relationship between Christ and his bride, but in heaven the bridegroom and bride will be united for eternity.[169] There is no need for an image of a thing when the real thing is at hand.

Dr. Jerry Walls, a co-editor of this volume, has written an inspiring account of heaven in his book on the Christian doctrine of the afterlife, *Heaven, Hell and Purgatory: Rethinking the Things That Matter Most.*[170] He too discusses the genre of romantic comedy, but instead of criticizing it, embraces it. He writes:

> The Alpha who created us for happiness is the Omega who is the foundation of happiness. This is the foundational truth that holds out the delicious prospect that the human story is destined for a glorious end that will surpass our wildest imagination.[171]

In Walls' account there is a fairy tale ending to the human drama. In Revelation 21:2, we again find the imagery of marriage: "And I saw the holy city, new Jerusalem, coming down out of heaven from God, made ready as a bride adorned for her husband." In heaven we will find

---

[168] Mark 12:25

[169] See Revelation 21:9-11, "'Come here, I will show you the bride, the wife of the Lamb.' And he carried me away in the Spirit to a great and high mountain, and showed me the holy city, Jerusalem, coming down out of heaven from God, having the glory of God. Her brilliance was like a very costly stone, as a stone of crystal-clear jasper."

[170] Jerry Walls, *Heaven, Hell and Purgatory: Rethinking the Things that Matter Most* (Grand Rapids, Michigan: Brazos Press, 2015). The chapter this section is based on is entitled "Heaven, Trinity and the Meaning of Life."

[171] Ibid., 27.

a relationship and life that is ideal—that will represent a permanent, never disappointing, happy ending. It is a testimony to the power of our current romantic relationships that one of the images used to describe heaven is that of a bride appearing before her groom on her wedding day. So there is something right about the image of paradise and fairy tales, though to see what is right we need to look forward with expectation, as opposed to seeking it only in our relationships with each other.

Concluding Suggestions

Our movies, books, songs, and TV shows are filled with theological ideas. This volume is a testament to the fruit we can find in exploring well-executed artistic expression. I would suggest that while there is much theology in our media, there is far less biblical theology. That is, as we have seen in this essay, there is a raising of important questions in media, but the answers are often given without much theological specificity and usually outside any given particular religious tradition. I do not believe this is because of a deliberate attempt to marginalize Christians or anything of that sort. Rather, I think it is because there is a lack of understanding about what the Bible, for example, has to say about important matters, and a general unease about portraying any particular religious tradition as having the right answer.

I mention this because the picture I give for marriage has profound implications on our current debates in sexual ethics. In these debates, the minority of Americans currently holds the traditional Christian understanding.[172] Given the scope of this essay it would be too much to wade into the debates about the role of women and men in marriage, divorce, sex outside of marriage, homosexuality, and gender. For now, let me gesture at what I take to be a promising way forward for our

[172]See, for example, John Mark Reynolds' essay "On Minority Status in Sexual Ethics," Eidos, a blog on Patheos.com, http://www.patheos.com/blogs /eidos/2014/07/on-minority-status-in-sexual-ethics/ (accessed 2014).

understanding of these issues. Too often our debates on these issues are divorced from an understanding that sexual ethics in the Christian tradition are not just founded on a verse or two, but rather are a consistent narrative throughout Scripture that marriage reflects a deeper reality. For example, many would struggle to understand why many Christians have opposed a loosening of attitudes toward divorce or why they hold standards on sexual practice that are very hard to live out, especially as the average age of marrying couples rises. Perhaps those positions may find a greater resonance and meaning in the framework of marriage presented in this discussion. In sex and marriage we find a way to serve God by reflecting his love for us. Love is not a tragedy or a fairy tale. It is a biography, the true story of Christ's death and resurrection for us.

11

THREE STORIES ABOUT ONE STORY: POSTMODERNISM AND THE NARRATIVE STRUCTURE OF *PULP FICTION*

John McAteer

Quentin Tarantino's *Pulp Fiction* is a quintessentially postmodern film. As such, it can help us see the relevance of postmodernism for theology. In this chapter, I will explore *Pulp Fiction*'s postmodern claims about the ambiguity of the world and the necessity of narrative to interpret the meaning of events. I will connect this to the role of Scripture in interpreting the true meaning of the world, historical events, and our lives.

Postmodern Filmmaking

All of Tarantino's films are about the movies. They all take place in a world Tarantino supposedly calls the "movie-movie world."[173] They don't take place in the real world or the imaginary world of Hollywood films; they take place in a cartoon world in which Hollywood clichés are exaggerated so far they take on a reality of their own. Not only do Tarantino's films take place in such a world, they are *about* that world. They are self-reflective celebrations of exaggerated movie clichés. In this, they are quintessentially postmodern.

Postmodernism is a slippery concept that is used to describe many contradictory phenomena and ideologies. For our purposes it will be most helpful to approach postmodernism from the perspective of art theory. Postmodernism is the rejection of at least four trends in modern art. (1) Modernist art—including modernist film—is art about the nature of art. Just as modern philosophy began when Descartes turned his consciousness upon itself and began to reflect on the foundations of thought, so modern art self-consciously explores the nature of art. For example, modernist film explores the nature of cinematic representation and the medium of film itself. (2) Along these lines modernism also emphasizes the concept of the avant-garde and the idea of artistic progress, for example, toward the goal of "pure" cinema that perfectly expresses the nature of cinema itself. (3) Moreover, modern art, especially painting, rejects realism and the classical theory of art as representation, tending instead toward abstraction and formalism. These modernist trends can be seen in avant-garde cinema such as the later films of Jean-

---

[173] A quote often attributed to Tarantino has him saying: "There's my realer-than-real movies like *Reservoir Dogs*. And then there's my movie-movies. And *Kill Bill* is definitely one of those. It's the movies that Jules and Vince would go and see." But that distinction seems primarily designed to explain why some characters are able to cross over between films but others are not. Really, all Tarantino films take place in the same hyper-real world based on exaggerated movie clichés. *Pulp Fiction* (purportedly a "realer-than-real" world film) has as many or more cinematic allusions than *Kill Bill*.

Luc Godard, a French filmmaker who influenced Tarantino.[174] Godard's films are the cinematic equivalent of a Picasso cubist painting. They place cinematic technique and form in the foreground, abstracting from the sort of representational content—such as an intelligible story with sympathetic characters—emphasized by classical Hollywood movies. (4) Finally, and perhaps most importantly for our purposes, according to modernism, an artist constructs meaning within an autonomous self and expresses it by imposing order on an objective/meaningless nature. From this assumption Godard and his fellow French film theorists developed the "auteur theory" of film criticism, which emphasizes the role of the director in constructing the meaning of a film.

Postmodernist art, on the other hand, is art that rejects modern appeals to "the true nature" of art. For postmodernism, art is a "social construction," so there are as many kinds of art as there are societies, and none should be seen as better or more "pure" than any other. Thus postmodernism does not privilege elitist, avant-garde "high art" films like Godard's over populist "low art" like Hollywood movies. Moreover, postmodernism rejects the existence of an autonomous self and the ability of the artist to impose absolute meaning. Postmodernism aims to deconstruct itself, revealing itself to be just another construction. Thus postmodern art is not about the *nature* of representation but the *fact* of representation. It reveals artistic representation *as* representation and revels in the artifice of artistic representation. It is about the content of artistic cliché, not the medium.

These aspects of postmodern art should be familiar to fans of Tarantino, for they are present in all of his films, though perhaps most obvious in *Pulp Fiction*. One of *Pulp Fiction*'s most often cited (and most influential) postmodern elements is its self-aware and ironic use of pop

---

[174] Tarantino named his production company after Godard's 1964 film *Bande à Part*.

cultural clichés and references. This sort of technique is associated with many terms in academic jargon: pastiche, homage, intertextuality, bricolage, metafiction, etc. One thing all these concepts have in common is the attempt to "deconstruct" or reveal the artificiality of conventional boundaries—for example between high art and popular culture, between genres, between tragedy and comedy, between audience and author, between irony and sincerity, between reality and fiction, etc. The fundamental philosophical assumption beneath all of this is that reality is ambiguous, that reality must be interpreted or "constructed," but that all constructions are always only partial, contingent, and open to deconstruction.

It should be obvious that *Pulp Fiction* is all about interpretation and ambiguity as it starts with two different definitions of the word *pulp*. Right from the opening title, the film emphasizes the multiplicity of possible meanings, and it ends with a discussion of an ambiguous event that may or may not have been a miracle. In between, the characters have conversations about everything from the cultural relativity of language (in the "Royale with Cheese" scene) to the ambiguous social construction of sexuality (in the "foot massage" conversation), etc. *Pulp Fiction* constantly forces us to think about the inescapability of interpretation and the ways we construct meaning out of the ambiguous events of our own lives. In this, it is a quintessentially postmodern film.

Narrative and Intelligibility

When film theorists call *Pulp Fiction* a "postmodern" film, they are often referring to its unconventional narrative structure. Narrative is a central concept in postmodern art. In his seminal work *The Postmodern Condition*, French philosopher Jean-Francois Lyotard famously defined postmodernism as "incredulity to metanarratives."

However, he wasn't rejecting narratives altogether.[175] On the contrary, he insisted that narratives are inescapable. But because narratives are inescapable, all truth claims must be interpreted from within a narrative. So postmodernism isn't necessarily incredulous toward all narratives, just *meta*narratives. Metanarratives are claims to "absolute" truth that pretend not to be narratives and pretend, rather, to be objective, scientific facts—history rather than story. Lyotard's favorite examples are Marxism and Hegelianism, but we might add Darwinism or any other worldview that claims to have the only *possible* complete system of facts, a system which must be accepted by any rational observer. But postmodernism reveals that "objectivity" is just another story we tell ourselves, just another limited interpretation of reality. According to postmodernism, the world is ambiguous. Another way to put this is that reality is *pulp*—it is a soft and shapeless mass that must be formed into something meaningful. Reality in itself is not meaningful; rather we must give it meaning. And our tool for giving meaning to reality is narrative.

Narrative is essential for the intelligibility of events and actions.[176] We cannot identify an action *as* an action (in contrast to a mere bodily movement) without locating it in a narrative of intentions. For example, imagine you are standing on the corner of Fletcher Drive and Atwater Avenue in Los Angeles when you see a white 1980 Honda Civic crash into a large African-American pedestrian carrying a box of doughnuts. You might offer to go to court for the injured man, believing the driver was "a drunken maniac." It wouldn't occur to you that the crash was intentional, because intentional actions are actions done for reasons. In other words, they are teleological, or goal-oriented. You can't understand

---

[175] See James K.A. Smith, *Who's Afraid of Postmodernism: Taking Derrida, Lyotard, and Foucault to Church* (Grand Rapids: Baker Academic, 2006), ch. 6.
[176] My argument here follows Alasdair MacIntyre. See *After Virtue*, 3rd ed. (Notre Dame: University of Notre Dame Press, 2007) especially Chapter 15.

an action until you can understand *why* the agent performed the action. But what reason could the driver have to crash his car into a pedestrian?

Moreover, narrative is essential for the *identity* of actions. You can't even know *which* action the agent performed unless you know the agent's goal. For you to understand what *happened* and to conceptualize which behavior the driver actually performed—to decide whether, for example, the crash was an accident, attempted murder, self-defense, etc.—you would need to know the driver's particular intentions. Hence, for the car crash to become intelligible you would need information about the past interactions between the driver and the pedestrian as well as information about their conflicting future goals. You would need a narrative context: a future end toward which the past and present aim.

Narratives can always be extended in ways that re-contextualize individual events. For example, if you knew the pedestrian was gangster boss Marsellus Wallace and the driver was boxer Butch Coolidge who had cost Marsellus a large sum of money by not throwing a fight as ordered, then you could understand that Marsellus wanted Butch dead and Butch crashed his car into Marsellus in an effort to protect himself. So within this narrative context, the action Butch performed was "trying to protect himself from a gangster." But if you expanded the narrative to include Butch's relationship with his girlfriend Fabienne, you might see that the reason Butch didn't throw the fight was so he could make enough money to quit boxing and start a better life with his girlfriend. In this wider narrative context, the action Butch performed becomes something like "trying to start a new life." The wider narrative context changes the meaning and even the *identity* of the action.

The narrative context can be extended still further. If you include Butch's entire life story all the way back to his childhood, including the formative event of receiving an heirloom gold watch that his father,

Major Coolidge, had smuggled through a concentration camp, then the action takes on yet another meaning. The watch represents a family history of pride and honor for Butch. It is a symbol of manhood for Butch and the toughness that allowed Major Coolidge to pass on this "birthright" to his son. A watch is something that keeps time and orients us to the past and future, thus a symbol of heritage. Dreaming of the watch inspired Butch to win the fight. His masculine sense of honor wouldn't let him intentionally lose. Despite the fact that he tells the taxi driver that American names don't mean anything, Butch does in fact live up to his macho name. Continuing the story, the reason Butch is driving down Atwater Avenue is that he went back to his apartment to get the watch before leaving town. So in this context the action he is performing in the car crash narrative is something like "trying to live up to his father's image of manhood." Moreover, this wider narrative explains what happens later still, after the car crash. When Butch unexpectedly risks his life to save Marsellus, his actions are unintelligible unless seen within the narrative of the gold watch. Again, Butch's sense of honor and manhood won't let him leave Marsellus behind. In his life story, he sees himself playing the role of hero.

So events are always ambiguous because the narrative context can always be extended in new directions. We can't even limit the relevant narrative context to our physical life (birth to death) because, as the example of Butch's father shows, the intelligibility of Butch's life requires knowledge of things Major Coolidge did before Butch was born. Likewise, Major Coolidge's action of hiding the gold watch in his rectum is made intelligible by his own past heritage and the future life of his son Butch. Moreover, events are ambiguous, because there is always more than one way to tell the story of the narrative connections between the events. The narrative of "The Gold Watch" segment of *Pulp Fiction* is only one way to tell the story of Butch's life. Even Butch himself might not tell the same story. He dreams of the watch before his big fight, but perhaps he is only subconsciously aware of how it has influenced the way he constructs his self-identity. Butch later comments that he rarely ever remembers his dreams.

Playing a Role in a Narrative

As we have seen, all events must be understood narratively, but smaller narratives (like Butch's crash into Marsellus) must be understood in a larger narrative (like Butch's relationship with his father). A Grand Narrative that was able to embed all other narratives would be able to provide the final meaning of everything. It would be a "metanarrative." But only God could have such a narrative. Christian theologians are sometimes wary of postmodernism, because they see it as an attack on all truth claims. Postmodernists often attempt to justify their rejection of metanarratives by asserting the impossibility of a "God's-eye view." But if there is a God, then there must be a God's-eye view, and we need not be incredulous toward all metanarratives. Indeed, if God has revealed the Truth to us through Scripture, then it seems we have access to the most credible metanarrative one could ask for.

But this is a mistake. Even if we have the outlines of the one true narrative revealed to us in Scripture, we still can never know with final certainty how all the smaller narratives fit together. As new events happen, we constantly have to reinterpret the past to construct new narratives. The problem of intelligibility is especially clear in the problem of evil. Events we call "evil" are *unintelligible*—they don't fit with our narrative of God's love and Providence. Suffering for a good reason (e.g., the pain from exercising that will make us healthier and thus prevent future pain) is not evil. Only unintelligible suffering is evil. The Christian response is hope that there is a larger narrative (God's narrative) in which all things become intelligible. But since we can't know the details of that narrative, we're constantly revising and reinterpreting our life stories as we go along.

Yet we can't create just any narrative for our lives. Unless we are massively self-deceived, we will have to be accountable to the narratives of those whose lives intersect ours, as well as our own past actions. We may reinterpret our past in light of new experiences, but we cannot simply ignore it. For example, Marsellus can't plausibly interpret himself as merely an innocent victim in the car crash. His narrative is accountable to Butch's narrative of being coerced into throwing the fight and then being threatened with death.

Moreover, we must interpret ourselves from within the conceptual resources of our culture. Our culture provides certain characters or social roles that operate as ideals for us and give us a framework within which we may construct our self-identities in relation to others.[177] Even if we choose to reject our culture's dominant roles, we nevertheless define ourselves in relation to them. We have already noticed how Butch's self-identity is built from the role of Manly Man that his father bequeathed him, a role influenced by the old Hollywood war movies and westerns Tarantino references throughout the story of "The Gold Watch." In fact, all of Tarantino's film characters are built out of cliché movie roles. Butch is clearly playing the role of washed-up boxer (a la Marlon Brando in *On the Waterfront*), but he draws upon many other movie roles as well. We are not trapped in any particular role, but because human beings are social animals, we cannot create a role from scratch in isolation from a society. So there is a balance between freedom and determination. To use Heidegger's term, we find ourselves "thrown" into a culture and must construct a character for ourselves out of the material we find

---

[177] Ibid., ch. 3.

there.[178] Butch didn't choose to be born in America; he didn't choose for his father to die in a war; he didn't choose for Marsellus Wallace to control the boxing clubs in Los Angeles; but Butch did choose what sort of person he would become in this context.

Part of the reason we can't know the final metanarrative is that it hasn't been written yet.[179] Scripture reveals that God has determined the outlines of the story, and we know God will bring about a "happily ever after" ending someday; nevertheless, we are co-authoring the details of the story as it unfolds. Scripture provides a fixed narrative context for our lives, and it teaches us to play certain roles—disciple, martyr, prophet, etc.[180] The crisis events of our lives—the turning points in the narrative—are points where we contribute to the narrative by determining what sort of characters we will be. *Pulp Fiction* is largely about precisely this need to construct a character for oneself. The film portrays a number of characters trying to decide what kind of role they want to play and what kind of story they want to be a part of.

Consider the opening scene in the diner with Pumpkin and Honey Bunny (later called "Ringo" and "Yolanda").

Honey Bunny: You want to rob banks?

Pumpkin: I'm not saying I want to rob banks. I'm just illustrating that if we did, it would be easier than what we've been doing.

Honey Bunny: And no more liquor stores?

Pumpkin: What have we been talking about? Yeah, no more liquor stores.

Honey Bunny: Well, what, then? Day jobs?

---

[178] See Heidegger, *Being and Time*, trans. John Macquarrie and Edward Robinson (New York: Harper & Row, 1967), I.5, section 29, 174.

[179] I am assuming an Arminian view of free will, according to which our choices are not determined by God.

[180] Compare 1 Cor. 12:28.

Pumpkin: Not in this life.

Honey Bunny: What, then?

They're trying to decide which way their life is going to go: Liquor Stores, Banks, or Day Jobs. Consider also the contrast in the way Pumpkin and Honey Bunny talk to each other—especially the way Honey Bunny says sweetly, "I don't want to kill anyone"—with their sudden shift into the role of "robber." Tarantino's published screenplay calls it their "robbery persona." Compare this to when Jules tells Vincent "let's get into character" just before they go into the apartment to get the briefcase back. Vincent is normally very talkative, but his "hit man" persona is quiet. These personas are roles the characters consciously set for themselves, but *Pulp Fiction* suggests that our ordinary lives are roles as well.

Flash forward to the rest of this scene in the diner, which actually comes at the very end of the movie. This time the events are seen from Jules and Vincent's point of view. Like Pumpkin, Jules is talking about a career change: he says he's "in a transitional period." Jules repeats his big speech (allegedly) from Ezekiel 25:17, but he sees it very differently than he did earlier in the movie.

> **Jules:** The path of the righteous man is beset on all sides by the iniquities of the selfish and the tyranny of evil men. Blessed is he who, in the name of charity and goodwill, shepherds the weak through the valley of darkness.

He continues:

> Now I'm thinkin', maybe it means you're the evil man. And I'm the righteous man. And Mr. 9mm here, he's the shepherd protecting my righteous ass in the valley of darkness. Or it could mean you're the righteous man and I'm the shepherd and it's the world that's evil and

selfish. I'd like that. But that shit ain't the truth. The truth is you're the weak. And I'm the tyranny of evil men. But I'm tryin', Ringo. I'm tryin' real hard to be the shepherd.

So Jules is trying to figure out which role he should play in the world. Note that he thinks there is a set narrative that he has to fit into. He's not creating his character from scratch, but finding his place in a traditional story.

It is significant that this is not an actual quotation from Scripture. It is similar to several biblical passages, but it is actually a direct quote from a 1970s kung fu movie starring Sonny Chiba. Jules himself mentions that he is going to "walk the earth" and "get in adventures…you know, like Caine in *Kung Fu*." So Jules is modeling himself on fictional heroes. In some way he seems to dimly recognize that he is a stock character in a stereotypical gangster movie. He sees that there are certain roles available to him in his social context, and he is trying to choose the best one.

Now, since both parts of the diner scene that frames *Pulp Fiction* are about choosing your role in a narrative, it is not too much of a stretch to suggest that this is the main theme of the movie. And, indeed, the theme shows up in all of the stories: Vincent has to choose whether to be loyal to Marsellus or not; Butch first has to choose whether to throw the fight, and then he has to choose whether to go back and heroically help Marsellus escape from the hillbillies. In the end, all three sub-stories are structured around redemption: the main characters of each story get to show that they "have character" in the moral sense. As Winston "The Wolf" says, "Just because you *are* a character doesn't mean you *have* character."

Three Stories about One Story

This point about each story being structured around redemption raises another interpretive problem: what significance does the movie's unique plot structure have? I think a good way to approach this problem is to ask, *How many narratives are there in* Pulp Fiction? The title page of the published script says the film is "Three stories about one story," but the overall meaning of the movie depends on whether you emphasize the "three" part or the "one" part.

If there is only one narrative, then that narrative looks jumbled up and meaningless. It looks incoherent and does not resemble a single set of events aimed at a single conclusion. This is the typical interpretation of those theologians who see postmodernism as nihilistic. From this perspective, the point would be that the world is meaningless pulp— "a soft, moist, shapeless mass or matter"—and any apparent narrative structure you see in your life is merely "fiction" imposed on the chaos. So by editing and arranging the story this way, Tarantino can ironically give the illusion of meaning while simultaneously deconstructing that artificial meaning through its disjointed structure and making sure we remember that the un-interpreted events are meaningless. Needless to say, if this is the message of the film, then it is obviously not compatible with Christianity. It is essential to Christianity that God is in control of the world, that God created the world for a purpose, and that God is guiding history toward a meaningful end.

But the nonlinear interpretation is not the only way to read the structure of the film. *Pulp Fiction* can just as easily be read as three perfectly linear short stories. It is only if you take the whole movie as "one story" that you feel disjointed. If you recognize that the film is comprised of three short stories—an homage to the pulp anthology magazines popular in the early 20th Century—then there is nothing unusual about these narrative structures except that there are three of them in a row. Each short story is a perfectly straightforward and linear narrative. Indeed, the film clearly marks off the three stories with separate titles, and frames them all with the diner scene. On this "anthology" interpretation, the film's structure seems like an attempt to point out the fact that each of us is really the hero of our own life narrative. In other words, it is an attempt to reflect a necessary fact of human existence: we each find ourselves living in a story. The point of the movie, then, would be that despite seeming like meaningless pulp, the world is actually meaningful and ordered, though the larger narrative context that connects the small narratives of our individual lives can be hard to discern. Thus, by editing the movie the way he does, Tarantino is not making up an artificial narrative structure; he's helping us see what was there all along. Butch's life, for example, really was organized around his relationship with his father (symbolized by the gold watch), but in a traditional Hollywood narrative, we might not have realized that. It wasn't until Butch—a minor character in Jules' story—was narrated as the protagonist of his own story that we began to see his true significance. Likewise, in our own lives we must see ourselves as the hero of our life story in order to make meaningful choices about the sort of character we are to have. But only within the larger narrative framework of Scripture can we understand the full significance of our lives.

Ambiguity and Interpretation

Pulp Fiction, like the real world, turns out to be ambiguous. The film can be interpreted in two very different ways, depending on how one thinks about its narrative structure, but this is true for any set of events in our lives. So *Pulp Fiction* actually serves to draw our attention to an inescapable feature of our world. In fact, the ambiguity of the world is actually the subject of the debate between Vincent and Jules in the diner at the end of the movie.

> **Jules:** I just been sittin' here thinkin'.
> **Vincent:** About what?
> **Jules:** The miracle we witnessed.
> **Vincent:** The miracle *you* witnessed. I witnessed a freak occurrence.

Jules takes the theistic viewpoint that there is a meaning and order to the things that happen, while the atheistic Vincent thinks the world is just random events. The two characters locate the same event in different cosmic narrative contexts. The film doesn't resolve this ambiguity for us.[181] Has the film been an ingenious demonstration that even the most inane gangster movie clichés can reveal deep existential truths? Or has the film been a cynical exercise in nihilism? We each have to choose how we will give shape to the pulp.

---

[181] On the other hand, Vincent is the only main character to die. Is this a comment on the fact that he was unable to appreciate the miracle? Moreover, all of the stories involve freak occurrences that could be interpreted as miracles. Is it just luck that the adrenaline shot revives Mia? Is it just luck that Vincent is in the bathroom when Butch returns to his apartment?

LIKE A MAN:
RESERVOIR DOGS, AUGUSTINE'S PEARS, AND MASCULINITY

Russell Hemati

In his *Confessions*, Augustine recounts his experience at sixteen years of age, when he and a group of his friends stole pears from a nearby farm. He analyzes his motives and the motives of his friends, trying to understand how they did a crime together that none of them individually would have performed. Quentin Tarantino's first film, *Reservoir Dogs*, explores a similarly toxic camaraderie, which pushes each member of the band of thieves to perform their crimes without regret and under a dreadful kind of necessity. In this chapter, I will use the categories Augustine develops to better understand the interplay of characters in *Reservoir Dogs*, and by doing so, show the concept of masculinity as the principle means by which this toxic camaraderie coheres.

Sin—When Stealing Is More Than Just Theft

Let us begin by first describing sin, because within Christian theology, sin is more than the mere transgression of divine commands. Though it often is depicted as a set of rules that one does or does not violate (as in the Ten Commandments or the various dietary restrictions in *Leviticus*), sin is more complex. It warps and subverts the whole of human behavior, distorting good practices and relationships. For example, within the family, sin can change fathers into tyrants, mothers into cold manipulators, and siblings into enemies. Or in one's personal profession, it can turn a career from service for the community to service of oneself. When sin has its full effect, it kills us all. When considering the tyrannical father, the power of sin is not most manifest in the transgression of a command like "Thou shalt not be an angry, difficult husband." Rather, it is the power of sin undermining the goodness of creation and turning what should be a beneficial, loving relationship into something twisted and harmful where sin's power is most heavily felt. In the same way, one of God's greatest gifts, friendship, which can bring out the very best of virtues, can be twisted through sin into a factory for vice. Augustine provides a helpful example from his own life to help us understand how this happens and to see clearly the negative effects that follow.

St. Augustine was one of Christianity's earliest psychologists, exploring the mental effects of sin and holiness on the personality. In order to show the tendency of sin to push us toward vanity (or emptiness) he recounts an incident from his wild adolescence. Augustine's teenage crime seems quite mild: he and his friends steal a quantity of low-quality pears from a farmer, then proceed to throw them at pigs. It is the kind of incident we might write off as mere hijinks or teenage boisterousness, but for Augustine it is a far more serious crime. In his estimation, this incident reveals much about his moral state in particular and about crime and transgression in general. Contrary to the commonly held theory that people do wrong due to confusion or by inappropriately choosing lesser goods rather than greater goods, Augustine reminisces that he committed the crime *because* it was wrong. "I was seeking not to gain anything by shameful means,"[182] he writes, "but shame for its own sake." He could find no rational motive for it, since he did not consume the pears or even keep them. He acted only for the enjoyment of doing the crime.

Inverted Community

This desire to do wrong for its own sake is deeply puzzling. Generally speaking, it isn't the *wrongness* of an act that makes it attractive, but rather the perceived benefits of the action. According to this line of thinking, stealing is explained by the desire for the object (whether that be gold, cash, or in this case, fruit) that overwhelms the desire to be an honest citizen. Since Augustine considers all wrong actions ultimately harmful, no one, in theory, should consciously choose to do wrong. If they did, they would be consciously choosing to harm themselves every time. Logically, then, since people act on their desire to benefit themselves, their ability to do wrong must be due to confusion or ignorance. After all, no one would put their hand on a hot stove if they knew the stove to be hot. Yet this is not what happened when Augustine stole the pears. He was neither confused nor ignorant of his moral transgression. He did it, he says, because he wanted to do something wrong. But why? What does he benefit? Augustine's answer is that he gained the respect of his friends, all of whom stole the pears together.

At the end of his tale Augustine considers the friendship with the

---

[182] This and other quotations from Book II of Augustine's *Confessions*, trans. Henry Chadwick (New York: Oxford University Press, 1991).

other perpetrators a necessary condition for his actions. "Friendship," he states, "can be a dangerous enemy... As soon as the words are spoken, 'Let us go and do it,' one is ashamed not to be shameless." Without his friends to urge him on, there would be no transition from idea to action—no way to connect the passing thought of theft with a decision to *actually* go and steal. If he were by himself he would have to decide if it were worth the trouble and risk of getting caught. Not so in a group. Once someone says "Let's do it," it is not possible to back down without losing the respect of the group. In Augustine's estimation, it would have been harder to accept the shame of weakness than to actually do something shameful. It was easier to commit a pointless crime than be thought to have a conscience. For Augustine, the horror of his crime is that he can give himself no excuses. Though he does not mention it in *Confessions*, it's likely his friends felt the same way and thus the theft was truly in vain.

A Pack of Dogs

It is the desire to gain the approval of his "pack" that pulls Augustine to theft. This same desire plays a crucial role for the men of *Reservoir Dogs* as they commit their crimes, with pack approval and dynamics becoming an obsession within the story. Examples are legion, and once this pattern is detected the evidence is present in nearly every scene. Below I examine a few of the most paradigmatic.

Reservoir Dogs is a movie saturated with machismo. The tone is set early on with the opening scene. The men, using their pseudonyms, banter with each other over breakfast. They talk, as in many Tarantino films, about seemingly insignificant or off-topic issues. The scene begins as Mr. Brown is deep into an analysis of Madonna's "Like a Virgin," theorizing about the singer's many sexual partners, and then closes with Mr. Pink explaining why he is opposed to tipping the waitress. Mr. Brown reduces the love song to an extended metaphor for penis size while Mr. Pink, played with infectious intensity by Steve Buscemi, rejects any compassion for the waitress.

It is tempting, though I think incorrect, to read this scene as a mere misogynistic display of bravado. This temptation strengthens when we later discover that Mr. Pink's manliness is already in question. He is given the pseudonym "Pink" because Joe, the contractor, thinks he is gay and says so to the group during a planning session. "Pink" asks to be "Mr. Purple" instead, which is possibly a wink to the audience that Joe is correct about Mr. Pink. As Pink explains, "Mr. Pink sounds like Mr. Pussy." It is important for Pink to define himself as something other than feminine and weak, lest he lose the respect of the pack— even if the alternative is Mr. Purple, which still sounds opulent and luxurious next to the plain, no-nonsense colors of his fellows. Again, on the surface this scene seems to indicate that the thieves are misogynistic and homophobic. However, I think this incident is not so much about Brown's and Pink's disregard for femininity, but about their desire and ability to lead the pack. For these men, leadership means asserting oneself and causing the others to back down.

This ability to cause the other person to back down is central to the opening scene at the breakfast table. Consider a play-by-play of the scene: Mr. Brown succeeds in forcing the group to listen to his analysis of Madonna, exercising his will over the group. He is then one-upped when Mr. White causes Joe, the boss, to back down when Mr. White takes Joe's book and refuses to return it. Their tone is more playful than aggressive, but there is no question that Mr. White is asserting himself as equal to the boss, or at least enjoying special privileges as he shows his lack of deference to the boss. This does not sit well with Mr. Blonde, who then offers, perhaps still playfully, to shoot Mr. White for taking the book. Blonde is, in effect, casting his vote for the leader of the pack and demonstrating his loyalty. As we discover later, Blonde is not independent like the other men. He owes Joe his livelihood and comparative freedom and cannot allow Joe's dominance to be questioned, especially by a stranger. Mr. White again one-ups the table with his boast that if "you shoot me in a dream, you better wake up and apologize," and Eddie, Joe's son, changes the subject. Mr. White's point has been made and Eddie's role is to keep things from escalating too far during these chest-beating displays.

Mr. Pink, not to be outdone, attempts the same maneuver when he refuses to tip. He surprises everyone at the table with his uncompromising stance on tipping waitresses. Mr. Orange claims to be convinced by Pink's argument and tries to take his dollar back but is stopped by Eddie, the same person who changed the subject when Mr. White took Joe's book. When Joe returns, he tells Mr. Pink to tip a dollar. Pink, nervously looking from side to side, realizes he doesn't have the support of the group. Unlike White, Pink has failed in his attempt to be macho. Instead of coming across as tough and assertive, he merely sounds like a miser. His display of dominance is foreign and confusing to the other men at the table, which Pink realizes in time to find an excuse to tip (in this case, that he didn't pay for his own breakfast anyway). He chips in his dollar and they leave.

Conforming to the Paradigms of Masculinity

There is a delicate balancing act that these men must perform. They have to challenge each other in order to determine their pecking order, but they have to do so in ways that the others will accept. But these signals are not always understood, as Pink continually shows. Not only does he fail to give himself a non-feminine name (Pink vs Purple), but he confuses "tough" with "stingy" in a group likely to boast about how much money they have lavished on their female companions. Later on he attempts to sidestep the dominance maneuvers by asking everyone to be "professional," that is, to replace the macho game with calculation. It is his most ingenious gambit for leadership. Surely the calculation game is one in which he can succeed, and in fact he already has with his forward-thinking concealment of the stolen goods. Not surprisingly, his pleas to act "professionally" fall on deaf ears since the group is preoccupied not with completing the job, but with finding out who insulted and betrayed them, and who has to take orders from whom. Unlike Mr. Orange, who in an earlier scene rehearsed the mannerisms and attitudes he would need in order to gain acceptance, Pink failed to do enough homework to be able to fit in successfully with this pack.

The thieves must retain the respect of the group by appearing to each other as proper criminals, but they seem to be unsure of how exactly to do so. Thus they affect the mannerisms and attitudes of their movie icons. Mr. Orange is taught to channel Marlon Brando in order to convince the thieves that he is a legitimate tough-guy. After a particularly tense exchange between White, Pink, and Blonde, Mr. Blonde compares Mr. White's intensity to Lee Marvin. In his Madonna analysis, Mr. Brown references both the prolific pornographic actor John Holmes and the action/western hero Charles Bronson. It is as if the characters are unaware of what it looks like to be a man, and must take their cues from portrayals, whether artistic or pornographic. Aping these portrayals will convey the appropriate manly bona fides to the other men, since they will all recognize in each others' mannerisms these revered macho images. Channeling the movie portrayals of criminality affords their behavior instant recognition with the rest of the group.

The best way to appear manly is, as it was with Augustine and his friends, to always meet a challenge, always take the dare. The ability to never back down is even explicitly stated as *the* masculine characteristic when Eddie tells the others that Mr. Blonde, who was being accused of double-crossing Joe, did his time "like a man" and never accepted the likely numerous offers to provide evidence against his employers. The police and prosecutors could not bend the will of Mr. Blonde, thus proving Blonde's status as a "real" man. The captured police officer, representing all of Mr. Blonde's experience with all police and corrections, is the recipient of Blonde's vengeance. Blonde tortures the officer as a final act of defiance against those who tried to break him. Interestingly, his actions are done in private. He has no audience of thieves to impress. There is no real contest of wills between a torturer and his victim, especially since Blonde wishes for only the pleasure of brutalizing his victim. No information is needed, and it serves no strategic aim. We will return to this particularly disturbing scene soon.

The brutality of Mr. Blonde is quite opposite to the tenderness of Mr. White. When there is no audience of thieves, Mr. White becomes compassionate and comforting. He consoles and encourages the frightened and mortally wounded Mr. Orange. He holds his hand, responds positively to Orange's request to be held, and protects him from the suspicions of the other men. Far from his earlier bravado of "you shoot me in a dream, you better wake up and apologize," he responds with personal anguish when Orange's betrayal is revealed. Clearly Mr. White must put on an act in order be taken seriously by the pack, much as Jules and Vega must remind each other to "get into character" in the opening apartment scene in *Pulp Fiction*. The standoffs, the macho leading man references, the bickering over pseudonyms, the refusal to tip: these are all efforts by the characters to "get into character" and convince each other that they are real desperados. Real men.

Even the cold and violent Mr. Blonde must convince the boss that he retains his manliness. In a flashback, we see Blonde newly released from prison and sitting in Joe's office. Their meeting is cordial and respectful until Eddie arrives and the two taunt each other playfully, as old friends. Blonde cannot carry on such banter with Joe, since he needs Joe to vouch for him as a non-rehabilitated criminal and Joe is in a more respected, senior position. But Eddie, as Joe's son and Blonde's old chum, is a suitable target. Blonde and Eddie accuse each other of being homoerotically attracted to each other, and both deny it forcefully enough, eventually settling the playful dispute with a wrestling match right in front of Joe's desk. They are all smiles throughout the exchange, but one feels a certain tension and is never quite sure if real fisticuffs may break out, though they never do.

Blonde is indebted to Joe in a way that the other men at the breakfast table at the beginning of the film are not. It is Blonde, after all, who offers to shoot White when White initiates a mild challenge to Joe. It is White's ability to challenge Joe without impunity that lends so much weightiness to Blonde's famous line from later in the film, "Are you going to bark all day, little doggie, or are you gonna bite?" At the point when that line emerges, Joe, to whom Blonde must show proper allegiance, is no longer around, so Blonde can challenge White openly. And at this point in the story the stakes have been raised severely. They are no longer hiding behind half playful acts of impish mischief such as swiping a book; this standoff could mean life or death. One of them must back down, and the one who doesn't is the real man, the alpha leader.

Cops and Competition

Now we can return to Blonde's particularly intriguing interaction with the policeman. Presumably a career criminal and former inmate, Blonde has no respect for officers of the law, possibly having been the recipient of their brutality and neglect. He explains that he enjoys torturing police, and that he intends to do so without the aim of acquiring information, but merely for the pleasure of causing another person pain. This is consistent with the thieves' view of police officers that explicitly denies their value and humanity. For example, when Mr. White is trying to find out how many deaths they caused in the heist-gone-wrong, Mr. Pink asks if any "real people" were harmed. Mr. White responds that no real people, "only cops" were shot. But Blonde's treatment of the hostage police officer is much worse than the disregard White and Pink display, or Eddie's casual callousness.

The hostage cop incites Mr. Blonde's sadism for two reasons. First, he functions for Mr. Blonde as a symbol of someone else telling him what to do. Immediately prior to torturing the cop, Mr. Blonde tells him that he has no boss. The policeman, as a representative of all the traditional structures of authority and boundaries, poses a special challenge to someone like Blonde whose credibility within his band of criminals hinges on his willingness to do whatever he wants. Confronted with a person whose very identity is telling others what to do, Mr. Blonde beats him, cuts off his ear, and attempts to set him on fire.

Second, the police officer offers a very different image of a "real" man. The police officer detains criminals and keeps his neighborhood safe, all for relatively low wages. At their best, police officers accept a life of danger in exchange for the satisfaction of bettering their communities. When Blonde relishes mutilating the policeman, he is taking this different image of manliness and treading it underfoot. This is more than the silencing of a witness or the too-harsh attempt to discover the identity of their infiltrator. It is the annihilation of an alternate vision of masculinity (to protect and defend) to preserve his own: to do what one wishes and not give place to a rival.

Pack and Necessity

When acting as a pack, the Reservoir Dogs are in a kind of feedback loop. They must one-up each other in order to prove their masculinity. They cannot back away from perceived disrespect, and they cannot, without risking being a "bitch" or a "pussy," be the person who declines when one of them says, "Let's do it." Yet it would be a mistake to think that they act without moral responsibility. They are not, as it were, in the grip of a power so great that their free will is destroyed. After all, they choose to be a part of the heist, choose to return to the rendezvous location instead of run, and so on. At any moment, any of them could walk away. Certainly it is *possible* for them to act otherwise. However, the pack framework answers crucial questions regarding who they are and what their relative value is. It tells them who is in charge and where they must place their loyalty. The loss of these answers is not an easy thing to bear, especially when, in the case of Mr. Blonde, it has kept him steadfast even in prison, and in the case of Mr. White, has been the steady part of his life that has outlasted even romantic companionship.

Because of its intense focus on the relationships between the men, *Reservoir Dogs* highlights the social aspect of wrongdoing in a way unusual in crime films. Heist films tend to show protagonists as playful geniuses, using their creativity to pull off the perfect crime. See *Oceans 11*, *Gambit*, and *How to Steal a Million* for films of that sort. But in *Reservoir Dogs* the thieves look to each other for affirmation, posturing and snapping at each other to establish their dominance.

The sociality of wrong that *Reservoir Dogs* displays so vividly is also found in Old Testament wisdom literature. The Psalmist writes: "Blessed is the one who does not *walk in step* with the wicked or stand in *the way that sinners take* or sit *in the company* of mockers."[183] The opening chapter

---

[183]Psalm 1 (NIV). Emphasis mine.

of Proverbs warns against falling in with those who plan to assault and steal from others. Yet we often mistakenly think of sin within the context of a single person. We ask what that one person did that was wrong, and since all actions are performed by *someone*, this is a legitimate route of inquiry. But the dynamism of a group can push people toward actions that would not have been tempting alone, and that dynamism can create a feeling of necessity.

Like Augustine many centuries prior, the thieves of *Reservoir Dogs* cannot allow themselves to show reticence. Instead of being ashamed of their immoral actions, they are ashamed of caring about the morality of their actions. Pink and White *must* beat up their hostage, even though Pink is obviously unaccustomed to punching people. Blonde *must* show that he's even more brutal than the two men he does not respect. Like Augustine, the thieves care more about their standing within their association than they do about what was stolen. Once one of them escalates, they all must follow or lose respect. Like Augustine, the thieves are driven by what they believe the other men think about how true manliness appears. Augustine shows the emptiness of sin, and how that emptiness seeks only further emptiness. The men in *Reservoir Dogs* display that emptiness in their discussions, their macho posturing, and their crimes.

Augustine eventually rejected a masculinity based on "Let us go and do it," in favor of a life characterized by service and contemplation, so we do not know how his life of never backing down would have concluded. The men of *Reservoir Dogs* give us a vivid image of just that sort of life, and show us why it is unlivable.

LIFE LESSONS FROM *KILL BILL* (AND OTHER TARANTINO FILMS)

Abernathy McGraw

When life gets tough, you probably don't turn to Tarantino films for advice, even if you use them to escape for a moment to a cathartic world of spectacle and violence. It's just not practical to use the Black Mamba as a role model for problem solving; after all, Pai Mei isn't around anymore to teach you the Five-Point Palm Exploding Heart Technique. I suspect no matter how much you cheer on Uma Thurman's kick-ass character, and no matter how much your boss or ex–significant other gets on your nerves, you're just not that into killing people. In that case I applaud the distinctions you make between art and life, between cinematography and ethics.

While we're on the subject of conflict resolution, there's a chance you didn't expect a film featuring a sexy-as-hell assassination squad and a title as blunt as *Kill Bill* to be saturated with insights into the value of human life. At least I didn't expect that—but I've since come to notice strong impulses toward life and redemption behind much of the killing in the movie. Sure, it's a revenge flick, but it's also more than that. Although "revenge" may be the first word to appear on screen, it's not the last.[184] In a special features interview, Uma Thurman said that *Kill Bill* was about "justice and redemption"; neither of these is simply "revenge." Since Uma played such a critical role in the film through the creation and portrayal of the Bride, I would like to consider these themes more deeply. Along the way, I'll mention a few life lessons that keep appearing in Tarantino films.

By "life lessons" I don't mean "instructions for behavior." A movie is not a driver's manual for the road of life, even if art can reflect life, and vice versa. Part of the attraction of a Tarantino film is the sheer spectacle, the outrageous action, the shock value of the extraordinary event, the impossibly clever dialogue—the art—but another integral dimension is a psychological realism that includes depth of insight into the human heart, complex characterization, and themes that provoke both thought and wonder, promoting a view of life that points to something vastly bigger than ourselves or the decisions we make.[185] In this essay, rather

---

[184] The last word of *Vol. 1* is "alive," spoken when Bill asks the mutilated Sophie Fatale if Beatrix knows her child is living. The last phrase of *Vol. 2* is "Thank you," which Beatrix tearfully whispers in the bathroom as she is reunited with her daughter. As I write this, I realize I'm at a disadvantage, not able to see if anything will come of plans for a possible *Kill Bill: Vol. 3*. But the conclusions of both Vols. 1 and 2 emphasize hope and life. Tarantino has said that there are many different *Kill Bills*, as seen not only in the differences between the Asian version and the international version (cut with queasier American stomachs in mind) but also in script variations and in the imaginations of its creators. In this essay, unless otherwise noted, I refer to the international version of the film.

[185] When this wonder deals with spiritual and eternal questions and themes, we approach what the great Italian poet Dante Alighieri referred to as the anagogical level of meaning—a level that he puts higher than the literal or historical or moral levels in interpreting a work of art. In other words, to imagine and ponder eternal ideas and truths is a higher order of responding to art than simply approving, accepting instruction from, or judging the actions of the characters. Self-appointed moral arbiters of the silver screen frequently accuse Tarantino of encouraging real-life violence through his films. Such charges (which Tarantino has sometimes ignored, sometimes flatly rejected) hinder a more nuanced inquiry into the way art bleeds into life, insulting not only the director but the viewers by implying they have no choice but to imitate the violence they see. Tarantino at least does

than trying to tell anyone how to live his or her life according to some unauthorized Gospel of Quentin, I hope simply to draw attention to certain aspects of the film that have led me to reflection and wonder. The world of *Kill Bill* is, after all, a place where the most fantastic things can happen—from geysers of blood spurting out of head wounds to direct flights between El Paso and Okinawa—but it also wrestles with some very recognizably human ideas and impulses.

Life Lesson #1: The World as a Stage

If there's one thing that all Tarantino films seem to share—and this includes aestheticized violence, samurai swords, and subtitles—it's his signature use of meta-cinema and artistic self-awareness. We see examples of meta-cinema in his use of extravagance, exaggeration, distortion, animation, cameo roles, film references, overt dramatic irony, the showing of movies within movies, and the breaking of the "fourth wall" separating audience and characters. From Ordell Robbie's use of "Chicks Who Love Guns" as a marketing tool, to Vincent Vega's reference to the show *Cops* to dismiss a miracle as a freak occurrence, to Beatrix and B. B.'s cuddling to *Shogun Assassin*, Tarantino's characters live in a world that engages with, and depends on, film.[186] In *Inglourious Basterds*, the actress Bridget von Hammersmark patiently explains the distinction between character and creator to her German drinking

not reduce his audiences to mere products of their environments.

[186] The most striking of these instances of meta-cinema is the movie Shosanna and Marcel create for the *Nation's Pride* premiere in *Inglourious Basterds*. Shosanna has at least half of Tarantino's passion for 35 mm film, but she's ready to burn her aunt's nitrocellulose collection for the Allied cause, creating a fearsome backdrop to her message for Germany. But the showing of *Stoltz der Nation* also exemplifies how art can move us in surprising ways. It's only after seeing his military exploits represented on the silver screen as entertainment and propaganda that Frederick Zoller admits his distaste for reliving past strife. And after Shosanna shoots her unwelcome suitor in the back, she first looks at the Nazi soldier onscreen, alone in his bird's nest, and only then does she turn to him in that fatal moment of compassion. The film inspires a surprising act of empathy, and its power is not erased by the consequence—that she too, having let down her guard, is shot and killed.

buddies at *La Louisianne* tavern: "The character is the character. Hamlet is not British, he is Danish." Von Hammersmark speaks for herself, not necessarily for Diane Kruger or Quentin Tarantino, yet there are layers of creative performance. The characters come from the mind of the creator, and they are also involved in their own self-creation and role-play. When this happens in Tarantino films, this isn't just a cute artistic game. Frequently, the success of a character's performance becomes a matter of life and death.

Consider, for example, the ethical questions raised by the need not to break character in *Django Unchained* and *Reservoir Dogs*. In order for Django to convince Calvin Candie that he is a cutthroat mandingo expert, he has to watch a pack of dogs rip away the flesh of an escaped slave. Without intervening. Without flinching. Without so much as a look of compassion. And in *Reservoir Dogs*, for Mr. Orange not to blow his cover, he chooses to watch the mutilation of a young officer at the hands of a psychopath. As Tim Roth's character slips in and out of consciousness, slowly bleeding to death from a bullet to the gut, he faces many moments of silent dilemma. He has to hold the success of his undercover mission, his deteriorating physical condition, his will to live, his duty to support a fellow officer, and the foolhardy loyalty of Mr. White in delicate balance. Mr. Orange and Django keep up their act while lives are lost, because some mission of greater importance to them is at stake.

In *Kill Bill*, the Bride does her own share of purposeful acting: hiding her knife from Vernita Green's four-year-old daughter, pretending to be a ditzy American tourist in Okinawa, charming Tommy Plympton under the alias "Arlene Machiavelli," playing dead when B. B. shoots her with a toy gun. She is coolly self-aware, waiting in the dark before she strikes, cooperating before she kills, accepting an order of sushi before ordering what she really wants—a Hanzo sword. She breaks character when appropriate, revealing that even in her role-play she keeps her endgame in mind: She's fighting to the death.

Before the wedding chapel massacre at Two Pines, however, she acts and fights for life—for the life of her daughter. Love for her child leads Beatrix to commit to a lifelong charade. Her new role is charged with all the honor of motherhood, but the Bride could never be simply Arlene Plympton, the used record store employee with nothing spectacularly good or evil about her. She admits this to Bill under the influence of the Undisputed Truth serum. She knows her life in El Paso will be a performance, not a metamorphosis.

But while Beatrix and Bill agree she could never really become Arlene, there is some dispute over her true identity. Professionally, as the deadliest viper in the Deadly Viper Assassination Squad, she is Black Mamba. With the handle "Death Incarnate" she is the picture of relentless, merciless, and sometimes gargantuan forces of destruction. But she is also Beatrix Kiddo, the name important enough to bleep out for its first few occurrences. She used to raise her hand to that name in elementary school, and this side of her hints at the more childlike aspects of her character. She remains the "Kiddo" Bill affectionately regales with stories of Pai Mei by a campfire. "Beatrix" means "giver of blessings" or "bringer of happiness," and we see something of this in her desire to protect and provide for her daughter. But it's not that simple. Bill thinks Beatrix always has been and always will be Black Mamba. She's a natural born killer, he says, which means she herself doesn't have the clean slate that she wanted to give—and wasn't able to give—to her own daughter.[187] And she continues that way, he argues,

---

[187] It's quite motherly that Bea wants to protect her child from the taint of evil. It's quite human of her that she can't. Beatrix is extraordinary—in some cases superheroic, even—but she faces some universal problems. One of these corresponds with the theological doctrine of original sin—that we are all born imperfect, none of us completely

because she admits taking pleasure in the killing that led her to the final showdown. Her primary role shifts from deadly assassin (Black Mamba) to shrewd, protective parent (Mommy), to a superheroic avenger with the relentless memory of Miss Havisham (the Bride), but in all these she remains a fighter. The docile Arlene Plympton is merely her cover and her critique of the human race.

All this meta-cinema and self-conscious acting reinforce the old trope that "all the world's a stage," the idea that we're all actors and our lives are performances. One implication of this metaphor is that there will be a time after our life where we will truly be ourselves, and our performances will be evaluated. And here's a twist: Thinking of our life as a performance can actually reinforce our awareness of the importance of how the play is acted.[188] Our acting is part of human innocent of evil. We can wrong others without any good reason, as when B. B. takes Emilio out of his fishbowl and stomps on him. Protective parents might succeed for a while in safeguarding their children from the worst of the outside world, but they can't shelter children from their own internal battles. The ongoing struggle between selfish impulses and the greater goodness of loving God and others is part of what the apostle Paul described as the Old Man/New Man fight, a fight with some similarities to *Kill Bill*. Having in a past life worked for the most notorious crime boss in the world, the Christian who acknowledges Jesus Christ as Lord still has to fight off old patterns of thought and action. See Romans 6:6, Ephesians 2:15, Ephesians 4:22–24, and Colossians 3:9–11.

[188] Shakespeare eternized the phrase "All the world's a stage" in *As You Like It*, but I am also thinking of Sir Walter Raleigh's poem "What is our Life? A play of passion," which provides a different example of the world-stage analogy, emphasizing the conclusion that this world is not all there is. Some might assume that belief in an afterlife leads to scorn for the present life, to an attitude that says, "Who cares what happens here? I'll get my reward after I die." And indeed there are strains of Christianity that downplay the value of earthly life. Disregard for the present world can lead, for example, to annoying platitudes at funerals, to pat remarks that don't acknowledge real loss and real grief. But that sort of insensitivity doesn't have to happen. Consider the example of Jesus Christ in the gospel of John. When Jesus' friend Lazarus dies, Lazarus' sister Martha acknowledges her belief in the afterlife. "I know everyone will rise again at the last day," she says (John 11:24). Jesus affirms her belief with one of his strongest recorded statements: "I am the resurrection and the life" (vs. 25). Then he performs one of his greatest miracles—he brings Lazarus back from the dead. But Jesus, in the midst of these promises of the immortality of the soul and the resurrection of the body, still cries—weeps, even—at the death of his friend. He grieves for the dead on the very occasion that he demonstrates his power over death. His tears validate both the value of this earthly life and grief as an appropriate response to the loss of it. Life may be a stage, but it's an important one.

And there's another reason why earthly life is precious even in the midst of the most dignity, freedom, and choice, and a decent actor, like Mr. Orange, Django, or the Bride, knows that there are real-life consequences to the performance.[189] When the charade is dropped, or the curtain falls, or the credits roll, these consequences continue. We face applause or disapprobation from the only Critic who counts. The only problem is— and this leads to my next reflection—we all fall short of his standards.

#2: The Response to Injustice

In Oscar Wilde's *The Importance of Being Earnest*, a ridiculous character, Miss Prism, explains the ending of a very bad novel she has proudly written, along with her quaint writing philosophy: "The good ended happily, and the bad unhappily. That is what Fiction means." Oscar Wilde is wittily reminding us that in real life, people don't always get their deserts. He's also ridiculing the cheesy, predictable, moralizing fiction of his day. Similarly, Tarantino rejects the cheesy, predictable, and moralizing aspects of '80s cinema.[190]

For one thing, he's aware the world is not starkly divided between the virtuous and the vicious. The first Nazi soldier we see cudgeled to death by the Bear Jew in *Inglourious Basterds* demonstrates the extraordinary

---

profound assurances of eternal life to come. Most people who believe in an afterlife, who expect that a part of them will somehow live on after the death of their physical bodies, believe that in this afterlife there will be some accounting for how one lived one's earthly life. Christianity focuses on the role of Jesus Christ in restoring our relationship with God, but it's not a passive religion. It also has many, many verses that give encouragement and guidelines for life decisions and for responses to God's generous gift of eternal life. According to the New Testament, salvation comes from Jesus Christ alone, but this doesn't mean that human action is irrelevant. See, for example, Matthew 7 and 22, Galatians 5, Philippians 2:12–13, and James 5:7–11.

[189] All analogies are imperfect, and the comparison of life to a stage is inexact in that an actor may be praised for portraying an excellent villain, while presumably how well one acts on the stage of life depends upon moral as well as artistic choices. Nevertheless, it is interesting that young children tend to shy away from villains in costume even after the performance is over.

[190] See "Quentin Tarantino: Keeping Morality Out of the Question," YouTube video clip from an interview by Lynne Hirschberg of *The New York Times*, http://www.youtube.com/watch?v=8jakMHGv2yE.

bravery for which he was decorated—a far cry from the Führer's spastic, red-faced guffawing at dying soldiers in the *Nation's Pride* premiere. You can't separate the heroes from the villains by race, nationality, or uniform. Hitler, Hans Landa, and Frederick Zoller each wear their swastikas differently. Both Kate Fuller, preacher's daughter and vampire slayer in *From Dusk Till Dawn*, and Buck, the sexual predator upon the comatose in *Kill Bill*, wear a cross necklace. And within individual characters, there's also a mixture of good and bad. Tarantino's "bad guys" often have admirable qualities, and his "good guys" are rarely law-abiding citizens. Seth Gecko, the thief, looks pretty good to Kate in comparison with the pure evil of the vampires they've been fighting all night long. And when Seth turns down her offer to accompany him to El Rey at the end of the movie, we admire him for not wanting to corrupt her. "I may be a bastard, but I'm not a fucking bastard," he explains. That statement could apply to quite a few of Tarantino's characters.

In a world where nobody's perfect and everyone is eligible for redemption, justice gets complicated. Even if readers and moviegoers desire a happy ending, too simple of a resolution will be rejected as inauthentic. Making sense of the world is also a messy project because bad things happen to nice people, and vice versa.[191] The theological conundrum that arises from questioning this unfairness is called theodicy, or the inquiry into the justice of God in a world where evil exists.

Enter Beatrix Kiddo, who has her own ideas about divine justice. She admits the temptation to attribute her success to divine approval: "When Fortune smiles on something as violent and ugly as revenge, it seems proof like no other that, not only does God exist, you're doing

---

[191] Incidentally, that's often the case in the Bible, too. Characters like Job, David, and Jeremiah all know that there's no simple explanation for bad things happening to decent people, and that sometimes the bad guys seem to be the only ones to live well and prosper. (See Psalm 73, Job 9, Job 21, and Jeremiah 12; see also Luke 13:1-5 and John 9:1-3 for Jesus' comments on undeserved misfortune.)

his will." Like Beatrix, we may prefer coincidences to be purposeful and expect God to have some part to play in vengeance and retribution. Call it karma or divine intervention, we tend to assume that when people get what we think they deserve, some higher power must be orchestrating matters according to plan. It's tempting to think we have a role to play as executors of that plan. The gun in the cereal box misses Bea; maybe this means her quest for retribution is divinely authorized and protected.

Retribution as a species of justice is broader than an individual desire to "get even" and calmer than a "roaring rampage of revenge." It's civic and legal rather than personal and vindictive. It's as old as the laws of Hammurabi or Moses—an eye for an eye, tooth for tooth, life for life.[192] Beatrix has personally suffered, but she doesn't just desire to make others pay for the betrayal, the beatings, the sexual violations, or the lost years of motherhood. She half-believes that she acts on behalf of her daughter and of God. If true, this would transform her quest from simple revenge to retribution.

But Beatrix tentatively states that her success *seems* proof her mission is authorized. She may be wrong. For Bea, hunting down her attackers is obvious and instinctive, and the story is told in such a way that we want her to win. But she herself is far from innocent. Budd puts it best: "That girl deserves her revenge, and we all deserve to die. But then again, so does she. So, we'll just have to wait and see, won't we?"

The pervasiveness of injustice does not mean it shouldn't be fought, even by the imperfect, at times even with force, and even with life and death in the balance. Most people, after all, aren't readily reasoned or sweet-talked into curbing their villainy or paying their dues. Sometimes a little violence is warranted. I'll go on the record saying it was okay for Bea to bite Buck's tongue off when he approached her with a perverse

---

[192] See Exodus 21:22–25, Leviticus 24:19–21, Deuteronomy 19:16–21. These laws of retaliation are often explained using the Latin term *lex talionis*.

grin and a grimy jar of Vaseline. And what if you're caught in one of Tarantino's signature "us or them" situations?[193] Beatrix Kiddo is willing to sacrifice her career and lifestyle for her unborn child, but she's no martyr. From the first fight scene with Cottonmouth to the last fight scene with Bill, Beatrix knows that she fights to the death. Who could blame her (or her opponent) for wanting to be the one to survive?

Conflict isn't just an indicator of the world's problems; sometimes it is an appropriate response to those problems. Even if evil is ineradicable, fighting back is worthwhile. The difficulty lies in deciding which battles are worth fighting, and the answer usually involves, somehow, love, because love requires being willing to struggle, suffer, and make personal sacrifices for the sake of the loved one, as Django does for Broomhilda, or Beatrix for B. B., or even Mr. White for Mr. Orange. While the world would clearly be better off without lying, deceit, violence, breaking vows, betraying allegiances, or surrendering refugees over to the unmerciful, Tarantino's films would be worse without them, because conflict is both interesting and human. A good story must have conflict, and for the conflict to be effective, the underbelly of the real world must be acknowledged. Attempts to create a utopia, from Plato's *Republic* to Candieland in *Django Unchained*, require the exploitation of others. Dr. Schultz knows that sometimes we can't just shake hands and get along with the enemy, and riding away into the sunset prematurely might be construed as tacit approval of evil. Even Hattori Hanzo realizes that nonviolent retreat, despite its zen-like allure, isn't always an adequate

---

[193] In the opening diner scene to *Pulp Fiction*, Honey Bunny tells Pumpkin, "I'm not gonna kill anybody." He responds, "I don't wanna kill anybody either. But they'll probably put us in a situation where it's us or them." At the end of the Beaumont sequence in *Jackie Brown*, Ordell explains to Louis why his car trunk contains the body of "an employee [he] had to let go." He concludes, "Now that, my friend, is a clear case of him or me. And you best believe it ain't gonna be me." Louis gets the message. Jackie also knows she is caught in a "him or me" situation with Ordell, so she forgives Ordell for trying to kill her and then manipulates him into thinking they both can win.

response to injustice.[194]

#3: The Importance of Family

One of those cases where fighting is not only permitted, but also expected, is when it is done on behalf of a family member. Acknowledging the importance of family is more than condoning clannish egotism, for family creates one of the most immediate—and often most challenging—spaces for the practice of love. Otherwise bland or unlikeable characters can secure an audience's goodwill by demonstrating family loyalty. We see this in Clarence's father in *True Romance*, or Nice Guy Eddie in *Reservoir Dogs*. It's also intriguingly hinted at when Mr. Orange slips on his wedding ring before walking into danger. In *Death Proof*, because Rosario Dawson's character is a mother, her friends respectfully give her the chance to opt out of a deadly game of Ship's Mast. One thing that makes Jackie Brown so aloof—and so alone—is that we do not meet any of her family members. Max Cherry is a little scared of her. Humans are social creatures. Beasts and gods live alone.

Love of family motivates many actions in *Kill Bill*. Although the relationship is strained, evidence of Bill's love for his brother is etched into the glinting steel of a priceless Hanzo sword: "To my brother Budd. The only man I ever loved." Fraternal feelings go both ways, evidently. Before letting the coffin lid fall on Bea with a deadening thud, Budd explains, "This is what you get for breaking my brother's heart." He acts

---

[194] Hattori Hanzo seems to accept some measure of responsibility for the way Bill used the knowledge he gained from him in the art of the samurai—enough to craft a priceless sword pro bono for the Yellow-Haired Warrior. "Philosophically I'm sympathetic to your aim," he admits, and so he breaks an oath to God never to make another instrument of death. But what first seizes his attention is the name of Beatrix's target—his former student, Bill. Hanzo is the artisan. He fashions the sword, and may even train the wielder. But is he indeed accountable for the actions of those he arms? Is the weapon supplier any more responsible for the actions of the weapon user than the artist that provides a portrait of violence? The Hattori Hanzo scenes reexamine the question of artistic responsibility, but it's worth remembering that Hanzo officially announces his philosophical sympathy rather than any moral obligation as the reason for his priceless gift.

on behalf of the sibling he seemed to have forgotten.

Consider how family connections affect the portraits of the other assassins on the Death List. The origin of O-Ren Ishii is told in brilliant anime. We join in her stifled whimper at the murder of her parents—and at least partially sympathize with the vengeance she exacts from Boss Matsumoto. We know heads will roll if her Chinese-American heritage is scorned. We see family pride in the decapitated Boss Tanaka too, but he himself said he put the illustrious council of Yakuza lords over his own children, so we don't waste tears over his geyser-spouting head. In the House of Blue Leaves fight sequence, Bea has some motherly sympathy for the young, or recognizes that they can still change for the better. She gives GoGo the chance to leave Cottonmouth. And when the silhouette of a young member of the Crazy 88s quivers in fear before the Black Mamba, she opts for spanking the boy with the broad side of her samurai sword, delivering a clear and humiliating message—"This is what you get for fucking around with Yakuzas!"—and sending him home to mommy. Beatrix and O-Ren each respect the family unit, with O-Ren's emphasis on her ancestors and the past, and Beatrix's emphasis on the younger generation. Their duel to the death is the most honorable one in the film.

Elle Driver, or California Mountain Snake, is the least sympathetic of the DeVAS, partly because she has no family mentioned and is given little backstory beyond the eye gouging by Pai Mei and her poisoning of him—a patricide of a sort. She is jealous, vindictive, and backstabbing, and makes her entrance to the freaky whistling in the background. Her ways of seeking love are poisonous and perverse; she's not above using a snake in a suitcase to kill Budd and frame Beatrix, a vicious attempt to remove her rivals for Bill's affection. Her lack of family background may not cause her villainy, but it doesn't make her any more relatable.

Granted, the encounter with Copperhead lets us know early on that

Bea's family-friendly side can only go so far. Although Bea assures Vernita Green of her intentions not to kill her in front of four-year-old Nikki Bell, nothing Copperhead has done since the El Paso wedding chapel massacre—including "getting knocked up"—is going to get her off the hook. "Getting knocked up," to be sure, is what puts this story in motion. That's the phrase Beatrix uses to explain herself to Bill on the front porch of the wedding chapel, and so its second occurrence invites us to draw comparisons between the two mommy-assassins. For both, having a daughter changes everything. Even while maintaining her tough-girl persona, Vernita can't help but ask for mercy and forgiveness for Nikki's sake. A little reflection, however, might have warned her that the subject is a sore one for Beatrix, who also speaks—and kills—for the sake of her daughter.

And the loss of her unborn child is indeed murder in Beatrix's mind. When Earl McGraw and Son #1 assess the carnage at Two Pines, they count nine bodies. They assume at first that the Bride is dead. When the recovering Bride assesses the damage, she also counts nine among the dead. Her unborn daughter, she assumes, is one of them. As Fabienne in *Pulp Fiction* tells us, "the difference is huge" between "a tummy and a pot"—between a little extra fatty tissue and the bulge of new life. One may reveal excessive self-indulgence and the other is harbinger of maternal self-sacrifice. Granted, Beatrix's first reaction to the blue strip on her pregnancy test is an obscenity, but soon after she interprets that all-important code—that blue strip on the pregnancy test—she prioritizes the life of her child over the death of her target. She cares enough for the wellbeing of her child to change her life and leave her lover, mentor, and boss. Beatrix explains that with Bill, B. B. "would have been born into a world she shouldn't have." As the screenplay elaborates, "She would be born with blood stains." But we don't always get the life we would choose, or that our mothers would choose for us. Beatrix's first words coming out of the coma are "my baby"— words that carry the agony of loss. The lines on her palm inform her of the years of life she has lost. The single scar line on her flat abdomen informs her of another life entirely ripped away from her. It's not just the lost opportunity of motherhood she laments. The unborn child counts and is counted.

That's why almost everything changes when Beatrix realizes that B. B. is alive. In the presence of a child, the killer decides to play dead. Beatrix's final battle in *Vol. 2* is in one sense a destruction of the family unit just as we see the allure of its restoration. After all, there's nothing homier than two adults sparring in metaphor in the presence of an unwitting child. The couch looks comfortable enough, and Beatrix and Bill look rather cute together, as far as assassins go. But the practice of love is far from cute. Rarely is it equally requited and understood. Beatrix expected that Bill loved her enough to let her go. Bill bluntly tells her she thought wrong, and so begins one of the greatest custody battles of all time.

#4: The Limits of Revenge

One of the phrases Bea uses when she talks about getting revenge is "bloody satisfaction." In this use, satisfaction is not a feeling of contentment. "Satisfaction" comes from Latin words meaning "to make enough," and it contains the idea that the punishment fits the crime, that proper proportions between actions and consequences have been restored. It's compensation, vindication, restitution, payback, and settling score, but not pleasure. Bea does admit the killing feels good—and so it might, with each step bringing her closer to her ultimate target—but as she defeats her enemies one by one, or lets them defeat each other, her countenance remains somber, void of any hint of real happiness. Her smiles are reserved for when she has to play a part, pretend to be someone she's not. She kills with firm resolve, not the psychotic pleasure of Vic Vega in *Reservoir Dogs*.

She's unsatisfied in *Vol. 1* not only because she hasn't found Bill yet, but also because there's one thing revenge can never do: restore the lost. And so, after she defeats O-Ren Ishii, and as she tough talks Sophie Fatale in her car trunk, there's no relief, peace, or exultation. From her Pasadena home, Vernita admits to Beatrix, "You have every right to want to get even," but making things "square" doesn't make Bea a mother again. This obvious but difficult fact contributes to Bea's sparing of Vernita's husband and daughter. In *Death Proof*, Stuntman Mike meets his Judgment Day at the fists of three women in the film industry, but nothing the vigilantes do can bring back Butterfly, Jungle Julia, and the rest of his previous victims. Revenge cannot resurrect the dead.

Revenge also cannot provide closure. This uncomfortable fact is acknowledged when Nikki Bell appears in the kitchen entry after her mother's death. Sure, Beatrix doesn't intend to kill in front of the four-year-old. Sure, Vernita Green "has it comin." But if Vernita's death at the hands of Beatrix is justified, there's still an injustice in Nikki's loss of her mother. Killing Nikki as a preemptive strike against a potential avenger wouldn't close the loop, either—it merely broadens the circle of injustices that another might desire to avenge. Revenge begets revenge. And so the same woman who spares Nikki also offers her a challenge: "When you grow up, if you still feel raw about it, I'll be waitin.'"[195]

Like the narrative of *Pulp Fiction*, *Reservoir Dogs,* or *Kill Bill: Vol. 1*, "Revenge is never a straight line. It's a forest, and like a forest it's easy to forget where you came in." We all know those stories of family feuds lasting over so many generations that the original offense has long been

---

[195] Although a *Kill Bill: Vol. 3* may never materialize, the very fact that plans for *Vol. 3* were announced supports my argument that, well, the killing must go on, even if only in the imagination of this storyteller.

forgotten. Looking forward to an end point of the feud isn't any easier. One of the earliest stories exemplifying the thicket of revenge is the Greek *Oresteia* myth, where a young prince is plagued by furies because he killed his mother because she killed his father because he killed their daughter because he needed to sacrifice her before going to war to kill Trojans, including the one who stole his brother's wife. It's complicated. An even earlier story of bloodshed and revenge is the biblical account of Cain and Abel, two brothers, one killing the other in jealousy because God prefers Abel's sacrifice over Cain's. God calls Cain to account for his slain brother: "Listen! Your brother's blood cries out to me from the ground" (Genesis 4:10). Abel's blood cries for revenge, for bloody satisfaction. Cain is cursed, wanders restlessly, and is afraid that others will now kill him. In a surprising act of bittersweet mercy, God puts a protective mark on Cain that comes with a second curse: "Anyone who kills Cain will suffer vengeance seven times over" (v. 15). Sometimes the fear of another's revenge is the best preventative for our own acts of violence and vengeance. Then again, sometimes this just doesn't work. The next story in the book of Genesis introduces Lamech, whose big claim to fame is a song he composes about his own personal vendetta:

> I have killed a man for wounding me,
> a young man for injuring me.
> If Cain is avenged seven times,
> then Lamech seventy-seven times.
> (vv. 23-24)

Revenge is not resolution, and the threat of revenge is not enough of a deterrent to crime. On the contrary, anticipation of revenge can lead to a breakdown in the warrior's code of honor. Vernita's desperate situation leads her to forgo the midnight knife fight for a chance to catch Beatrix off guard, shooting at her through a box of "Kaboom!" cereal. If the ultimate goal is justice, revenge is not the way to get there.[196]

#5: The Cost of Redemption and the Way Out

The pursuit of justice is both noble and understandable. We naturally resist being treated unfairly. The impulse to revenge is also understandable, even if it can get out of hand. Awaiting the full strength of Beatrix's fury, Vernita asks her antagonist to be rational. "It's mercy, compassion, and forgiveness I lack," Beatrix responds, "not rationality." Cold reasoning is well suited for impartial enforcement of the law, and retribution itself is a reasonable desire for the victim. Budd acknowledges this when he tells Bill, "I don't dodge guilt and I don't jew out of paying my comeuppance." Antisemitic remark aside, there's some nobility in

---

[196] One might even say that the continual search for justice and equitable treatment for all is exemplified over the course of Tarantino's career with respect to the different people groups and personalities represented in films. In *True Romance*, Sicilians get a bad rap, and Clifford Worley's racism against black people doesn't do much for older Anglo-Americans. In *Reservoir Dogs*, Vic Vega doesn't do much to help out the Italian image, but the unreliability of Italian stereotypes is more fairly presented in *Inglourious Basterds*. Germans get a rough treatment in *Inglourious Basterds*; reparation is made not only with a few redeemable Nazis but with the good Dr. Schultz and the Brunhilde/Siegfried story in *Django Unchained*. The beautiful homage to blaxploitation films in *Jackie Brown* and Tarantino's tendency to create impressive black male characters like Marsellus Wallace, Jules Winnfield, Marcel, or Django is surprisingly tempered by putting Samuel L. Jackson in the role of Stephen, the obsequious servant to Calvin Candie. A southern plantation owner becomes the most despicable of villains, but I wouldn't be surprised to see a new Tarantino film with a southerner treated sympathetically. The chain of justice continues.

Tarantino also draws attention to racism by having his characters try to make sense of other characters using obviously unsuitable stereotypes. Lt. Aldo Raine is a hero for the Allies, but he confines his understanding of a brave enemy soldier to an enemy with a "wiener-schnitzel lickin' finger" and a craving for a "sauerkraut sandwich." He thinks a story about mountain climbing is a good cover for a German actress who prefers smoking and drinking and ordering in restaurants. As Hans Landa knows, Lt. Raine's imitation of the Italian tongue is ridiculous, and Utivich's exaggeration of the musicality of the language equally reveals their imposture. Raine wants his Nazis always in uniform because he doesn't want to think of them as anything other than Nazis, and to him, "a Nazi ain't got no humanity." The Nazis ignorantly stereotype their enemies, but so do some of the Americans. Tarantino can elicit a laugh from his audience with a racial slur and then, with a masterful twist, remind us that the slur is utterly inappropriate.

Budd's admission of guilt and his resolve to accept his fate when that day of settling scores should come. He knows the blood of the innocent is crying out for vengeance.

I suspect that most people would prefer not to be held accountable for every selfish thought, hurtful word, and wrong action they've done. According to the Bible, the cost for sin is death, the debt each mortal must pay. The good news is that all humanity is offered forgiveness, not

because the fine was waived, but because it was paid by someone else, Jesus Christ. The story of Christianity is a reminder not just that God is love, but that redemption is costly. The author of the Book of Hebrews, drawing an analogy between the Jewish laws of sacrifice and the sacrificial death of Jesus, states that "without the shedding of blood there is no forgiveness of sins" (Hebrews 9:22). The writer doesn't disregard the impulse of retribution and the demand for bloody satisfaction. He doesn't ask God to ignore our sins, reach out, shake our hand, and act as if everything's okay. What Dr. Schultz refuses to do for Calvin Candie, God cannot do for us, because he is holy and just. The need for bloody satisfaction is acknowledged, but this satisfaction is then completed in a surprising way—through self-sacrifice of the Son of God, motivated by a love none of us deserve. Jesus gives "the sprinkled blood that speaks a better word than the blood of Abel" (Hebrews 12:18-24). Abel's cry for vengeance, reasonable enough, is satisfied by Christ's astounding sacrifice and silenced by his call to mercy, compassion, and forgiveness. In Jesus' most famous sermon, the simple code of justice that would leave everyone blind and toothless is supplanted by instructions to "turn the other cheek" and to "love thy enemy" (Exodus 21:14, Matthew 5:38-39), but this doesn't make him a wimp. He backs up his words with actions, and spills his own blood.

Now, we wouldn't have a movie if Beatrix forgives her betrayers and walks away from her past after waking from her coma. Such a passive retreat would be colder than the killing spree she goes on, simply because as an assassin and a mother this quest for bloody satisfaction is her character's most natural course of action. There's goodness in Beatrix's desire to redeem her honor and avenge the death of nine innocent people. But her quest for redemption and justice is mixed up in revenge, and as we've noted, revenge is messy.

As Beatrix and B. B. drive away with the prospect of a happy life together, we might mentally return to Chapter 1, aware that somewhere out there Nikki Bell is growing up. The only way to get off the revenge carousel is to acknowledge the injustice, yet forgive, and be forgiven. This is psychologically healthy, but hard to do sincerely, and it often seems irrational, risky business. It requires ignoring an enemy's status as enemy and giving up the vengeance to which you feel justly entitled. In theological terms, this would be a move from retributive justice to mercy. This is definitely not what Beatrix does...but that's okay. The fact that the film is not heavy handed or moralistic in its treatment of retribution paves the way for some surprising turns.

I return to Uma Thurman's comment that *Kill Bill* is about redemption as well as justice. Whereas revenge implies some personal offense suffered by the avenger, agents of justice or redemption usually act on another's behalf. In redemption, the person bearing the grievance or expecting the fulfillment of an obligation is given satisfaction, and in that sense redemption is as evenhanded and fair as justice. But redemption can create a new and greater obligation: a debt of gratitude to the redeemer by the redeemed. This debt is not settled and forgotten with exchange of blows or money or favors; it's too precious for that. And this is the debt Beatrix incurs when all her efforts to redeem her own honor and avenge the deaths of others become dwarfed by an unexpected gift of life and new awakening.

Beatrix has been to hell and back. A mosquito sucking her blood wakes her from her coma, sending her on her own bloody quest. Her waking is startling, as if brought from death to life, but to a life of intense sorrow and anger. Her will to live is fueled by energy drawn from these emotions. In *Vol. 2* there is another "resurrection" scene as Beatrix emerges, zombie-like, from the lonely grave of Paula Schultz. But being undead is not quite the same as being alive. On her vengeful killing spree, the Bride is an energetic Angel of Death moving in a sequence of dreamlike environments. It's only after the bond between Beatrix and B. B. is restored that Beatrix can say, "I'm wide awake, pretty girl." This is her true resurrection, and the fact that it happens is utterly out of her control.

Beatrix's last words are "thank you," whispered as she cries on the bathroom floor, clutching a teddy bear, her child happily watching cartoons in the next room. But for whom are those words of gratitude uttered? Bill, surprisingly, is a candidate. Beatrix may be thinking of how Bill didn't kill her in the hospital or in his hacienda when he could have, or how he took custody of B. B., tenderly cared for her for four years, and was willing to fight fairly to keep her. Alternatively, she may be thinking of her debt to Pai Mei for her training, or to Hattori Hanzo for Japanese steel. Or Bea could be thanking God for this unexpected and bittersweet end to her journey. She could be acknowledging that some higher power, some divine artist, was at work weaving a story with an ending that reunites lioness and cub, where all is right in the jungle. Regardless of who is foremost in Beatrix's mind at this moment, her "thank you" registers her awareness that she is a mommy again because of kindly forces beyond her control. No amount of bloodshed can bring a baby back to life. It's the surprising discovery of something she could not control—that B. B. is alive—that brings about the happy, if temporary, conclusion.

Texas Ranger Earl McGraw called the El Paso wedding chapel a "house of mercy," but there Beatrix hoped to settle for a mercy bought too cheaply, under a false identity, and it just didn't work. If Beatrix thought she could get away with breaking the heart of a self-proclaimed murdering bastard, she thought wrong. The irony is that the *coup de grâce*—the stroke of grace—is not mercy killing but accidental survival. And so begins Bea's violent, sometimes ugly, somehow beautiful quest for revenge. At its end, she no longer lacks mercy, compassion, and forgiveness, not because she has shown them, but because they have been shown to her through the restoration of her child. No act of revenge can earn this redemption. A twist of a sword might remove an enemy and a punch of the fist might destroy a coffin lid, but the movement from Nikki's "Kaboom!" cereal to B. B.'s Lucky Charms isn't a tale of revenge, cold reason, karma, comeuppance, or even justice. It's a story of waking up, of redemption and precious grace—precious not only because it is costly, but also because it is priceless.

ABOUT THE EDITORS

Jonathan L. Walls lives in Los Angeles with his beautiful wife, Emily, where he works in the film industry. He recently wrote and directed his first independent feature film, *Couch Survivor,* completed in 2015. His next independent film project, *Extracurricular,* is currently in development. He is the editor of *The Legend of Zelda and Theology* (Gray Matter Books, 2011) and co-wrote an essay for *The Ultimate Harry Potter and Philosophy* (John Wiley & Sons, 2010). He studied media communications at Asbury University and studied film at the Los Angeles Film Studies Center. He has lexical gustatory synesthesia, which he modestly refers to as his "superpower."

Jerry L. Walls, who has a PhD from the University of Notre Dame, is Professor of Philosophy and Scholar in Residence at Houston Baptist University. Among his dozen or so books is a trilogy on the afterlife. Most recently, he wrote a popular level book that synthesizes the key insights of the trilogy, namely, *Heaven, Hell and Purgatory: Rethinking the Things That Matter Most* (Brazos Books, 2015). He thinks Tarantino could do a great movie about purgatory and/or hell.

ABOUT THE AUTHORS

Ben Avery is a children's minister, puppeteer, and comic book writer. He has written comics for publishers as diverse as Zondervan, Random House, Image, and Marvel, and the subject matter and genre of those comics are just as diverse, from adapting George R. R. Martin's *The Hedge Knight* into comic book form to writing a twelve-issue life of Christ that puts the events of all four Gospels in chronological order. He also hosts a podcast about the intersection of faith and sci-fi & fantasy. *Jackie Brown* is his favorite Tarantino movie, but only after writing his contribution to this book. He can be found at www.benavery.com and www.strangersandaliens.com.

Josh Corman teaches English in Central Kentucky. A graduate of the University of Kentucky (BA English Literature) and Asbury University (MA English Education), Josh also serves as a contributing editor at Book Riot, where he hosts the Riot Read podcast. He totally knows what was in the glowing suitcase, by the way, but you should probably tell him what you think it was, just so he can know for sure if you're right.

Jeffrey Green is Assistant Professor of Philosophy and Dean of the School of Christian Thought at Houston Baptist University. He earned his PhD in Philosophy from the University of Notre Dame and his BA in History and Philosophy from Southern Methodist University. His main research interests are in metaphysics and epistemology and the intersection of those areas with questions in philosophy of religion. He has published papers in philosophy of religion and just war theory.

Russell Hemati is the chair of the Philosophy department at Houston Baptist University, where he thinks long and hard about how to teach philosophy and how to bring the insights of the medieval world into the 21st century. He studied St. Augustine's philosophy of divine omniscience at Baylor University, where he received his PhD. He lives life on two wheels and thus was pleased that Butch knew the difference between a motorcycle and a chopper.

Emma Hinds-Greenaway has an MA in Theology and English, and an MLitt in Imagination, Theology and the Arts from the University of St. Andrews, Scotland. Most recently she achieved an MLitt in Creative Writing, and continues to write south of the Scottish border, in England. She is currently having pieces of her creative work developed for theatre in Manchester, where she lives with her husband and their books. She loves Chuck Berry and doing the Twist.

Kevin Kinghorn received his D.Phil from the University of Oxford and is Professor of Philosophy and Religion at Asbury Theological Seminary. He is the author of *The Decision of Faith* (T&T Clark, 2005) and a forthcoming book on the nature of The Good. He has also published articles about an earlier film master, Alfred Hitchcock, who, like Tarantino, entertained (and scared) a generation of cinema fans— although he did it with less hair.

John McAteer is assistant professor at Ashford University, where he serves as the chair of the liberal arts program. Before receiving his PhD in philosophy from the University of California at Riverside, he earned a BA in film from Biola University and an MA in philosophy of religion and ethics from Talbot School of Theology. His scholarly work has appeared in the journal *Film and Philosophy*, and he regularly writes cinematic apologetics for *Christian Research Journal*. He once sat at a table next to Quentin Tarantino in the Wendy's on Sunset Boulevard in Hollywood.

Brett McCracken is a film critic for *Christianity Today* and managing editor of *Biola Magazine* at Biola University, where he also teaches as an adjunct professor. He received a BA from Wheaton College, an MA in cinema and media studies from UCLA, and is currently pursuing an MA in theology from Talbot School of Theology. He is the author of *Gray Matters: Navigating the Space Between Legalism & Liberty* (Baker Books, 2013) and *Hipster Christianity: When Church and Cool Collide* (Baker Books, 2010). Five of his top ten favorite films of all time are the work of one filmmaker: Terrence Malick.

Abernathy McGraw is the pen name of an assistant professor of literature at Houston Baptist University. Excepting this pseudonym, she has yet to make a name for herself. She holds a PhD in literature from the University of Dallas. She has a unicorn t-shirt. And she's tryin' real hard to be the shepherd.

Lawson G. Stone is Professor of Old Testament at Asbury Theological Seminary in Wilmore, Kentucky, where he has taught since 1987. He received his PhD from Yale University. His most recent publication is a commentary on the book of Judges in the *Cornerstone Biblical Commentary* series (Tyndale Press, 2012), which, along with scholarly articles on Joshua and Judges, seeks to integrate the Old Testament's use of warfare and violence into biblical theology. He is the proud owner of an exact replica of a Late Bronze Age battle sword. And he knows how to use it.

Philip Tallon (PhD, University of St. Andrews) is an Assistant Professor of Theology at Houston Baptist University, where he chairs the Apologetics Department and teaches in the Honors College. He is the author of *The Poetics of Evil,* and the editor of *The Philosophy of Sherlock Holmes* (with co-editor David Baggett). He is also the father of four children (with co-parent Karen Tallon). You can find him on Twitter @ philiptallon.

Rebecca Ver Straten-McSparran holds an M.Div. from Fuller Theological Seminary and is currently a PhD Candidate in theology and film at King's College London, writing her thesis/dissertation on the prophetic voice of the film auteur, a comparative analysis of Lars von Trier and Ezekiel. She is currently director of the Los Angeles Film Studies Center (CCCU). In addition to being a conference speaker and published writer, she won a senator's award for her work as head of arts for the Mid-City West district of Los Angeles. An ordained pastor, she remembers with deep fondness the years she spent working with urban youth, gang members and taggers who were all too familiar with blood.

CPSIA information can be obtained
at www.ICGtesting.com
Printed in the USA
FSOW01n1728221015
12480FS